LET THEM

Eat

CAKE

CLASSIC, DECADENT DESSERTS

with VEGAN, GLUTEN-FREE

& HEALTHY VARIATIONS

LET THEM

Eat

CAKE

CLASSIC, DECADENT DESSERTS

with VEGAN, GLUTEN-FREE

& HEALTHY VARIATIONS

More Than 80 Recipes for
Cookies, Pies, Cakes, Ice Cream, and More!

GESINE BULLOCK-PRADO

Photographs by **TINA RUPP**

STEWART, TABORI & CHANG | NEW YORK

Published in 2015 by Stewart, Tabori & Chang
An imprint of ABRAMS

Library of Congress Control Number: 2014930934

ISBN: 978-1-61769-080-8

Editor: Elinor Hutton
Designer: Chin-Yee Lai
Production Manager: Denise LaCongo

The text of this book was composed in Akzidenz-Grotesk Pro, Filosofia, Guadalupe Essential Gota, School Script, Engravers' Roman, and ChevalierStripesSCD.

Printed and bound in the United States
10 9 8 7 6 5 4 3 2 1

Stewart, Tabori & Chang books are available at special discounts when purchased in quantity for premiums and promotions as well as fundraising or educational use. Special editions can also be created to specification. For details, contact specialsales@abramsbooks.com or the address below.

ABRAMS
THE ART OF BOOKS SINCE 1949
115 West 18th Street
New York, NY 10011
www.abramsbooks.com

Dedication 〉 For the Fabulous Jasmin 5

table of
CONTENTS

PIES

P. 101

CAKES

P. 143

ICE CREAM *and* CANDY

P. 191

INTRODUCTION

My mother was a dietary contradiction. She was a strict vegetarian, a health-food nut unparalleled. Her Virginia kitchen was a mecca to all things whole grain and sugar free; my school lunches were legendary for their whole-grain, soy-centric weirdness, and I didn't try a Coke until my Nanny slipped me a sip when I was seven. I didn't get another taste until high school.

Yet every summer when we traveled back to my mother's hometown of Nürnberg in Germany, we feasted with glee on pork bratwurst nestled in bleached white-flour buns. She was at once strident in her dietary convictions for everyday meals and supremely tolerant of the most egregious culinary morsels. A perfect example was her love of puff pastry, that white flour–based, butter-engorged patisserie staple: You'd think she'd consider it anathema. But she understood the beauty and joy of a well-made pastry and actually gloried in the caramelized goodness of a *palmier*.

Now that I have the pleasure of being a grown woman in charge of her own dietary landscape, I realize that I am my mother's daughter. I recognize the need to live a healthy life but, man, if that croissant doesn't look damn good. And having had a pastry shop of my own, I found that more and more customers were walking in the door asking for treats that wouldn't put Junior into anaphylactic shock, or that wouldn't pull them into a morass of regret the second they'd polished off a cookie. I had customers who wanted a healthier version of my wares with all the soul satisfaction of the classic. I was confronted with the need to make things gluten free, dairy free, egg free, even vegan. So I made it a mission to keep making the tastiest of treats with all the traditional ingredients in play, but then also figuring out how I could jury-rig them for someone who has celiac disease or suffers lactose intolerance or is sidled with an egg allergy or high cholesterol. To be perfectly honest, sometimes the healthier version *is* my favorite version (I'm talking to you, Chocolaty Chippy Chunk Cookies) and there are times when a vegan cake just blows me away (that's a tip of the hat to you, Figgy Pistacho Upside Down Cake).

With this book, I'm giving *everyone* an option to celebrate with cakes, pies, ice creams, candy, cookies, brownies, and more. Each of the more than eighty recipes here is a classic, at least in my book, and I've included the tastiest, no-holds-barred version of it. Then I have converted each of those recipes into healthier iterations, in which the glycemic index is lower and the fiber and nutrients are higher. You'll also find gluten-free and vegan versions of each tasty morsel. For every Killer Coffee Cake (page 82), there is a Vegan Killer Coffee Cake, and a Gluten-Free Killer Coffee Cake, and a Healthier Killer Coffee Cake. You get the idea.

In other words, everyone gets to have their cake and eat it too.

What does "healthier" really mean? Can't you just swap gluten-free flour mixes for traditional flour one for one? And why the vegan option?

First, you'll see a "healthier" variation for each recipe. These aren't calorie free and fat free, of course. They do, however, feature fiber- and nutrient-rich flours and mineral-dense sweeteners that are lower on the glycemic index than refined white sugar. Instead of empty calories and fat, these sweet and scrumptious treats offer nutritional benefits.

Next, in the gluten-free variations, you'll notice that there are subtle changes to ratios of the ingredients. That's because if you simply do a one-to-one swap of gluten-free flour mix for wheat flour without addressing the moisture and protein levels in the remaining ingredients, the baked goods can be gummy or dry. Follow the recipes closely for the best results.

Finally, you may notice, as you snuggle by a cozy fire, reading through the entirety of this book in a single sitting (as I assume you will), that I have a vegan option instead of a dairy-free or egg-free option. If this tome is catering to those with food allergies, why not address those issues individually? Well, by creating a vegan option I kill two (figurative) birds with one stone: I provide an alternative for those who choose an entirely plant-based vegan diet due to an ethical or dietary choice while also providing a safe harbor for those who suffer from dairy, casein, whey, and egg allergies or intolerances. This means that the vegan options are, of course, also allergy friendly (except for those in which tree nuts and peanuts are used).

Here are some of the perhaps less familiar ingredients that you may need when swapping out more traditional ingredients in the recipes in this book:

The Egg Replacement Compendium

Eggs perform myriad tasks in baking. When eggs are called for in a baked good, it is very difficult to find a substitute. Eggs act as leavening agents. The most extreme example of their leavening power is when egg whites are beaten into peaks and the resulting fluff is baked on its own into meringues or folded into the ingredients of an angel food cake to make it light and delicate. Eggs also act as binding agents, keeping the ingredients stuck together: Yolks act as emulsifiers, allowing fats to be suspended within the structure of a baked good, building moisture, and the protein in egg whites builds structure. So you can imagine, with one ingredient doing so much work, it's a tough act to follow.

Each of the egg replacement options listed performs a relatively specific function, and none can simulate every aspect of the egg. I've given recommendations for how to replace the eggs in the individual recipes, carefully choosing the right replacement based on how the eggs work in the traditional recipe.

Here are some of the egg replacements I use most in this book:

Bananas, prune puree, or applesauce: ¼ cup (60 ml) applesauce or prune puree, or ½ large banana, mashed = 1 large egg

These ingredients don't provide leavening or the needed protein to provide structure but they do act as emulsifiers, and they impart wonderful moisture in quickbreads and some heavier cakes. They can also be used as fat replacers in the same kinds of recipes.

Ener-G egg replacer: 1½ teaspoons egg replacer powder stirred or whisked thoroughly with 2 tablespoons warm water = 1 large egg

This mixture is often lumpy, so it's worth running the finished mixture through a fine sieve before using. You can use this mixture immediately. This egg replacer is wonderful when more than one egg is called for. It is relatively flavorless and contains a measure of leavening (it's gluten free as well). It acts as both a leavening agent and a binding agent.

There are other products that are labeled "egg replacer" but the ingredients are varied and cannot be substituted with Ener-G one for one.

Flaxseed meal: 1 tablespoon flaxseed meal mixed thoroughly with 3 tablespoons hot water = 1 large egg

To drain, cut the tofu into three pieces, place the tofu on a sheet pan lined with paper towels, place paper towels on top of the tofu, cover with another sheet pan, place heavy books or cans on the top sheet pan, and let sit for about 1 hour.

Versawhip 600K: The application and amount varies depending on the recipe.

Versawhip is an egg white replacement product made from "pure enzymatically treated soy protein" (as it's described in the Versawhip literature). It's a foaming agent that can replace egg whites in cold foams and in baked goods but cannot be used in conjunction with fats or it deflates. As a cold foam—a meringue-like topping for pies or even berries, for example—it keeps its shape for only about 15 minutes, unless you stabilize it with a gelatin-like setting agent like powdered agar, so plan accordingly (actual gelatin is not considered vegan). Versawhip is available for purchase online on Amazon.com.

Flours and Flour Alternatives

There are many ways to de-flour a pastry these days. But not every flour alternative will be right for every job. So keep in mind what the traditional flour is supposed to accomplish in a recipe and choose your gluten-free or healthier alternative from there. Of course, the recipes in this book have specific directions as to which flour alternative works best for each recipe when making it gluten free or healthier. I have my own tried-and-true variations that I've developed based on the flavor and texture I want in a particular baked good. Also, I wrote the recipes in this book with an eye toward keeping the specialty ingredients to a minimum: You won't have to invest in a pantry full of expensive flours to make these desserts.

In healthier recipes, I like to combine a mix of whole-grain flours and gluten-free alternatives. My focus is to provide fiber and nutrition where white flours provide none.

I get many of my flour substitutes at the good ol' grocery store. You'd be surprised how well stocked they are now with gluten-free and alternative options. I also sometimes turn to the Internet: King Arthur Flour's website, in particular, and my go-to source for all things nuts and alternative flour, Nuts.com.

Before using, allow the mixture to stand until it obtains a gel-like consistency, about 10 minutes. I use flaxseed meal to replace eggs when only 1 or 2 are called for. Flax meal doesn't act as a leavening agent and doesn't contain enough protein to provide much structure, but it does a great job of binding ingredients. It's perfect for some cookies and many quickbreads. I keep flax meal refrigerated as it can go rancid if left out for long periods of time.

Silken tofu: Silken tofu, blended in a food processor or blender until smooth. The amount varies depending on the application.

Tofu is most often used to simulate cooked eggs, as in vegan egg salad and quiches, but it's also the go-to ingredient for many "ice creams" and mousse-like recipes, providing structure and texture.

Here are some of the flours and flour alternatives I use most in this book:

Brown rice flour, finely milled (gluten free): I prefer this to white rice flour for its flavor and lack of grit in baked products.

Coconut flour (gluten free): Ground from dried, defatted coconut meat, coconut flour is high in fiber and low in digestible carbohydrates. It does have a subtle coconut flavor, so it's best used in products that are suited to being coconutty.

Gluten-free flour blends: I prefer the ones from King Arthur Flour and Thomas Keller's Cup4Cup blend. Remember that with most gluten-free flour blends, you'll have to add a certain measure of xanthan gum to your recipe. There are some gluten-free blends that do include xanthan, including King Arthur Flour's Gluten-Free All-Purpose Baking Mix and Cup4Cup.

Nut flours (gluten free): Nut flours are simply very finely ground nuts, nothing else. You can grind your own in a food processor, but it's tough to get the "flour" as fine as those that are commercially milled. This is a lovely way to bring both structure and flavor to a baked product. I use nut flours in both gluten-free applications and traditional applications because they are so delicious. All nuts can go rancid, so keep your nut flours tightly sealed after using. You can also refrigerate or freeze them for a longer shelf life.

Spelt flour (contains gluten): Spelt flour is a whole-grain flour that is highly water soluble, so its nutrients are easily absorbed. Adding spelt to your flour mix can really up both flavor and nutrition.

Sprouted flours (contain gluten): These flours are made from whole grains that are first sprouted and then dried at low temperatures to retain the highest percentage of active enzymes, nutrients, and vitamins in the grain. Truly the healthiest of gluten-containing flours, these often bring a lovely texture and nutty taste to the proceedings. They are traditionally very dark, so keep that in mind when adding to cake batters if you want to maintain a lighter colored crumb.

Fats

I am of the firm belief that butter is better. It really is. For taste and for texture and for doggone general goodness, I'm butter's biggest fan. However, I understand that it's not on everyone's dietary agenda. It's worth doing a taste test to see what fats appeal to you best. Here are some options:

Canola oil: Canola oil is low in saturated fat and has a high proportion of monounsaturated fat. It's also pretty tasteless, so it's a great oil for allowing other flavors in a quickbread or cake to take predominance.

Clarified butter or ghee: If your inability to eat butter is due to lactose intolerance or an allergy to casein, fear not: You can bake with clarified butter or ghee. In butter and ghee those elements have been removed, creating a wonderful alternative to butter that's actually the real thing.

Coconut oil: It's an oil, but you're forgiven for being confused when you actually see the stuff because it's solid at room temperature—not what you'd expect of an "oil." Coconut oil has health benefits, like reducing cholesterol and combating bacteria and viruses, and can have benefits to thyroid function and hormone levels. It's also heat safe, which makes it great for both cooking and baking. The best way to work with coconut oil is to melt it and measure it per the recipe and then to let it resolidify either at room temperature or in the fridge. Refined coconut oil isn't obviously "coconutty" in taste, so you'll be fine using it even when there are coconut haters in the vicinity.

Earth Balance Vegan Buttery Sticks: Another buttery alternative is Earth Balance's Vegan Buttery Sticks, a combination of non-GMO, non-dairy, trans fat–free, nonhydrogenated, ALA omega-3–rich oils. Yes, it's still fatty, but it is a very decent alternative to butter, at least in mouthfeel (even if it doesn't taste like butter).

Grapeseed oil: High in vitamin E, grapeseed oil, a by-product of wine production, is at once touted as the healthiest of all oils and lambasted as full of toxins from the chemicals used in the wine production. That's why I use organic grapeseed oil. Grapeseed oil is a great fat to use in cakes and quickbreads because it has a neutral flavor.

Vegan shortening: Vegetable shortenings and palm oil shortenings are a wonderful alternative to butter, as they add very little to no taste to the pastry. You might think that's a disadvantage, but you'd be surprised how many things that claim to taste like butter really just taste like shoe. You can melt or freeze shortening and it cuts into flour easily. Please note that these are not necessarily healthy alternatives to butter: Traditional vegetable shortening contains unhealthy trans fats. Palm oil shortening is trans fat free and works just as well as any vegetable shortening, however, you might want to consider the fact that the harvesting of palm oil has endangered rainforests and the wildlife they sustain.

Sweeteners

The first order of business when jury-rigging a pastry with a view to making it healthier is to address the sugar content. At least

that's how I address the conundrum. After years of experimenting, I've created a few firm but certainly not fast rules about substituting sugar. First, rid yourself of the notion that brown sugar, whether light or dark, is healthier than traditional granulated sugar. It's simply granulated sugar saturated with varying degrees of molasses (white granulated sugar is made through the process of extracting molasses from the sugar cane, leaving us with the snow-white stuff).

It's also worth noting that the filtering process used for white cane sugar is often achieved using charcoal, some of which is made from animal bone and is therefore not vegan. This isn't true of granulated sugar extracted from sugar beets. Turbinado, organic evaporated cane juice, organic dehydrated cane juice, and organic cane sugar are all vegan. (See the "Things You Thought Were Vegan or Gluten Free That Might Not Be" below for more information on vegan sugar.)

As a rule, I don't use artificial sweeteners. Not only are they chemical wastelands (and not healthy), they also taste horrible in baked goods. That holds true for the completely natural sweetener, stevia, which tends to taste like a shrub when it's not cut with another sweetener. There are now sugar/stevia baking blends available that attempt to address that problem and are worth trying.

Here are some of the sugars and sugar substitutes I use in this book:

Agave syrup: This is a great alternative to honey for vegans. Its traditional form is a syrup, something that works well in mousses and fillings but is not the best in cookies.

Blackstrap molasses: I also like to use blackstrap molasses in appropriate recipes due to its wonderful flavor, deep chocolate color, and the significant dose of minerals it brings to the party.

Maple syrup and sugar: These add great flavor and sweetness. If you love maple, it's worth replacing up to half the sugar called for in a recipe with maple sugar. It is sweeter than sugar, tablespoon for tablespoon, so a little goes a long way.

Organic granulated palm sugar: My favorite "healthy" sweetening option is granulated palm sugar. It's a sugar wrangled from the nectar of the flowers that grow atop coconut trees, but it doesn't taste like coconut. In fact, it has a lovely caramel flavor, both rich and sophisticated. Palm sugar has a very low glycemic index, which means it is absorbed into the bloodstream at a much slower rate than granulated sugar. It's also full of vitamins and minerals while still behaving like granulated sugar in the way it melts and cooks.

Sucanat: Sucanat is a minimally processed cane sugar and possesses trace minerals that are otherwise stripped from granulated sugar. It maintains a slightly molasses flavor.

Things You Thought Were Vegan or Gluten Free That Might Not Be

There are a host of innocuous ingredients that you'd assume were vegan or gluten free but that often aren't. I'll refer you to this page throughout the book to remind you that these ingredients may not be vegan or gluten free. When sugar is called for in a vegan recipe, make sure you use a vegan sugar; when baking powder is called for in a gluten free recipe, make sure it is a gluten free type; and so on! Here are the biggies:

Baking powder: Check the label of your baking powder container to be sure it's specifically designated "gluten free."

Chocolate: Chocolate is almost always gluten free. It is sometimes labeled vegan and sometimes not. An indication that the chocolate is vegan when it's not explicitly labeled as such is when all the following phrases are used: casein free, whey free, and dairy free. Sometimes it's not apparent from the label but the chocolate is still vegan. When in doubt, look at the ingredient list. On occasion, the ingredient list will indicate that the chocolate does not contain dairy but the manufacturer will include a warning that the production of an otherwise vegan chocolate is either sharing a machine or made in close proximity to milk chocolate production (which by its very nature is full of dairy). Those chocolates are not, therefore, guaranteed to be completely dairy free.

Both Trader Joe's–brand chocolate chips and Green & Black's chocolate (with the exception of the milk chocolate) are vegan.

The same holds true for Callebaut and Cacao Barry dark chocolates. (Of course, always check the label, even when buying trusted brands, as occasionally their formula or process will change.) There's a very good chance that if you're buying very good quality semi- or bittersweet chocolate, it will be dairy free. And then there are the chocolate angels who make it easy, like the Chocolate Dream brand, which says right on the front of the semisweet baking chips label "dairy free" and "gluten free."

Food dye: Most commercial dyes are tested on animals and thus might not be appropriate for a vegan diet. There are natural dyes that are clearly labeled "cruelty free." These dyes are often truly natural, using pigments from beets and spinach. If you choose to go this route, keep in mind that the hues won't be as vibrant as traditional food dye and depending on the amount of natural dye used, they may or may not taste of beets or spinach.

Gelatin: Gelatin is made from animal bone. There are alternatives like agar agar and Genutine, a vegetarian gelatin.

Nonstick baking spray: What makes a baking spray a baking spray is the inclusion of flour in the mix. So it's obviously not gluten free. Instead, use traditional nonstick cooking spray.

Oats: Make sure that the oats and oat flour that you buy are labeled "gluten free"—oats themselves are indeed gluten free but some manufacturers' oats are cross-contaminated with wheat products.

Sugar: Sugar is gluten free but often it's not vegan. The problem isn't in the ingredient itself, it's with the processing. Modern-day processing of cane sugar very often makes use of charcoal from cow bones (called bone char) to whiten the sugar. Brown sugar made from cane sugar isn't vegan because it's made from processed white sugar to which molasses is added. The good news is that sugars derived from sugar beets are safe for vegans, as are most sugars labeled "organic" because they're minimally processed. You need only look at the ingredient list, which up to now probably seemed a ridiculous thing to do on a sugar package, to see whether the sugar in question is derived from sugar cane or from the sugar beet. Other sugars that are safely vegan are turbinado sugar, organic evaporated cane juice, organic dehydrated cane juice, and organic cane sugar.

Vanilla and other extracts: Check the bottle to make sure it indicates that the extract is gluten free. Many manufacturers use additives that contain gluten. And while we're at it, check the ingredient list to see whether the extract lists cane sugar as one of its ingredients. If it does, there's a good chance it isn't vegan (see "Sugar" above).

A FEW WORDS AND PHRASES YOU SHOULD GET FAMILIAR WITH BEFORE YOU START BAKING

Bain marie/double boiler: The terms bain marie or double boiler are often used interchangeably, although technically they are two separate things. A double boiler is used on the stovetop and is simply a container of simmering water upon which you set a heatproof pot or bowl containing ingredients; the steam from the simmering water below is used to slowly and evenly cook or melt those ingredients. The simmering water should fill the container only halfway in order to produce the most even and gentle heat (you do not want the top pot or bowl to touch the simmering water, just be resting in its steam). A double boiler is most often used to melt chocolate. A bain marie is used in the oven: A batter- or custard-filled pan is placed in a larger baking dish that contains hot water reaching just over halfway up the sides of the inner container, which helps the baking temperature remain steady. It's often used when baking cheesecake so it doesn't crack or dry out.

Coconut cream: For a great vegan whipped topping that mimics whipped cream, I call for the use of something called "coconut cream." You can find coconut cream when you open a can of full-fat coconut milk: It's that really thick stuff that is separated from the liquids in the can, the "cream" of the coconut milk. To use it, you want to separate it completely from the liquids. Recently, outfits like Trader Joe's have begun to sell coconut cream all by itself, which makes planning for desserts much easier because you're guaranteed a specific measure of coconut cream; when opening up a can of coconut milk, you can't depend on how much cream is going to be hanging around inside. See page 126 for more information.

Coconut cream is not to be confused with cream of coconut, which is a highly sweetened coconut milk and won't whip. Cream of coconut is used in some cake batters and many a tropical drink.

Convection versus conventional ovens: Many modern ovens have both a conventional setting and a convection setting. The difference is that on the convection setting, a fan circulates the hot air in the oven, which speeds up the process of cooking or baking. This book is written with conventional ovens in mind. If you wish to use your convection setting, simply reduce the oven temperature by 25°F and bake for the same amount of time as indicated.

Creaming: Creaming is a kind of mixing. When you beat butter (or other fats) and sugar together until the mixture is light, airy, and fluffy, you are creaming the ingredients together. The sugar granules act as little grenades, blowing holes in the butter and creating pockets of air that give the leavening a foothold to do its work. You can use either the paddle or whisk attachment to cream ingredients. So don't run around looking for cream in the ingredient list when you see that word in the instructions, but do get ready to spend a few minutes in front of the mixer while it does its work.

Docking: This isn't sailor's lingo for parking a boat. This is about punching tiny little holes in dough to let hot air circulate around and under the dough. I almost always suggest that once you've lined a pie pan with dough you dock it: Take a fork (you can also use a specialty docking tool, but you've already got a fork and it does the same thing) and use the tines to make holes all over the bottom crust. Make sure the tines go all the way through.

Folding: Folding an ingredient into a batter simply requires you to be delicate and ladylike when incorporating, say, beaten egg whites, into a heavier mixture. What's required of you is both a specific piece of equipment, normally a large rubber spatula, and a very gentle, ballet-like physical motion. Instead of using your rubber spatula to stir vigorously, you use it in a sweeping motion, like the paddle of a boat, to sweep the ingredients throughout the batter so as not to release any air that's been incorporated into the batter.

Ribbon stage: When beating together whole eggs and sugar or egg yolks and sugar, there is a stage in the process when the mixture starts to "ribbon." That is, the mixture thickens, lightens in color, and increases in volume, and when you lift the whisk, the mixture will fall in thick ribbons from the whisk into the bowl, leaving a clear trail on the surface of the mixture in the bowl that will slowly melt away.

Silpat: A Silpat is a nonstick silicone baking mat used in lieu of parchment paper. It tolerates very high heat and has the distinction of being genuinely nonstick; it can be used in candy making and baking. (Silpat is actually a brand name that's become synonymous with the thing itself, much like Kleenex.)

Tempering: Tempering refers to two things in baking. The first refers to a process by which a hot ingredient and a cool one are introduced to each other. For instance, when making a mousse, you might temper a warm gelatin mixture with a cold whipped cream by incorporating a small portion of the whipped cream into the gelatin; using a small amount means that the cool cream won't "shock" the gelatin and make it harden, so now you can incorporate the gelatin into the larger portion of whipped cream more smoothly. You might also temper a mixture of room-temperature eggs with a hot, melted chocolate by adding just a small portion of the hot chocolate to the eggs so as to gently combine the two without cooking the eggs; once a small amount of the hot ingredient is incorporated (raising the temperature of the eggs a bit), you can slowly add the rest.

Tempering also refers to the process of heating and cooling chocolate that ensures that the cocoa butter in the chocolate hardens uniformly.

Spoon-and-level method (or how I measure flour): Get ten people to measure a cup of flour in a dry cup measure and then weigh the results, and you'll likely get ten different weight measurements. Everyone seems to have a different method of putting flour into the same small container, and this can lead to some wonky results in a finished baked product if you don't know how the baker who created the recipe measured the flour. So let me tell you how I do it: I use a very large spoon to gently scoop flour into the cup measure. I continue filling until the flour just starts to mound in the cup. Then I use something to level the cup and knock off the excess mound of flour, like the flat side of a dinner knife. Don't wiggle the cup or stomp it down on a work surface, as that makes the flour settle and pack more into the cup than intended—this would result in a heavier weight measure than what I came up with when I measured the flour my way.

Vanilla bean paste and vanilla extract: You'll notice that I call for the use of vanilla bean paste throughout this cookbook. If you're familiar with the stuff, you're thinking, "Hell, yeah!" If you aren't, get ready for a treat because if you've ever dropped twenty-five bucks on a few vanilla pods just to wrangle that dry bean open to scrape a meager few specks from it, this paste is what vanilla dreams are made of. It's made of vanilla seeds suspended in a vanilla-extract syrup. It's readily available at fine food stores and on the Internet, but if you can't find it you can use regular vanilla extract in a one-for-one swap. Never use imitation vanilla. It's better to use no vanilla at all than that metallic, artificial malarkey.

Whipping cream and heavy cream: For a cream to "whip," it needs to contain at least 30% fat; the more fat, the better it whips. Whipping cream, on average, contains 30 to 36% fat and whips up into soft, light peaks. It often contains whipping agents or stabilizers like carageenan to help the whipping along. Heavy cream must contain at least 36% fat (and local dairies in my area have some that are more than 40%!). Heavy cream whips up more stiffly and holds a firm shape well. It's great for piping on top of cakes and pies. When whipped, both are called "whipped cream." It can be a bit confusing, but it's always delicious. I often ask for heavy cream to be pre-whipped in the ingredient list so that it's immediately available to be incorporated into the batter without wasting any time and, possibly, compromising the batter. Simply pour the cream into a large bowl and whisk until medium-stiff peaks form when you lift the whisk from the cream. Don't over-whip to the point that the cream starts to look chunky.

THE BIG
WINOOSKI

Chocolaty Chippy Chunk Cookies

SALTY DOG OATS   COCONUT MACAROONS

PEANUT BUTTER SANDWICH COOKIES

THE MIGHTY MINT *Maple Cookies*

MACARON   MAPLE MADELEINES

ALMOND COOKIES *Lime Meltaways*

SPEKULATIUS COOKIES

PEANUT BUTTER TOGA COOKIES

Bergamot Fortune Cookies   SAMOAS

HAZELNUT LINZER HEARTS

STARRY STARRY NIGHTS

Rugelach

COOKIES

When most people think of my work—my oeuvre, if you like—cookies aren't usually the first things that come to mind. I'm the fancy-schmancy pastry person. I do the cakes with the crazy, complicated stuff in the middle. I do laminated dough and spun sugar. But cookies are where I started my professional pastry life. Macaron were my first commercial venture way back in 2004, years before they became as popular as cupcakes, and while they may be fancier cookies than most, they are still cookies. At my pastry shop, cookies were as big a priority as mousse cakes. It's the ultimate "treat yourself" confection. They're also the most comforting thing to share. My chocolate bomb, called the Big Winooski, was coveted by Vermonters near and far. The petite morsels that are Starry Starry Nights are a fan favorite as well, with their naturally gluten-free nature and their trufflelike texture. And who doesn't love childhood favorites like crisp peanut butter sandwich cookies and caramel-and coconut-infused samoas? Everyone deserves to enjoy a beautiful cookie.

Chocolaty Chippy Chunk Cookies

Peanut Butter
Toga Cookies
(PAGE 25)

One of the rare sweets my mother kept tucked away in the freezer were bittersweet chocolate morsels. Being the sugar addict I was (and still am), I'd razor open the seam and slip out a handful. I'd crazy glue the bag right up, thinking it appeared unsullied. If unsullied is permanently affixed to the freezer door and half empty, then my efforts were a raging success! It shouldn't surprise you that any special-occasion chocolate chip cookies that got made in our house were skimpy on the chocolate chips. Now I buy my chocolate in bulk, in twenty-pound blocks in fact, so I always have enough for emergency cravings *and* cookies.

Chocolaty CHIPPY CHUNK COOKIES

{ MAKES 20 MEDIUM-SIZED COOKIES OR 12 GIANT COOKIES }

Procedure

- Preheat the oven to 375°F (190°C). Line two sheet pans with parchment paper.
- In a large bowl, whisk together both flours, the baking powder, baking soda, and salt for 30 seconds to evenly distribute the leavening. Stir in the grated unsweetened chocolate.
- Melt the butter in a saucepan over low heat. Simmer until the butter starts to brown and gives off a nutty aroma. Pour the hot butter into a bowl, leaving and discarding the darkest brown bits in the pan. Cover the butter and let cool completely and resolidify (this can take quite a while at room temperature, so you can stick in the fridge for 20 minutes to speed the process along).
- In the bowl of a stand mixer fitted with the paddle attachment, cream together the cooled butter and sugars until light and fluffy. Add the eggs one at a time, mixing until just combined. Scrape down the bowl and add the vanilla and briefly mix. Add the flour mixture and mix on low speed until the dough just comes together. Add the chocolate chips and chopped bittersweet chocolate and mix until just combined. Cover with plastic wrap and refrigerate for at least 20 minutes to allow the dough to hydrate.
- Scoop the dough with a medium (1½-ounce/45-ml) or large (3-ounce/90-ml) cookie scoop and place on the prepared sheet pans 3 inches (7.5 cm) apart. Bake until lightly golden on the edges, 10 to 12 minutes for the medium cookies or 12 to 15 minutes for the large; halfway through the baking time, slam the sheet pans down on the counter to deflate the cookies a bit and rotate the pans for even browning.

Ingredients

2 cups (260 g) all-purpose flour

1 cup (120 g) pastry flour

1 teaspoon baking powder

1 teaspoon baking soda

2 teaspoons fine sea salt, or 1½ teaspoons table salt

3 ounces (85 g) unsweetened chocolate, grated with a Microplane (freeze the chocolate before grating)

1½ cups (3 sticks/340 g) unsalted butter, at room temperature

1½ cups (330 g) light brown sugar, packed

1 cup (200 g) granulated sugar

2 large eggs, at room temperature

1 tablespoon vanilla bean paste or vanilla extract

8 ounces (225 g) dark chocolate morsels (like Nestle Toll House Dark Chocolate Morsels)

3½ ounces (100 g) bittersweet chocolate (like Lindt 70%), coarsely chopped

Check page 16 before proceeding for additional details on ensuring your recipes are gluten free and/or vegan.

VEGAN

Confirm that all the chocolates are vegan. Replace the butter with Earth Balance Vegan Shortening, but don't melt and brown it. Replace the eggs with 2½ tablespoons golden flaxseed meal and 6 tablespoons (90 ml) water; stir and let gel before adding to the sugar-shortening mixture.

GLUTEN FREE

Replace the flour with 2½ cups (400 g) finely milled brown rice flour, ½ cup (70 g) sweet white sorghum flour, and 1½ teaspoons xanthan gum. Increase the granulated sugar to 1½ cups (300 g) and decrease the brown sugar to 1 cup (220 g).

HEALTHIER

Replace the pastry flour with organic whole-wheat pastry flour and increase by ½ cup, to total 1½ cups (150 g) whole-wheat pastry flour. Replace the all-purpose flour with 2 cups (240 g) spelt flour. Replace the butter with ½ cup (1 stick/115 g) unsalted butter, ½ cup (120 ml) prune puree (I use organic baby food, such as Plum Organic's Just Prunes), and ½ cup (120 ml) organic unrefined virgin coconut oil. Replace all of the sugar with 2 cups (320 g) organic granulated palm sugar. Forgo the melting of the butter and just cream together the butter and coconut oil with the palm sugar until light and fluffy. Add the prune puree before adding the eggs. Reduce the oven temperature to 350°F (175°C) and bake until the edges of the cookies just begin to brown, 12 to 15 minutes, watching very carefully as palm sugar will burn more readily than white.

---

a note from my sweet tooth

AN OPEN APOLOGY TO VEGANS

I've been known to get snarky about veganism, scoffing at perfectly lovely humans' choice not to consume eggs and dairy. As a pastry chef, butter and cream (any animal product, for that matter) are the building blocks of my existence, and there was a time when I'd become unbearably cranky when someone asked whether my pastry cream was vegan. (Fine: I still get cranky at that question, if only because it's called pastry *cream*.) I've since come to the realization that I have no right to question anyone's decision to adhere to a dietary construct that's dedicated to protecting animal life and, in many cases, improving human health as well. I've also evolved just enough to understand that exploring vegan baking options is a way to address many severe dietary allergies all at once. Not only that, but undertaking the challenge to transform an otherwise dairy- and egg-laden treat into something entirely without . . . well, that's exactly the kind of adventure for which we chefs live. So forgive me for having been a closed-minded putz. I hope to make it up to you in this book.

As we were renovating the space that would become my erstwhile pastry shop, Gesine Confectionary, I put "teaser" products in the shop window to let Vermonters know what was soon to come. Of all the pastries I displayed, a jar of peanut butter cookies received the most gawkers. More than filigreed wedding cakes, more than a caramel-bedazzled croquembouche, and more than a tower of macaron. Something about those homey, fork-marked beauties brings out the moon-eyed, cookie-loving kid in all of us. But before you think this is your workaday peanut butter cookie, take a quick gander at the ingredient list. What's that strange addition? What in the hell is *nanami togarashi*? Well, it's a traditional Japanese seasoning (available in Asian markets and online) composed of various chiles, sesame seeds, and orange peel. It gives a subtle kick to the cookie. Nothing alarming, mind you, just a nudge.

Peanut Butter **TOGA** COOKIES

(MAKES ABOUT 22 COOKIES)

Procedure

- In the bowl of a stand mixer fitted with the paddle attachment, cream together the brown sugar, butter, and honey until light and fluffy. Add the peanut butter and continue mixing on medium speed until incorporated. Add the whole egg, egg yolk, and vanilla and mix on medium speed until incorporated.
- In a small bowl, whisk together the flour, baking soda, salt, and nanami togarashi for 30 seconds to evenly distribute the leavening. Add to the mixer bowl and mix on low speed until the flour is completely incorporated. Cover with plastic wrap and refrigerate for at least 30 minutes.
- Preheat the oven to 325°F (165°C). Line two sheet pans with parchment paper.
- Using a medium (1½-ounce/45-ml) cookie scoop, scoop the dough onto the prepared pans at least 2 inches (5 cm) apart. Using the palm of your hand, flatten the cookies. Use a fork to mark the cookies with the tines twice to get the traditional crosshatch design. Bake until the cookies just start to brown on the edges, about 15 minutes.

Ingredients

1 cup (220 g) dark brown sugar, packed
¾ cup (1 ½ sticks/170 g) unsalted butter
¼ cup (60 ml) honey
¾ cup (195 g) smooth peanut butter
1 large egg
1 large egg yolk
1 tablespoon vanilla bean paste or
    vanilla extract
2 cups (260 g) all-purpose flour
1 teaspoon baking soda
1 teaspoon salt
1 ½ teaspoons *nanami togarashi*

Check page 16 before proceeding for additional details on ensuring your recipes are gluten free and/or vegan.

VEGAN

Replace the butter with ¾ cup (170 g) Earth Balance Vegan Shortening or Spectrum Organic All Vegetable Shortening. Replace the honey with ¼ cup (60 ml) organic agave syrup. Replace the whole egg with 1 large egg's worth of prepared Ener-G egg replacer (see recipe, page 12) and the egg yolk with 1 large egg's worth of flaxseed meal mixed with water (see page 12).

VEGAN

FOR THE COOKIES: Replace the butter with an equal amount of Earth Balance Vegan Buttery Sticks. Replace the egg with 1 large egg's worth of flaxseed meal mixed with water (see page 12). FOR THE FILLING: Replace the butter with an equal amount of Earth Balance Vegan Buttery Sticks and replace the honey with an equal amount of organic agave syrup.

GLUTEN FREE

Replace the flour with 1¼ cups (200 g) finely milled brown rice flour, ½ cup (70 g) sweet white sorghum flour, ¼ cup (20 g) peanut flour, and 1 teaspoon xanthan gum.

GLUTEN FREE

FOR THE COOKIES: Replace the all-purpose flour with 1 cup (160 g) finely milled brown rice flour and ½ teaspoon xanthan gum.

HEALTHIER

Replace the brown sugar with 1 cup (160 g) organic granulated palm sugar. Add 2 tablespoons almond milk to the batter just after adding the eggs. Replace the flour with ½ cup (40 g) peanut flour and 1½ cups (180 g) white whole-wheat flour. Use organic unsweetened smooth peanut butter, such as Arrowhead Mills creamy peanut butter.

HEALTHIER

FOR THE COOKIES: Replace the sugar with ⅓ cup (60 g) organic granulated palm sugar. Make sure to use organic unsweetened smooth peanut butter such as Arrowhead Mills creamy peanut butter. Replace the all-purpose flour with 1 cup (160 g) finely milled brown rice flour and ½ teaspoon xanthan gum. FOR THE FILLING: Make sure to use organic unsweetened smooth peanut butter such as Arrowhead Mills creamy peanut butter.

As a kid, I had to commit grand larceny to procure anything resembling a pack-aged goodie. The poor Colemans. They were our neighbors across the street. Their larder was nirvana. All manner of name-brand, sugar-blasted, not-found-in-nature colored treats were to be found in the Coleman kitchen, and I may or may not at one time have put a box of Oreos under my shirt and made a run for it. Oreos, of course, are the obvious choice for a Cookie Desperado, but I also came to love the underappreciated Nutter Butter thanks to that very kind and forgiving family. Now I bake the sweets I once pilfered and, what do you know, I kinda like them even without the additives and colorants.

Procedure

MAKE THE COOKIES

- In the bowl of a stand mixer fitted with the paddle attachment, combine the butter and sugar and cream on high speed until light and fluffy. Add the egg and mix until incorporated. Scrape down the sides of the bowl. Add the peanut butter and vanilla and mix until incorporated.
- In a small bowl, stir together both flours, the salt, and baking powder for 30 seconds to evenly distribute the leavening. Add all at once to the mixer bowl and mix until just combined. Cover with plastic wrap and refrigerate for 20 minutes.
- Preheat the oven to 350°F (175°C). Line a sheet pan with parchment paper.
- Using a teaspoon cookie scoop, place two scoops of cookie dough next to each other, leaving a ⅛-inch (3-mm) gap between the scoops, on the prepared cookie sheet. Gently press down on each round to flatten slightly and so that the two rounds touch each other and form a peanut shell shape. Use the tines of a fork to make a crosshatch design on each scoop. This will be one cookie. Continue with the rest of the dough, plac-ing the cookies about 1 inch (2.5 cm) apart. Bake until the edges just start to brown, 15 to 20 minutes. Let cool completely.

MAKE THE FILLING

- Stir together the peanut butter, butter, honey, and salt. Spread about 1 teaspoon of the filling onto the bottom of one cookie and sandwich with another. Continue making sandwiches with the remaining cookies and filling.

{ MAKES 10 SANDWICH COOKIES }

Ingredients

FOR THE COOKIES

4 tablespoons (55 g) unsalted butter,
    at room temperature
⅓ cup (65 g) sugar
1 large egg
¼ cup (65 g) smooth peanut butter
1 teaspoon vanilla bean paste
1 cup (140 g) all-purpose flour
½ cup (40 g) peanut flour (see page 14)
1 teaspoon salt
¼ teaspoon baking powder

FOR THE FILLING

½ cup (130 g) smooth peanut butter
1 tablespoon unsalted butter, at room
    temperature
1 teaspoon honey
Pinch of salt

The BIG WINOOSKI

{ MAKES 14 COOKIES }

Ingredients

½ cup (40 g) Dutch-process cocoa powder
(like Cacao Barry Extra Brute)
¼ cup (35 g) all-purpose flour
½ teaspoon salt
¼ teaspoon baking powder
3 large eggs, at room temperature
½ cup (110 g) light brown sugar, packed
2 tablespoons honey
1 tablespoon instant espresso powder
1 teaspoon vanilla bean paste or
vanilla extract
3 tablespoons unsalted butter
10 ounces (280 g) bittersweet chocolate
(like Callebaut 60/40), finely chopped
1 cup (170 g) bittersweet chocolate chips

The Big Winooski is named after the river that ran behind our bakery (past tense not because the river has disappeared but because our bakery is no longer in that location). The river isn't big and it's not made of chocolate, but it is a charming little estuary with a great name. The cookie is a chocolate bomb, dense and fudgy, and was a customer favorite. So much so that our gentle villagers were clamoring for it by 7:30 a.m., as soon as we opened our doors.

Procedure

- Preheat the oven to 350°F (175°C). Line two sheet pans with parchment paper.
- In a small bowl, whisk together the cocoa powder, flour, salt, and baking powder.
- In the bowl of a stand mixer fitted with the whisk attachment, combine the eggs, brown sugar, honey, espresso powder, and vanilla. Whisk on high speed until the mixture ribbons thickly.
- Put the butter and chopped chocolate in a heatproof bowl and set it over a saucepan of simmering water (to make a double boiler). Stir until melted.
- Using a sturdy wooden spoon, stir the flour mixture into the melted chocolate mixture until well combined. This becomes a very thick paste, but if you use your muscles, you'll get through it.
- Stir one third of the egg mixture into the chocolate mixture to lighten it; again, this takes a little muscle. Add the lightened chocolate mixture to the egg mixture in the mixer bowl and whisk on medium speed until the batter is smooth and shiny. Using a wooden spoon, fold in the chocolate chips.
- If the dough isn't already firm, cover the bowl with plastic wrap and refrigerate until scoopable, about 1 hour.
- Dip a medium (1½-ounce/45-ml) cookie scoop in hot water (don't dry off after dipping), then scoop leveled scoops of the dough and place them on the prepared sheet pans 1 inch (2.5 cm) apart. Dampen your hands with water and gently press down on the cookies with your palm to flatten them a bit. Bake until the cookies just begin to lose their shine on top (they'll still have a "sheen" but they will no longer be shiny), 12 to 15 minutes.

Check page 16 before proceeding for additional details on ensuring your recipes are gluten free and/or vegan.

VEGAN

Omit the ingredients in the master recipe entirely and use the following instead:

    1 cup (140 g) all-purpose flour
    ½ cup (40 g) Dutch-process cocoa powder (like Cacao Barry
        Extra Brute)
    1 tablespoon instant espresso powder
    1 teaspoon baking powder
    ½ teaspoon salt
    5 ounces (140 g) bittersweet chocolate (like Callebaut 60/40),
        finely chopped
    1 cup (200 g) sugar
    ½ cup (120 ml) canola oil
    2 tablespoons organic agave syrup
    ¼ cup (60 ml) plain almond milk
    1 large egg's worth of prepared Ener-G egg replacer (see recipe,
        page 12)
    1 teaspoon vanilla bean paste
    1 cup (170 g) bittersweet chocolate chips

- In a small bowl, whisk together the flour, cocoa powder, espresso powder, baking powder, and salt.
- Put the chopped chocolate in a heatproof bowl and place over a saucepan of simmering water (to make a double boiler). Stir until melted. Set aside.
- In the bowl of a stand mixer fitted with the whisk attachment, whisk together the sugar, oil, and agave syrup. Add the almond milk to the prepared egg replacer and stir to combine. Add the egg replacer mixture and vanilla to the sugar mixture and whisk to combine.
- Add the flour mixture and, using a wooden spoon, stir until a thick paste forms. Add the melted chocolate and stir until thoroughly mixed. Fold in the chocolate chips. Form and bake as per the master recipe.

GLUTEN FREE

Replace the flour with ¼ cup (30 g) cornstarch.

HEALTHIER

Replace the flour with ¼ cup (40 g) Nuts .com's Sprouted Super Flour (see page 220). Replace 1 of the eggs with 1 large egg's worth of flaxseed meal mixed with water (see page 12) and stir into the melted chocolate mixture. Replace the brown sugar with ½ cup (80 g) organic granulated palm sugar. For the finely chopped chocolate, use Green & Black's organic 85% bittersweet chocolate and ½ cup (40 g) Green & Black's organic unsweetened cocoa powder. You'll notice that I've not opted for an alternative to the butter. You can substitute prune puree (I use organic baby food, such as Plum Organic's Just Prunes) for some of the butter (tablespoon per tablespoon), but sometimes being happier makes you healthier. And the small amount of butter in this recipe packs a lot of happy into it. Leave out the extra chocolate chips.

Chocolate is a beautiful thing. A Swedish study found that women who consumed 45 g of chocolate every week had a 20 percent lower risk of stroke than those who consumed 9 g or less each week. Huzzah! Chocolate also has anti-inflammatory properties that, among other things, reduce cardiovascular risk. Regular consumption of the dark stuff also has been linked to a reduced risk of diabetes, reduced stress, and increased blood flow. It's full of fiber and fills you up; it's full of skin-benefitting flavonoids; and chocoholics often have lower BMIs. Many chocolates are high in fat (which is not necessarily a bad thing) and sugar, but on the whole it's a healthy ingredient as far as I'm concerned.

The Big Winooski
(PAGE 28)

Peanut Butter Sandwich Cookies
(PAGE 27)

The Mighty Mint
(PAGE 32)

Salty Dog Oats
(PAGE 36)

Samoas
(PAGE 34)

The
MIGHTY
MINT

{ MAKES 30 SANDWICH COOKIES }

Ingredients

FOR THE COOKIES

1 cup (2 sticks/225 g) unsalted butter,
    at room temperature
1 cup (200 g) sugar
2 cups (260 g) all-purpose flour
¾ cup (60 g) Dutch-process cocoa powder
    (like Cacao Barry Extra Brute)
1 teaspoon instant espresso powder
1 teaspoon salt

FOR THE FILLING

3 tablespoons boiling water, or more if needed
3 tablespoons organic palm oil shortening,
    or more if needed
⅛ teaspoon peppermint oil
2 cups (200 g) confectioners' sugar, or more
    if needed
Pinch of salt

FOR THE CHOCOLATE COATING (OPTIONAL)

1 pound (455 g) semisweet chocolate chips
    (like Guittard Akoma Extra Semisweet
    Chocolate Chips)
1 tablespoon Spectrum Organic All Vegetable
    Shortening
Pinch of salt

I'm a sucker for the smooth combination of mint and chocolate. My aunt in Germany, Tante Christel, kept a "sweets" drawer and maintained a fresh supply of soft After Eight mints to serve along with après-dinner aperitifs. She had to stock up more often than I'm sure she'd have liked because I kept slipping open the drawer and shoving those delights into my pie hole, two at a time. But quite frankly, I'll eat any riff on the theme, from a firm Peppermint Pattie to the little nuggets known as Junior Mints. But my favorite variation is the one that combines a crisp chocolate cookie with a filling of soft, peppermint-infused nom. Please forgive me as I run off to bake a batch to curb my craving.

Procedure

MAKE THE COOKIES

- Preheat the oven to 350°F (175°C). Line two sheet pans with parchment paper.
- In the bowl of a stand mixer fitted with the paddle attachment, cream together the butter and sugar until light and fluffy.
- In a large bowl, whisk together the flour, cocoa powder, espresso powder, and salt. With the mixer running on low speed, add to the creamed butter and mix until the dough comes together.
- Turn the dough out onto a work surface and gently knead until smooth. Return to the bowl and cover with plastic wrap. Refrigerate for 20 minutes.
- Using a teaspoon cookie scoop, scoop balls of dough onto the prepared sheet pans and press them flat (about ⅛ inch/3 mm thick) with the palm of your hand or the bottom of a glass.
- Bake until the cookies lose their sheen, 12 to 15 minutes. Let cool completely. Reserve the parchment-lined sheet pans if making the chocolate coating.

MAKE THE FILLING

- In a small bowl, stir together the boiling water and shortening, allowing the shortening to melt completely. Add the peppermint oil.
- In the bowl of a stand mixer fitted with the paddle attachment, combine the confectioners' sugar and salt. With the mixer on low speed, add the shortening mixture, mixing until a paste forms. If needed, add 1 tablespoon more of hot water and 1 tablespoon more of shortening if the filling is crumbly. If too runny, add 1 tablespoon more of confectioners' sugar at a time.

continued

- To fill each cookie, take a scant teaspoon of filling, roll it between your hands to form a ball, gently flatten it, and place it on the bottom of one cooled cookie. Gently press a second cookie on top, being careful as the cookies break easily. Set the assembled cookies aside.

MAKE THE CHOCOLATE COATING (OPTIONAL)

- In a large heatproof bowl, combine the chocolate chips, shortening, and salt. Place over a large saucepan half filled with simmering water (to make a double boiler) and stir constantly until melted. Keep the melted chocolate coating over the simmering water to keep it from hardening while coating the cookies.

- Using a fork, lower an assembled cookie into the melted chocolate coating to cover. Take the coated cookie from the chocolate and gently tap it on the side of the bowl to release any extra coating. Place on the reserved lined sheet pans and continue with the remaining cookies. If you prefer you can dip only half the cookie in the chocolate or simply drizzle some chocolate over each cookie for a more delicate combination. Let the cookies stand until the coating is set, about 30 minutes.

OPTIONS

Check page 16 before proceeding for additional details on ensuring your recipes are gluten free and/or vegan.

VEGAN

FOR THE COOKIES: Replace the butter with an equal amount of organic palm oil shortening. FOR THE COATING: Guittard Akoma chips, while vegan per their ingredient list, are processed near their milk chocolate facility. If this concerns you, choose a semi-sweet or bittersweet chocolate chip labeled as vegan.

GLUTEN FREE

Replace the all-purpose flour with 2 cups (320 g) finely milled brown rice flour and 1 teaspoon xanthan gum.

HEALTHIER

Forgo the filling and coating altogether and make the cookies into mint chocolate cookies: Replace half of the butter with ½ cup (120 ml) organic grapeseed oil and replace the sugar with 1 cup (160 g) organic granulated palm sugar. Cream together the remaining ½ cup (1 stick/115 g) butter and the palm sugar, then add the grapeseed oil and ¼ teaspoon peppermint oil and mix to combine. Replace the flour with 1 cup (160 g) finely milled brown rice flour and 1 cup (100 g) whole-wheat pastry flour, whisk together with the salt, and add after the grapeseed oil and peppermint oil.

SAMOAS

(MAKES 2 DOZEN COOKIES)

Ingredients

FOR THE COCONUT SABLÉ

1 cup (140 g) all-purpose flour
½ cup (55 g) coconut flour
½ cup (45 g) shredded sweetened coconut
¼ cup (50 g) sugar
½ teaspoon salt
1 cup (2 sticks/225 g) very cold unsalted butter,
    cut into small pieces
1 large egg
1 tablespoon sweetened condensed milk
1 teaspoon vanilla bean paste

FOR THE CARAMEL-COCONUT MIXTURE

3 cups (270 g) shredded sweetened coconut
1 cup (220 g) light brown sugar, packed
1 cup (200 g) granulated sugar
6 tablespoons (85 g) unsalted butter, cut into very
    small pieces
2 tablespoons organic unrefined virgin coconut oil
½ cup (120 ml) light corn syrup
¼ cup (60 ml) sweetened condensed milk
1 tablespoon vanilla bean paste
1 teaspoon salt

TO FINISH

¼ cup (40 g) bittersweet chocolate chips, melted

There was a time when I couldn't stomach the *thought* of coconut, let alone consume it. I feel guilty for maligning such a lovely ingredient for all these years. All it took was a taste of that favorite Girl Scout cookie, the one that's just coated in the stuff, to convince me that it was worth experimenting with it in other applications. But first, let's revisit the cookie that first converted me into a girl who's cuckoo for coconut.

Procedure

MAKE THE COCONUT SABLÉ

- Preheat the oven to 350°F (175°C). Line two sheet pans with parchment paper.
- In the bowl of a food processor, combine the all-purpose flour, coconut flour, coconut, sugar, and salt. Pulse a few times to combine. Add the butter and pulse again until the mixture resembles coarse cornmeal.
- In a small bowl, whisk together the egg, condensed milk, and vanilla. Pulse the mixture in the processor while adding the egg mixture. Continue pulsing until the mixture looks uniformly damp but doesn't yet come together as a dough. Transfer the dough to a large piece of plastic wrap. Press the dough into a disk and wrap it up. Refrigerate for at least 20 minutes.
- Roll the dough out to between ¼ and ⅛ inch (6 mm and 3 mm) thick on a lightly floured surface. Using a 3-inch (7.5-cm) round cookie cutter, cut rounds from the dough and transfer them to the prepared pans, spacing about 1 inch (2.5 cm) apart. Leftover dough can be gathered together and rolled out one more time. Bake until lightly golden brown on the edges, 10 to 12 minutes. Let cool completely.

MAKE THE CARAMEL-COCONUT MIXTURE

- Preheat the oven to 300°F (150°C). Line a sheet pan with parchment paper.
- Toast the coconut by spreading it in an even layer on the prepared pan. Bake for a few minutes to brown. Stir the coconut and continue baking until the coconut is uniformly medium to dark golden brown; watch and stir frequently, as it burns quite easily. Transfer the coconut to a large mixing bowl.

continued

- In a heavy saucepan, combine both sugars, the butter, oil, corn syrup, condensed milk, vanilla, and salt and stir constantly with a wooden spoon over medium heat until the sugar is completely melted. Attach a candy thermometer and continue stirring until the caramel reaches 243°F (120°C). Pour the caramel into the bowl of coconut and stir until well coated. Let sit for 5 minutes to allow the caramel to set up a bit but don't allow to cool and harden.
- Scoop 1½ tablespoons of the caramel-coconut mixture onto the top of a cooled cookie and press down gently so that the mixture goes just to the edge of the cookie. Use your thumb to create an indentation in the center of the cookie. The mixture should be hot as you work with it; work quickly and wear a pair of nonlatex gloves to protect your fingers from the hot caramel as you work.

TO FINISH

- Melt the chocolate over a double boiler. Drizzle the topped cookies with melted chocolate. Let set, about 10 minutes.

Check page 16 before proceeding for additional details on ensuring your recipes are gluten free and/or vegan.

VEGAN

FOR THE COCONUT SABLÉ: Replace the butter with 1 cup (240 ml) organic unrefined virgin coconut oil that's been chilled and cut into small cubes. Replace the egg with 1 large egg's worth of flaxseed meal mixed with water (see page 12). Replace the condensed milk with 1 tablespoon full-fat coconut milk. FOR THE CARAMEL-COCONUT MIXTURE: Replace the butter with 6 tablespoons (90 ml) organic virgin unrefined coconut oil, chilled, to make 8 tablespoons (120 ml) coconut oil in total. Replace the condensed milk with ¼ cup (60 ml) full-fat coconut milk.

GLUTEN FREE

FOR THE COCONUT SABLÉ: Replace the flour with 1 cup (160 g) finely milled brown rice flour and ½ teaspoon xanthan gum. When assembling, press the caramel-coconut mixture gently onto the sablé, as it's very delicate.

HEALTHIER

FOR THE COCONUT SABLÉ: Replace the flour with 1 cup (100 g) organic whole-wheat pastry flour. Replace the sugar with ¼ cup (40 g) organic granulated palm sugar. Reduce the butter to ½ cup (1 stick/115 g) and add ½ cup (120 ml) chilled organic unrefined virgin coconut oil cut into small cubes. FOR THE CARAMEL-COCONUT MIXTURE: Replace the coconut with unsweetened shredded coconut. Replace both sugars with 2 cups (320 g) organic granulated palm sugar. Replace 2 tablespoons of the butter with 2 tablespoons organic unrefined virgin coconut oil for a total of 4 tablespoons (60 ml) coconut oil and 4 tablespoons (55 g) butter. Replace the corn syrup with organic agave syrup. Replace the condensed milk with ¼ cup (60 ml) full-fat coconut milk.

Salty DOG OATS

{ MAKES ABOUT 30 COOKIES }

Ingredients

1 ¾ cups (230 g) all-purpose flour
1 teaspoon kosher salt
1 teaspoon baking powder
¼ teaspoon baking soda
½ teaspoon ground cinnamon
¾ cup (1 ½ sticks/170 g) unsalted butter,
     slightly colder than room temperature
1 cup (220 g) light brown sugar, packed
½ cup (100 g) granulated sugar
2 large eggs
1 teaspoon vanilla bean paste
2 cups (160 g) rolled oats (not quick cooking)
1 cup (170 g) raisins
Extra-coarse-grain sea salt, to sprinkle on top

I'd never been much of an oatmeal-raisin cookie gal until I started making my own. Maybe it was simply that I'd grown older and my tastes had changed. Maybe it was because the cookie I made was just that good. Either way, it's always brightened my heart that even when this recipe is made "straight," without any jury-rigging, it's got a healthy dose of heart-loving oats to get your ticker thumping.

Procedure

- Combine the flour, kosher salt, baking powder, baking soda, and cinnamon in a bowl and whisk together for 30 seconds to evenly distribute the leavening.
- In a stand mixer fitted with the paddle attachment, cream together the butter and both sugars until light and fluffy. Add the eggs one at a time, mixing each until fully incorporated into the batter before moving on. Add the vanilla and mix.
- With the mixer on low speed, slowly add the flour mixture until just combined. Add the oats and mix for a few seconds on low, then add the raisins and mix until distributed throughout. Chill the dough in the refrigerator for at least 30 minutes.
- Preheat the oven to 350°F (175°C). Line two sheet pans with parchment paper.
- Scoop the dough with a medium (1 ½-ounce/45-ml) cookie scoop onto the prepared pans and press down on the dome of the dough to flatten just a bit. Sprinkle the top of each cookie with a wee bit of coarse salt. Bake, turning the pans halfway through the baking time to make sure the cookies brown evenly, 12 to 15 minutes.

Check page 16 before proceeding for additional details on ensuring your recipes are gluten free and/or vegan.

VEGAN

Replace the butter with an equal amount of Earth Balance Vegan Shortening or Spectrum Organic All Vegetable Shortening. Instead of the eggs, whisk together ½ cup (120 ml) warm oat milk with 2 tablespoons flaxseed meal and let sit for 10 minutes to gel before adding as instructed.

GLUTEN FREE

Replace the flour with 1¾ cups (280 g) finely milled brown rice flour and 1½ teaspoons xanthan gum.

HEALTHIER

Replace the flour with ½ cup (60 g) spelt flour, ½ cup (80 g) finely milled brown rice flour, and ¾ cup (90 g) whole-wheat flour. Replace 4 tablespoons of the butter with 4 tablespoons (60 ml) prune puree and add the prune puree (I use organic baby food, such as Plum Organic's Just Prunes) just before adding the eggs. Replace the brown sugar and granulated sugar with 1¼ cups (200 g) organic granulated palm sugar.

MACARON

{ MAKES ABOUT 20 SANDWICH COOKIES }

Ingredients

6 ounces (170 g) confectioners' sugar
4 ounces (115 g) pistachio or almond flour
3 large egg whites
¼ teaspoon salt
2 ounces (55 g) superfine sugar
2 drops gel food coloring (optional)
½ cup (120 ml) black currant preserves, or
    your preference

How is it possible to make macaron with anything but egg whites? Impossible, right? It's a cookie whose very nature is dependent on the special properties of egg whites. Well, there are a few tricks we can employ that will get you very satisfying results without the help of a hen and will let you participate in the wonderful world of meringue. And the master recipe is already gluten free. Another dessert win-win.

(Note: The ingredients for this recipe are given in weights. Macaron are finicky to begin with, so I implore you to weigh the ingredients to give yourself a fighting chance.)

Procedure

- Preheat the oven to 300°F (150°C). Line two sheet pans with parchment paper.
- In a mixing bowl, whisk together the confectioners' sugar and pistachio flour until combined. Sift the mixture two times after whisking and set aside.
- In the bowl of a stand mixer fitted with the whisk attachment, combine the egg whites and salt. Whisk on high speed until foamy. Slowly add the superfine sugar and continue whisking on high speed until the meringue is very stiff. Add the food coloring if using and whisk for 30 seconds to 1 minute more or until the color is evenly distributed.
- Fold the confectioners' sugar mixture into the meringue, using sweeping and smooshing motions. Continue folding and smooshing until the mixture flows like ketchup (this is called *macaronage*, and the fluidity of the batter is often described as "lavalike").
- Fill a large pastry bag fitted with a large plain tip with the batter. Pipe 1½-inch (4-cm) rounds, spacing them about 3 inches (7.5 cm) apart. Tap each pan on the counter a few times to release any large air bubbles and let stand, uncovered, for 40 minutes so that the macaron form a "skin."
- Bake on the middle rack of the oven for 16 minutes, turning the pans halfway through the baking time. Let cool completely.
- Place a scant teaspoon of preserves on a completely cooled cookie and sandwich with a second. Repeat until all the macaron are sandwiched.

Check page 16 before proceeding for additional details on ensuring your recipes are gluten free and/or vegan.

VEGAN

Omit the egg whites. In the bowl of a stand mixer fitted with the whisk attachment, combine 4 tablespoons (32 g) Ener-G egg replacer (not prepared) and 10 tablespoons (150 ml) water. Whisk until well combined and no clumps remain. Let sit for 3 minutes undisturbed. Add 1 teaspoon Versawhip 600K and ¼ teaspoon xanthan gum. Whisk until foamy. Slowly add the sugar and continue whisking until stiff peaks form but not so stiff that the "meringue" is dry (unlike the master recipe, you don't want the meringue to clump inside the whisk). Add the food coloring if using and whisk for 30 seconds more. Fold in the sifted confectioners' sugar mixture as described in the recipe. Pipe and let sit at room temperature at least 1 hour and up to 2 hours (the longer you allow a skin to form on these, the better the final texture). Bake as directed.

VEGAN

Replace the egg whites with 1 large egg's worth of flaxseed meal mixed with water (see page 12) and 1 large egg's worth of prepared Ener-G egg replacer (see recipe, page 12). Add ½ cup (50 g) almond flour. Put all the ingredients in a food processor and pulse until a smooth paste forms. Scoop onto the pan as in the recipe, but after gently pressing on the almonds, bake immediately. Bake for 15 to 20 minutes.

GLUTEN FREE

The main recipe is already gluten free.

GLUTEN FREE

Replace the flour with ½ cup (80 g) finely milled brown rice flour. Bake for 10 to 12 minutes.

NUT FREE

If you've been hankering for macaron but have a tree nut allergy, you can replace the nut flour with golden flaxseed meal or white chia flour. I suggest buying flax meals/flours that have already been milled, as they contain less oil than the freshly ground variety, which will result in flat macaron.

HEALTHIER

Sugar is integral to a well-made macaron, but we can replace half of the superfine sugar with 1 ounce (28 g) maple sugar and use organic confectioners' sugar.

HEALTHIER

Replace the ¼ cup (50 g) sugar used in the food processor with ¼ cup (40 g) organic granulated palm sugar. Reduce the sugar that goes into the whipped egg whites to 2 tablespoons. Replace the flour with 2 tablespoons spelt flour. Bake for 10 to 12 minutes.

This is an angel of a cookie. It's light. It's slightly crispy on the outside. Once you get into the meat of it, it's delightfully chewy and full of almond flavor. It's triply almondy, as a matter of fact: Almond paste, almond extract, and sliced almonds bring the nutty deliciousness home. It's also one of those cookies that tastes as if it should be much harder to make than it is. Let me tell you, it's so damn easy. And the baked cookies freeze well, too.

ALMOND COOKIES

{ MAKES 16 COOKIES }

Ingredients

8 ounces (225 g) almond paste
2 large egg whites
½ cup (100 g) sugar
2 tablespoons all-purpose flour
½ teaspoon almond extract
½ teaspoon vanilla bean paste
¼ teaspoon salt
¼ cup (20 g) sliced almonds

Procedure

- Line a sheet pan with parchment paper.
- In the bowl of a food processor, combine the almond paste, 1 of the egg whites, ¼ cup (50 g) of the sugar, the flour, almond extract, vanilla, and salt. Pulse until the mixture becomes a paste. Transfer to a large bowl.
- In a metal bowl, whisk the remaining egg white until frothy. Slowly add the remaining ¼ cup (50 g) sugar and continue whisking until you achieve medium-stiff peaks. Stir one third of the egg white mixture into the almond paste mixture to lighten it using a wooden spoon. Using a large rubber spatula, fold the remaining egg white mixture into the almond paste mixture until well combined.
- Using a medium (1½-ounce/45-ml) cookie scoop, scoop the cookie dough onto the prepared pan, spacing the cookies about 3 inches (7.5 cm) apart. Press an almond slice onto the center of each cookie. Leave the unbaked cookies, uncovered, out on your countertop for at least 2 hours to allow a "skin" to form on the outside of the cookies.
- Preheat the oven to 350°F (175°C).
- Bake the cookies for 12 to 15 minutes, until the edges of the cookies are golden brown.

Spekulatius Cookies
(PAGE 45)

Lime Meltaways

call your mother

Bergamot
Fortune Cookies
(PAGE 46)

These lovely tart nuggets do not disappoint—and do melt in your mouth. They are buttery, but the refreshing citrus notes eradicate any lingering guilt you may have harbored for eating so many cookies. I like to stamp each cookie with a rubber letter stamp to personalize these beauties, but you can leave them unstamped and they'll taste just as wonderful.

Procedure

- Preheat the oven to 325°F (165°C). Line two sheet pans with parchment paper.
- In the bowl of a food processor, pulse together the flour, cornstarch, confectioners' sugar, granulated sugar, lime powder, lime zest, and salt. Add the butter and pulse until the mixture resembles coarse cornmeal.
- In a small bowl, whisk together the egg, condensed milk, and vanilla. Slowly add the egg mixture to the flour mixture while pulsing; continue until the dough just begins to come together. Turn the dough out onto a lightly floured surface. Gently knead it until smooth.
- Using parchment paper, form the dough into a log 2 inches (5 cm) in diameter. Wrap the log tightly in the parchment then wrap tightly in plastic wrap. Tuck the log into an empty paper towel roll to keep a round shape or shape it into a long rectangle and place on a flat shelf in the refrigerator for at least 20 minutes and up to 2 hours; you can also freeze the dough for up to 2 weeks (no need to defrost—cut and bake straight from the freezer).
- Cut ¼-inch-thick (6-mm-thick) rounds or rectangles from the log, dip the edges in sparkling sugar, if using, and place on the prepared pans, ½ inch (12 mm) apart. Stamp with cookie letter stamps, if using. Bake until barely golden at the edges, about 10 minutes.

LIME
MELTAWAYS

{ MAKES 20 COOKIES }

Ingredients

2 cups (260 g) all-purpose flour
1 cup (120 g) cornstarch
½ cup (50 g) confectioners' sugar
¼ cup (50 g) granulated sugar
1 tablespoon lime powder (available online and at baking supply shops), or an additional 1 tablespoon lime zest
1 tablespoon lime zest (zested with a Microplane)
1 teaspoon salt
1¼ cups (2½ sticks/280 g) cold unsalted butter, cut into small pieces
1 large egg
3 tablespoons sweetened condensed milk
1 teaspoon vanilla bean paste
½ cup (100 g) sparkling sugar or Sugar in the Raw (optional)

Check page 16 before proceeding for additional details on ensuring your recipes are gluten free and/or vegan.

VEGAN

Replace the butter with 1¼ cups (280 g) Earth Balance Vegan Shortening; prior to using, cut the shortening into small pieces and freeze for at least 30 minutes. Replace the egg with 1 large egg's worth of flaxseed meal mixed with water (see page 12). Replace the condensed milk with 3 tablespoons full-fat coconut milk.

VEGAN

The cookies are already vegan.

GLUTEN FREE

Replace the flour with 1 cup sweet white rice flour (160 g), ½ cup (80 g) finely milled brown rice flour, ½ cup (70 g) tapioca starch, and 1 teaspoon xanthan gum. Bake for 12 to 15 minutes.

GLUTEN-FREE & HEALTHIER

Reduce the oven temperature to 325°F (165°C). Replace the brown sugar with ½ cup (80 g) plus 2 tablespoons organic granulated palm sugar. Use the grapeseed oil. Replace the all-purpose and graham flours with 1 cup (160 g) plus 2 tablespoons brown rice flour, ½ cup (50 g) quinoa flour, and 1 teaspoon xanthan gum. Use brown rice flour to dust the cookie stamp. Bake for 10 to 12 minutes.

HEALTHIER

Replace the flour with 1 cup (120 g) spelt flour and 1 cup (100 g) organic whole-wheat pastry flour. Replace both sugars with ½ cup (95 g) Sucanat. Replace half of the butter with 10 tablespoons (150 ml) organic unrefined virgin coconut oil that's been melted to measure and then resolidified; add both at the same time to the food processor. Replace the condensed milk with 3 tablespoons full-fat coconut milk.

Also known as speculoos, these crunchy, spicy wafer-thin cookies are both elegant and ridiculously addictive. In its "all out" iteration, it's already vegan. Graham flour adds a lovely nuttiness to the proceedings and is full of fiber. So this is a SPEK-tacular cookie in my book.

Procedure

- Preheat the oven to 375°F (190°C). Line two sheet pans with parchment paper.
- In the bowl of a stand mixer fitted with the paddle attachment, mix together the brown sugar, oil, coffee, ginger, cinnamon, white pepper, cloves, and nutmeg.
- In a small bowl, whisk together the all-purpose flour, graham flour if using, baking soda, and salt. With the mixer running on low speed, add the flour mixture to the mixer bowl all at once and mix until the flour is completely incorporated. Turn the dough out onto a lightly floured work surface and gently knead until completely smooth. Place the dough in a bowl and cover with plastic wrap. Refrigerate for 20 minutes to 1 hour.
- Using a teaspoon scoop, scoop and place the dough 2 inches (5 cm) apart on the prepared pans. Dust a 2-inch (5-cm) cookie or springerle stamp (see Resources on page 220) with flour and gently press down on each cookie to create a pattern, using more flour as needed to make sure the dough doesn't stick to the stamp. (This is a delicate dough and isn't the easiest to handle. Be gentle with it and place in the freezer for a few minutes if it gets too soft or difficult to handle to make stamping easier.) Trim any excess from around the cookie and put it into a scrap pile. Gather the scrap dough together, then scoop and stamp it. Don't use any trimmings a third time.
- Bake until the edges begin to brown, 8 to 10 minutes.

SPEKULATIUS COOKIES

{ MAKES 40 COOKIES }

Ingredients

¾ cup (165 g) dark brown sugar, packed
½ cup (120 ml) canola or organic grapeseed oil
3 tablespoons brewed coffee, at room temperature
1 teaspoon ground ginger
½ teaspoon ground cinnamon
¼ teaspoon ground white pepper
¼ teaspoon ground cloves
Pinch of freshly grated nutmeg
1½ cups (210 g) plus 2 tablespoons all-purpose flour, plus more for dusting
1 tablespoon graham flour (optional)
1½ teaspoons baking soda
1 teaspoon salt

Bergamot FORTUNE COOKIES

{ MAKES 1 DOZEN COOKIES }

Ingredients

Boiling water
1 Earl Grey tea bag
1 cup (200 g) sugar
¾ cup (105 g) all-purpose flour
¼ cup (30 g) cornstarch
½ teaspoon salt
3 large egg whites
5 tablespoons (70 g) unsalted butter, melted
12 handwritten fortunes, written on 2-by-
    ¼-inch (5-cm-by-6-mm) strips of paper

Fortune cookies are really just tuile cookies bent into a shape. The hardest part of making these is getting the hang of spreading the batter evenly and thinly. The second hardest part is twisting them into shape while they're still hot. If you have very delicate digits, I recommend that you only bake a few at a time so that you have the time to shape all the super-hot cookies before they cool and get too brittle to bend.

Procedure

- Pour a small amount of boiling water, a little over 3 tablespoons, over the tea bag and let it steep until the tea cools. Squeeze and discard the tea bag and keep the liquid. This creates a nice concentration of bergamot flavor. Set aside.
- Preheat the oven to 400°F (205°C). Line a half sheet pan with a Silpat and spray with nonstick cooking spray.
- In the bowl of a stand mixer fitted with the paddle attachment, combine the sugar, flour, cornstarch, and salt. Add the egg whites, butter, and tea. Mix together until a smooth paste forms.
- On the prepared sheet pan, spread 1 tablespoon of the batter with a small offset spatula into a 4-inch (10-cm) round. Until you get proficient at folding the cookies, make only two or three rounds of batter per sheet pan, spacing them evenly apart.
- Bake until the edges of the cookie just start to brown, about 6 minutes, turning the sheet pan halfway through the baking time. While the cookies are still hot, use an offset spatula to carefully pick up a round; quickly fold it in half but do not crease, slip a fortune into the tubelike opening, then bend the cookie at the center, drawing the two ends toward each other. Fold the remaining cookies while they are hot.
- Spray the Silpat with nonstick cooking spray again. Continue spreading, baking, and folding the cookies until the remainder of the batter is gone.

Check page 16 before proceeding for additional details on ensuring your recipes are gluten free and/or vegan.

VEGAN

Steep the tea in ¼ cup plus 3 tablespoons (105 ml) boiling water. Reduce the sugar to ½ cup (100 g). Reduce the flour to ½ cup (70 g), the cornstarch to 1 tablespoon, and the salt to ¼ teaspoon. Omit the egg whites. Replace the butter with ¼ cup (55 g) Earth Balance Vegan Shortening, melted. Stir together ¼ cup (60 ml) of the steeped tea with 1 tablespoon Energ-G egg replacer (not prepared) until smooth. Add the shortening, along with the steeped tea mixture to the flour mixture. Mix with a paddle attachment. Add the remaining tea 1 tablespoon at a time, if needed, until the mixture is a spreadable batter, still holding its shape but not watery. Bake until the edges are deeply golden brown and the middle of the cookie is baked through, 6 to 7 minutes. Fold as per the master recipe.

HEALTHIER

Replace the sugar with ¾ cup (115 g) maple sugar. Replace the flour with ¾ cup (75 g) organic whole-wheat pastry flour. Replace 2 tablespoons of the butter with organic refined virgin coconut oil (melted along with the butter). Reduce the oven temperature to 375°F (190°C) so the maple sugar doesn't burn. Fold as per the master recipe.

GLUTEN FREE

Steep the tea in 6 tablespoons (90 ml) boiling water. Replace the flour with ½ cup (50 g) finely milled oat flour, ½ cup (70 g) tapioca starch, and ½ teaspoon xanthan gum and stir together with the salt. Reduce the sugar to ¾ cup (150 g). Reduce the butter to 3 tablespoons. Mix the ingredients, along with the egg whites, per the master recipe. Instead of baking, spray a nonstick griddle with nonstick cooking spray and heat over medium heat on the stovetop. Spread a tablespoon of batter at a time on the grill into a 4-inch (10-cm) round, making sure that the batter is spread uniformly thin. Allow the edges to brown and the middle to become nicely golden brown, 4 to 5 minutes, then flip to cook through completely, an additional 1 to 2 minutes. Fold as per the master recipe.

Coconut Macaroons
(PAGE 51)

Starry Starry Nights

You know what I love about these cookies? They are the most delicious and chocolaty treats you'll ever eat. And they're gluten free from the get-go. When I first created them in 2004, it wasn't my intention to make a gluten-free cookie; I just wanted to get as close to a "baked truffle" as I could muster. I wanted a cookie that you could keep around for your chocolate fix but that wouldn't melt like a chocolate truffle. You can freeze them for up to a month after baking and just pop one in your mouth when you need a fix!

{ MAKES 50 SMALL COOKIES }

Procedure

- In the bowl of a stand mixer fitted with the whisk attachment, combine the eggs, ¼ cup (50 g) of the sugar, and the honey. Mix on high speed until the mixture ribbons thickly.
- Put the chocolate and butter in a heatproof bowl and set it over a saucepan of simmering water (to make a double boiler) until melted. Let cool slightly.
- In a small mixing bowl, whisk together the almond flour, cocoa powder, and salt. Add the melted chocolate and stir well. Add one quarter of the egg mixture to the chocolate to lighten it, stirring with a wooden spoon until no egg streaks are visible. Add the remaining egg mixture and gently fold with a large rubber spatula until completely incorporated. Cover with plastic wrap and chill until firm, 2 hours to overnight. It is imperative that the mixture is incredibly firm.
- Put the remaining ½ cup (100 g) sugar in a small bowl. Fill a heatproof mug with very hot water. Line a sheet pan with parchment paper.
- Using a teaspoon cookie scoop or a melon baller, first dip the scoop in the hot water and then scoop out a round of batter. Roll the ball in the sugar, then place it on the prepared pan (you can space them very close together to freeze; you will use another sheet pan to bake off). Continue to scoop and coat the balls. Cover the sheet pan with plastic wrap and freeze for 1 to 2 hours.
- Preheat the oven to 350°F (175°C).
- Line another sheet pan with parchment, remove the cookie-filled sheet pan from the freezer, re-dip each cookie in sugar, and place the cookies 1 inch (2.5 cm) apart on the new sheet pan, placing any cookies that didn't fit onto the sheet pan back in the freezer until their turn in the oven comes. Immediately bake for 10 minutes, turning the sheet pan after 5 minutes. The cookies will look slightly cracked but the sugar will not be browned when they are done baking.

Ingredients

2 large eggs
¾ cup (150 g) sugar
1 tablespoon honey
10 ounces (280 g) bittersweet chocolate (like Lindt 70%), finely chopped
2 tablespoons unsalted butter
1 cup (100 g) almond flour or very finely ground blanched slivered almonds
2 tablespoons Dutch-process cocoa powder (like Cacao Barry Extra Brute)
½ teaspoon salt

Check page 16 before proceeding for additional details on ensuring your recipes are gluten free and/or vegan.

VEGAN

Replace the eggs with 1 large egg's worth of prepared Ener-G egg replacer (see recipe, page 12) and 1 large egg's worth of flaxseed meal mixed with water (see page 12). Reduce the sugar to ½ cup (100 g) in the dough. Combine the egg replacers with the sugar and 1 tablespoon agave syrup (instead of honey). Whisk until combined. Replace the butter with 2 tablespoons Earth Balance Vegan Buttery Sticks. Increase the almond flour to 2 cups (200 g).

VEGAN

FOR THE MACAROONS: Omit the ingredients in the master recipe entirely and do the following instead: In a large bowl, toss together 3½ cups (315 g) unsweetened shredded coconut, ½ cup (55 g) coconut flour, ½ cup (100 g) sugar, and 1 teaspoon salt. In a small bowl, prepare 2 large eggs' worth of flaxseed meal mixed with water (see page 12). After the flax mixture has had time to gel, add ½ cup (120 ml) coconut cream and 1 teaspoon vanilla extract and stir to combine. Pour the coconut cream mixture over the shredded coconut mixture and stir with a wooden spoon until well combined. (You may have to use your fingers to ensure that the mixture is well combined.) Don't be delicate in shaping the macaroons. Press them firmly to hold their shape.

GLUTEN FREE

The cookies are already gluten free.

GLUTEN FREE

The cookies are already gluten free.

HEALTHIER

Replace the sugar with ¾ cup (120 g) organic granulated palm sugar or ¾ cup (145 g) Sucanat.

HEALTHIER

FOR THE MACAROONS: Replace the sugar with Sucanat or organic granulated palm sugar. Use organic unsweetened shredded coconut. TO FINISH: Use organic bittersweet chocolate.

Coconut macaroons are such simple cookies, it always amazes me how much pure delight they offer. I think their secret is the caramelized, browned goodness that gathers at the edges of the coconutty mounds as they bake. Macaroons are also, by nature, gluten free (hence their appearance on many a Passover dessert plate).

Procedure

MAKE THE MACAROONS

- Preheat the oven to 300°F (150°C). Line a sheet pan with parchment paper.
- In a heatproof bowl, combine the egg whites, coconut, sugar, coconut flour, vanilla, and salt. Set the bowl over a saucepan of simmering water (to make a double boiler) and stir occasionally to prevent the bottom from burning. Cook until the batter is hot and has thickened slightly, about 15 minutes.
- With a medium (1½-ounce/45-ml) cookie scoop, drop the batter onto the prepared pan; press the sides of each mound to flatten them, then pinch at the top to make a pyramid shape. Bake until the edges are dark golden brown, 15 to 20 minutes. Let cool completely.

TO FINISH

- In a microwave-safe bowl, combine the chocolate and shortening. Microwave at 50 percent power in 30-second bursts, stirring the mixture at each break, until melted. Dip the top of each cooled macaroon in the chocolate to create a capstone on each cookie. Place on a piece of parchment and allow the chocolate to set, about 10 minutes.

Coconut
MACAROONS

{ MAKES 20 MACAROONS }

Ingredients

FOR THE MACAROONS
4 large egg whites
3½ cups (315 g) sweetened shredded
    coconut
¾ cup (150 g) sugar
¼ cup (30 g) coconut flour
1 teaspoon vanilla extract
½ teaspoon salt

TO FINISH
3 ounces (85 g) bittersweet chocolate,
    finely chopped
1 teaspoon vegetable shortening

Rugelach

Hazelnut Linzer Hearts
(PAGE 55)

Rugelach are a sumptuous swirl of a cookie—a beautiful helix—and delicious to boot. This dough is cream cheese–based, giving the finished cookie a smooth and sumptuous mouthfeel. Rugelach are suited to any number of fillings, so you have limitless options, from berry jams to Nutella. I use Persian pistachios because the pop of bright green they offer is so stunning; they're worth seeking out, but you can certainly use regular pistachios instead.

RUGELACH

{ MAKES 36 COOKIES }

Procedure

MAKE THE DOUGH

- In the bowl of a stand mixer fitted with the paddle attachment, cream together the cream cheese, butter, sugar, and salt until creamy. Add the vanilla and milk and mix until incorporated.
- With the mixer running on low speed, add the flour at once and mix until just incorporated; don't overwork the dough.
- Turn the dough out onto a floured work surface and lightly knead until smooth. Divide the dough into three even pieces (if you're going to be exact, each piece will weigh 1 pound 1 ounce/485 g). Pat each piece of dough into a disk and cover with plastic wrap. Refrigerate for 1 hour.

ASSEMBLE THE COOKIES

- Preheat the oven to 350°F (175°C). Line two sheet pans with parchment paper.
- Roll each disk of cold dough on a lightly floured surface into a 12-inch (30.5-cm) round. Score the dough into twelve equal wedges. (Don't cut through just yet: Unless you have a pie marker, you won't be as good at this as you'd like and your pieces will be unequal—score first and you'll be able to make corrections.) Once you feel that your wedges are all equal, cut the dough all the way through into twelve wedges.
- Set aside 3 tablespoons of the pistachios. Spread ¼ cup (60 ml) of the preserves over the entirety of each round of dough, then sprinkle the three rounds with the remaining pistachios. Starting with the wide end, roll up each dough wedge, jam side in, toward its point. Place each on the prepared pans. Brush each with egg wash. Sprinkle each with the reserved pistachios and the Sugar in the Raw. Bake until lightly golden brown, 20 minutes.

Ingredients

FOR THE DOUGH

2 (8-ounce/225-g) packages cream cheese
2 cups (4 sticks/450 g) unsalted butter, at room temperature
1 cup (200 g) sugar
1 teaspoon salt
1 tablespoon vanilla extract
1 tablespoon whole milk
4 cups (520 g) all-purpose flour

FOR THE ASSEMBLY

½ cup (55 g) chopped Persian pistachios
¾ cup (180 ml) black currant preserves
1 large egg whisked together with 1 tablespoon water to make an egg wash
2 tablespoons Sugar in the Raw

Check page 16 before proceeding for additional details on ensuring your recipes are gluten free and/or vegan.

VEGAN

Replace the cream cheese with 1 (8-ounce/225-g) package vegan cream cheese. Replace the butter with 1 cup (225 g) Earth Balance Vegan Shortening. In the bowl of a stand mixer fitted with the paddle attachment, combine the vegan cream cheese, shortening, and sugar until smooth. Combine 2 tablespoons Ener-G egg replacer (not prepared) and ½ cup (120 ml) water in a bowl and stir until smooth. Add ½ cup (120 ml) full-fat coconut milk, the egg replacer mixture, and the vanilla to the vegan cream cheese mixture and mix until combined. Add the flour and salt and mix until the dough comes together. Replace the egg wash with ¼ cup (60 ml) plain soy milk.

GLUTEN FREE

Replace the flour with 3 cups (480 g) finely milled brown rice flour, 1 cup (135 g) sweet white sorghum flour, and 2 teaspoons xanthan gum.

HEALTHIER

Replace half of the butter with Earth Balance Vegan Buttery Sticks. Replace the sugar with 1 cup (160 g) organic granulated palm sugar. Replace the flour with 4 cups (480 g) white whole-wheat flour.

VEGAN

Replace the butter with 1 cup (225 g) Earth Balance Vegan Shortening. Replace the egg with 1 egg's worth of prepared Ener-G egg replacer (see recipe, page 12). Replace the condensed milk with 1 tablespoon full-fat coconut milk.

GLUTEN FREE

Replace the flour with 1½ cups (240 g) finely milled brown rice flour and ½ teaspoon xanthan gum.

HEALTHIER

Replace the flour with 1½ cups (150 g) whole-wheat pastry flour. Replace the sugars with 1 cup (160 g) organic granulated palm sugar. Use organic sweetened condensed milk (available at Trader Joe's). Add 1 tablespoon orange juice to the egg and condensed milk mixture.

Anything "linzer" reminds me of my *mutti*. My mother made *Linzerkuchen*, a simple Austrian tart from the town of Linz, for special occasions, especially as she fell ill and couldn't muster the energy to spend an entire day in the kitchen whipping up multicomponent delicacies. No matter its simplicity, when she made a linzer tart, it was always beautiful, sophisticated, and full of whimsy, just like my mother. I have turned her tart into individual cookie hearts in honor of her boundless spirit.

Hazelnut LINZER HEARTS

{ MAKES 10 SANDWICH COOKIES }

Procedure

- Preheat the oven to 325°F (165°C). Line two half sheet pans with parchment paper.
- In a large mixing bowl, combine the ground hazelnuts, all-purpose flour, cornstarch, salt, orange zest, baking powder, and cinnamon and whisk for 30 seconds to evenly distribute the leavening.
- In the bowl of a stand mixer fitted with the paddle attachment, cream together the butter and sugars until light and fluffy. Scrape down the sides and bottom of the bowl.
- In a small bowl, whisk together the egg and condensed milk. Add the egg mixture to the butter mixture and mix until combined. Add the flour mixture all at once and mix until the dough just comes together. Turn the dough out onto a lightly floured work surface. Gently squeeze the mixture together to form a disk and wrap in plastic wrap. Refrigerate for 30 minutes or until cold.
- Divide the dough in half. On a lightly floured work surface, roll out one half of the dough to a little thicker than ⅛ inch (3 mm). Using a 4-inch (10-cm) heart-shaped cookie cutter, cut out heart shapes from the dough and carefully transfer them to a prepared pan. Then, using a smaller heart-shaped cutter or a small round cookie cutter, stamp out the center of each cookie so that you are left with 4-inch (10-cm) hearts that have a cutout. These will be the "top" part of the cookie. Gently squeeze together any dough scraps and continue stamping out. Refrigerate the dough hearts.
- Roll out the second half of the dough to the same thickness and, using the same heart shape, stamp out additional hearts. Place the cookies 1 inch (2.5 cm) apart on the second prepared pan. Spread 1 teaspoon of the preserves over each cookie, leaving a ¼-inch (6-mm) border not covered with preserves, and top with the cookie hearts that have the cutouts. Press gently along the edges to seal. Bake until just golden brown around the edges, 12 to 15 minutes. Let cool completely.

Ingredients

1 cup (85 g) finely ground toasted hazelnuts, or 1 cup (100 g) almond flour
1½ cups (210 g) all-purpose flour
½ cup (60 g) cornstarch
1 teaspoon fine sea salt
1 teaspoon grated orange zest
½ teaspoon baking powder
¼ teaspoon ground cinnamon
1 cup (2 sticks/225 g) unsalted butter, at room temperature
½ cup (100 g) granulated sugar
½ cup (110 g) light brown sugar, packed
1 large egg
1 tablespoon sweetened condensed milk
¼ cup (60 ml) lingonberry preserves

MAPLE MADELEINES

{ MAKES 16 COOKIES }

Ingredients

½ cup (60 g) pastry flour
½ teaspoon instant espresso powder
½ teaspoon salt
¼ teaspoon baking powder
Grated zest of ½ lemon
¼ cup (50 g) granulated sugar
2 ounces (55 g) maple sugar
2 large eggs
1 large egg yolk
1 cup (2 sticks/225 g) unsalted butter,
     melted and cooled to room temperature
¼ cup (25 g) confectioners' sugar

Every spring, just as the temperature rises above freezing during the day but still dips below at night, we Vermonters tap our sugar maples. We collect the clear sap and start the great Green Mountain tradition of sugaring. Evaporating the sap yields the famous maple syrup (it takes four gallons of maple sap to make one quart of maple syrup). The lesser-known byproduct of the process is maple sugar, a silty, light brown beauty of a sugar that infuses baked goods with a hint of amber sweetness. Delicate madeleines are the perfect vehicle for its maple goodness.

Procedure

- Preheat the oven to 400°F (205°C). Spray a madeleine pan with nonstick baking spray.
- In a small bowl, whisk together the flour, espresso powder, salt, baking powder, and lemon zest.
- In the bowl of a stand mixer fitted with the whisk attachment, whisk together the granulated sugar, maple sugar, whole eggs, and egg yolk until light and fluffy and doubled in volume.
- Sift the flour mixture over the egg mixture and gently fold with a large rubber spatula until incorporated. Fold in the melted butter until incorporated. Cover with plastic wrap and let rest at room temperature for 10 minutes.
- Spoon the batter into the prepared madeleine pan so that the cavities are about three quarters full. Bake for 10 minutes, or until the cookies spring back when gently poked.
- Immediately sprinkle with confectioners' sugar and serve while still warm. (To mimic the photo, hold a piece of parchment over the lower bottom of cookie and sift the exposed area only.)

MAPLE MADELEINES

Check page 16 before proceeding for additional details on ensuring your recipes are gluten free and/or vegan.

VEGAN

Replace the flour with ½ cup (70 g) all-purpose flour and 2 tablespoons cornstarch. Replace the whole eggs with 2 large eggs' worth of prepared Ener-G egg replacer (see recipe, page 12). Replace the egg yolk with 1½ teaspoons golden flaxseed meal stirred together with 1½ tablespoons hot water, allowing it to sit 10 minutes to gel. Replace all of the butter with ½ cup (115 g) Earth Balance Vegan Shortening.

GLUTEN FREE

Use traditional nonstick cooking spray rather than baking spray (which contains flour). Replace the flour with ½ cup (80 g) finely milled brown rice flour and ½ teaspoon xanthan gum.

HEALTHIER

Replace the flour with ½ cup (50 g) whole-wheat pastry flour. Replace the granulated sugar with ¼ cup (40 g) organic granulated palm sugar.

MAPLE COOKIES

{ MAKES 3 DOZEN COOKIES }

12 ounces (340 g) European unsalted butter (like Plugra), at room temperature
¾ cup (180 ml) real maple syrup, preferably grade B
¾ cup (150 g) sugar
3¼ cups (435 g) all-purpose flour
¼ cup (30 g) cornstarch
½ teaspoon salt

Crisp. Slightly salty. Earthy sweet. These cookies are made for the first days of fall, when the air hints at briskness and the first leaves start to crunch underfoot. Please use real maple syrup in these and, if you can get your hands on it, use a darker syrup with a more robust flavor like a grade B.

Procedure

- In the bowl of stand mixer fitted with the paddle attachment, cream together the butter, maple syrup, and ½ cup (100 g) of the sugar until light and fluffy.
- In a large mixing bowl, whisk together the flour, cornstarch, and salt until fully combined. Add the flour mixture all at once to the butter mixture and mix on low speed until just incorporated. Turn the dough out onto a sheet of plastic wrap. Press the dough into a disk and wrap it up. Refrigerate for 1 hour.
- On a floured work surface, roll out the dough to ⅛ inch (3 mm) thick. Using a maple leaf cookie cutter, stamp out cookies and place ½ inch (12 mm) apart on the prepared pans. Press together and reroll the scraps one time. Sprinkle the cookies with a light, even layer of the remaining ¼ cup (50 g) sugar. Bake until the edges of the cookies are golden brown, 15 to 17 minutes.
- Preheat the oven to 350°F (175°C). Line two sheet pans with parchment paper.

OPTIONS

Check page 16 before proceeding for additional details on ensuring your recipes are gluten free and/or vegan.

VEGAN

Replace the butter with 1½ cups (360 ml) organic refined virgin coconut oil (melt the oil to measure, then allow to resolidify before proceeding). Bake the cookies for 10 to 12 minutes, until the edges start to brown.

GLUTEN FREE

Replace the flour with 2 cups (320 g) finely milled brown rice flour, ¾ cup (120 g) sweet white rice flour, ¼ cup (35 g) sweet white sorghum flour, ¼ cup (35 g) tapioca starch, and 1½ teaspoons xanthan gum.

HEALTHIER

Replace half the butter with ¾ cup (180 ml) organic virgin coconut oil (melt the oil to measure, then allow to resolidify before proceeding). Replace the all-purpose flour with 3¼ cup (325 g) whole-wheat pastry flour.

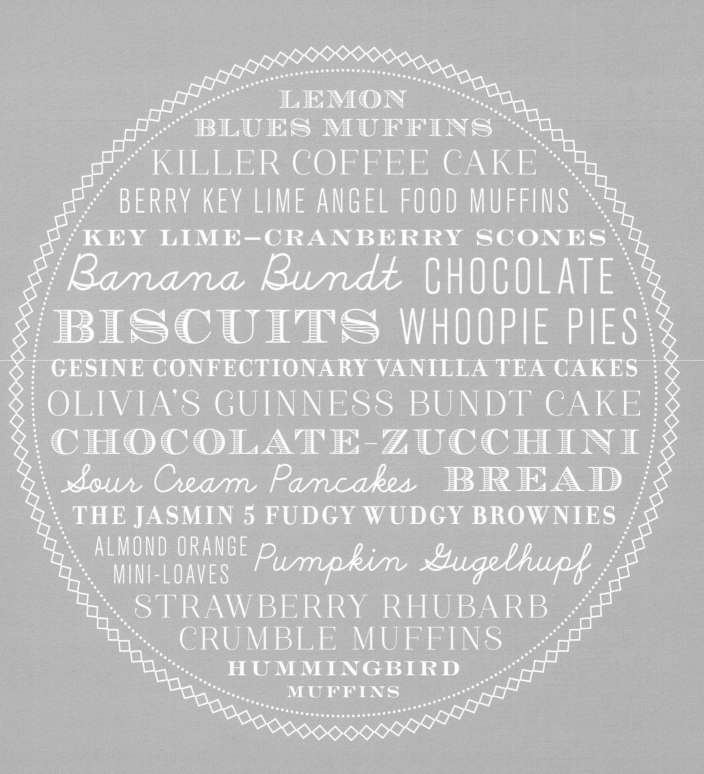

LEMON
BLUES MUFFINS
KILLER COFFEE CAKE
BERRY KEY LIME ANGEL FOOD MUFFINS
KEY LIME–CRANBERRY SCONES
Banana Bundt CHOCOLATE
BISCUITS WHOOPIE PIES
GESINE CONFECTIONARY VANILLA TEA CAKES
OLIVIA'S GUINNESS BUNDT CAKE
CHOCOLATE-ZUCCHINI
Sour Cream Pancakes BREAD
THE JASMIN 5 FUDGY WUDGY BROWNIES
ALMOND ORANGE
MINI-LOAVES *Pumpkin Gugelhupf*
STRAWBERRY RHUBARB
CRUMBLE MUFFINS
HUMMINGBIRD
MUFFINS

QUICK-
BREADS

Don't let the name fool you. Despite having the word *bread* in their name, quickbreads are most often sweet—think banana bread. What makes them quick is that they're leavened with artificial leavening agents like baking powder and baking soda as opposed to the leavening most associated with bread: yeast. Along with your baking powder or soda, quickbread batters are often mixed in very particular ways to increase your chances of creating lift, lightness, and tenderness in your final product.

One quickbread method is the biscuit method, wherein the dry ingredients are combined and the fat is cut into the dry ingredients until a coarse mixture is formed. To cut in the fat, most often your fingers are used, or a pastry cutter; you can also use a food processor. The liquid ingredients, having already been combined in a separate bowl, are combined with the dry/fat mixture until a dough *just* forms. Sometimes a little kneading is required for a dough to form. This method makes for flaky results, very much like—you guessed it—biscuits. It's also the most common method of making pie crusts and scones.

A muffin is also a type of quickbread. It's cake in a paper girdle; it's a cup-cake by a different name. The muffin method of mixing a batter is achieved by combining the dry ingredients in one bowl and whisking the liquid ingredients, along with the eggs, together in another bowl. The two are briefly stirred together to create a batter.

Last is the cake method, where the sugar and fat are creamed together until light and fluffy. The eggs are then added and the dry ingredients are mixed in. The initial creaming of the butter and sugar incorporates air into the batter, creating an airy finished product.

Each method has its place in different treats. While for the most part the type of treat matches the method you'll use to create it, sometimes, especially when altering and reconfiguring classic recipes to suit different diets, lifestyles, and allergies, a different method will work better. Sometimes it's best, for example, to use the cake method with a particular muffin recipe. Sometimes you have to change up the method depending on whether you're making a muffin with butter or with oil (butter usually requires the cake method and oil the muffin method). Getting to know the different methods and why they are used will help you immeasurably if you have to change up recipes yourself.

Key Lime-Cranberry Scones

Biscuits
(PAGE 65)

I've always wondered at people who've remarked that they have no love for scones. They describe them as stodgy and tough, essentially flour-based hockey pucks. Clearly these poor souls have never made these scones, because these beauties are tender and tasty. They are splendidly bright and buttery. It's all in how you handle the dough and shape the scones. Instead of manhandling the stuff, you divide the dough and gently pat it into two rough rounds, then just slice like a pie and you're ready to go!

Key Lime-
CRANBERRY
SCONES

Procedure

- Preheat the oven to 350°F (175°C). Line two half sheet pans with parchment paper.
- In a large bowl, whisk together the flour, granulated sugar, baking powder, and salt for at least 45 seconds to evenly distribute the leavening. Stir in the lime zest. Add the butter and, using the tips of your fingers, massage it into the flour mixture until the mixture resembles very coarse cornmeal. Stir in the cranberries.
- In a small bowl, stir together the buttermilk and lime juice. Whisk in the egg yolk. Pour the buttermilk mixture over the flour mixture and stir with a wooden spoon to incorporate the wet ingredients into the dry, continuing to mix just until the dough is uniformly wet and no dry patches remain; don't overmix.
- Turn the dough out onto a well-floured work surface. Divide the dough in two. Shape each piece of dough into a rough 6-inch (15-cm) round, then cut each round into 8 wedges, as if slicing up a pie. Place the wedges on the prepared pans, spacing them about 3 inches (7.5 cm) apart. Sprinkle each with Sugar in the Raw. Bake until the scones are golden brown and baked through, 25 to 30 minutes.

Ingredients

2½ cups (330 g) all-purpose flour
½ cup (100 g) granulated sugar
2 teaspoons baking powder
½ teaspoon salt
Grated zest and juice of 1 Key lime
¾ cup (1 ½ sticks/170 g) unsalted butter, at room temperature
1 cup (130 g) dried sweetened cranberries
¾ cup (180 ml) buttermilk
1 large egg yolk
¼ cup (50 g) Sugar in the Raw or sparkling sugar

Check page 16 before proceeding for additional details on ensuring your recipes are gluten free and/or vegan.

VEGAN

Decrease the baking powder to 1 teaspoon and add 1 teaspoon baking soda to the dry ingredients. Replace the butter with 6 tablespoons (85 g) cold Earth Balance Vegan Shortening. Replace the buttermilk and egg yolk with ½ cup (120 ml) full-fat coconut milk whisked together with ½ cup (120 ml) vegan sour cream, 1 tablespoon lemon juice, 1 tablespoon distilled white vinegar, and 1 tablespoon golden flaxseed meal; whisk together and let sit for 5 minutes before proceeding.

VEGAN

Replace the butter with ½ cup (115 g) Earth Balance Vegan Shortening, frozen and cubed, for a total of 1 cup (225 g) shortening. Replace the buttermilk with ½ cup (120 ml) almond milk stirred together with 1 tablespoon distilled white vinegar. Replace the egg with 1 tablespoon flaxseed meal (or finely ground white chia seeds) and 3 tablespoons water that have been whisked together well with the almond milk and vinegar. Proceed as in the main recipe.

GLUTEN FREE

Replace the flour with 1½ cups (240 g) finely milled brown rice flour, ⅔ cup (90 g) sweet white sorghum flour, ⅓ cup (45 g) tapioca starch, and 2 teaspoons xanthan gum. Increase the baking powder to 1 tablespoon. Reduce the buttermilk to ½ cup (120 ml). Use 2 whole eggs instead of 1 yolk.

GLUTEN FREE

Replace both the flours with 1 cup (160 g) finely milled brown rice flour, ¾ cup (105 g) tapioca starch, ¼ cup (35 g) sweet white sorghum flour, and 1 teaspoon xanthan gum, whisked together. Reduce the buttermilk to ¼ cup (60 ml). Increase the eggs to 2.

HEALTHIER

Replace the flour with 1½ cups (150 g) organic whole-wheat pastry flour and 1 cup (160 g) whole-grain teff flour. Replace the sugar with ½ cup (80 g) organic granulated palm sugar. Omit half of the butter and instead stir 6 tablespoons (90 ml) organic grapeseed oil into the buttermilk mixture.

HEALTHIER

Replace the bread flour with 1 cup (120 g) white whole-wheat flour. Use organic pastry flour. Replace the butter with ¼ cup (60 ml) organic refined virgin coconut oil, melted to measure and then resolidified and chilled. Work the coconut oil into the flour mixture along with the shortening as you would in the main recipe, but make sure that there are no large pieces of fat remaining in the dough. Proceed as in the main recipe.

I was in London with my husband. We ordered tea to be brought up to our room. I was concentrating intently on my work when it arrived, so I asked, "Ray, would you be mother?" Ray made my cuppa and handed it over. Without looking up, I asked, "Isn't there a biscuit?" At which point I grabbed a pencil and stabbed myself with it. There's a reason we Americans call cookies "cookies" and biscuits "biscuits": (1) We aren't British, (2) we had that little squabble in the 1700s, and (3) biscuits are delicious, flaky, and tender leavened breadlike nuggets that we eat with fried chicken and mac and cheese. British "biscuits" are not biscuits; i.e., this recipe is for the real biscuit, the American kind.

Procedure

- Preheat the oven to 375°F (190°C). Line a half sheet pan with parchment paper.
- In a large bowl, whisk together both flours, the baking powder, and salt for at least 45 seconds to distribute the leavening. Add the butter and shortening and, using the tips of your fingers, massage the fats into the flour until the mixture resembles very coarse cornmeal with some pea-sized chunks of fat still visible.
- In a small bowl, whisk together the buttermilk, egg, and maple syrup. Pour the buttermilk mixture over the flour mixture and stir with a wooden spoon. Continue stirring until the flour is evenly coated with moisture. Turn the dough out onto a well-floured work surface. Gently pat the dough into a rough rectangle ¾ inch (2 cm) thick. Using a 2-inch (5-cm) round biscuit cutter, cut rounds from the dough and place on the prepared sheet pan, at least 2 inches (5 cm) apart. Gently press and roll out any remaining dough scraps and cut more rounds from the dough. Bake until the tops of the biscuits are light golden brown, 10 to 15 minutes.

BISCUITS

{ MAKES 1 DOZEN BISCUITS }

Ingredients

1 cup (140 g) bread flour
1 cup (120 g) pastry flour
1 tablespoon baking powder
1 tablespoon salt
½ cup (1 stick/115 g) very cold unsalted butter, cut into ½-inch (12-mm) cubes
½ cup (115 g) Earth Balance Vegan Shortening, frozen and cut into ½-inch (12-mm) cubes
½ cup (120 ml) buttermilk
1 large egg
1 teaspoon maple syrup

Sour CREAM PANCAKES

{ MAKES 6 SERVINGS }

Ingredients

1½ cups (210 g) all-purpose flour
1 tablespoon baking powder
1 tablespoon sugar
1 teaspoon fine sea salt or ½ teaspoon
    table salt
1 cup (240 ml) whole milk or buttermilk,
    plus ¼ cup (60 ml) if needed
½ cup (120 ml) sour cream
1 large egg
1 tablespoon vanilla bean paste or vanilla
    extract
4 tablespoons (55 g) unsalted butter, melted

My little cousin from Bavaria visited me this past summer. She's the daughter of my first cousin, which makes her my first cousin once removed . . . or is it my second cousin? Either way, she's just twenty-one and is adorable. The kind of twenty-one and adorable that allows her to eat an entire batch of pancakes slathered in butter and maple syrup without any repercussions on the scale. She liked my recipe so much that she asked if she could try her hand at making them the next morning. And so it was, for the entirety of her weeklong visit with me, that we had these pancakes for breakfast, tacos for lunch, and burgers for dinner. Good times . . . until I stepped on the scale.

Procedure

- In a large bowl, whisk together the flour, baking powder, sugar, and salt.
- In another bowl, whisk together the 1 cup (240 ml) milk, the sour cream, egg, and vanilla until smooth. Slowly pour the melted butter into the milk mixture while you continue to whisk. Make a well in the flour mixture and pour in the wet ingredients. Stir with a wooden spoon until the batter is very smooth and has the pouring consistency of ketchup. If the batter is too thick, add more milk, 1 tablespoon at a time, until you reach the desired consistency.
- Spray a hot griddle with a very thin layer of nonstick cooking spray. Drop ¼-cup (60-ml) mounds of batter on the grill. When you see bubbles start to appear on the top of the pancake and the edges appear set, peek underneath it to make sure it's uniformly golden brown under there. If so, flip! Continue cooking until the second side is golden brown. Continue with the rest of the batter and eat immediately.

Check page 16 before proceeding for additional details on ensuring your recipes are gluten free and/or vegan.

VEGAN

Replace the milk with full-fat coconut milk. Replace the sour cream with vegan sour cream. Replace the egg with 1 large egg's worth of prepared Ener-G egg replacer (see recipe, page 12). Replace the butter with ¼ cup (60 ml) organic refined virgin coconut oil, melted.

GLUTEN FREE

Replace the flour with 1 cup (160 g) finely milled brown rice flour, ⅓ cup (45 g) sweet white sorghum flour, 3 tablespoons tapioca starch, and 1 teaspoon xanthan gum.

HEALTHIER

Replace the flour with 1½ cups (150 g) whole-wheat pastry flour. Replace 2 tablespoons of the butter with 2 tablespoons organic grapeseed oil. Increase the extra milk to ½ cup (120 ml)—you'll likely need it.

VEGAN

FOR THE MUFFINS: Replace the honey with ⅓ cup (60 g) organic granulated palm sugar. Replace the eggs with 2 large eggs' worth of flaxseed meal mixed with water (see page 12). FOR THE CRUMBLE: Replace the butter with ½ cup (120 ml) organic refined virgin coconut oil, melted.

GLUTEN FREE

FOR THE MUFFINS: Replace the honey with ⅓ cup (65 g) granulated sugar; you'll no longer need to microwave first. Increase the eggs to 3. Replace the oil and applesauce with ½ cup (1 stick/115 g) unsalted butter, at room temperature. In the bowl of a stand mixer fitted with the paddle attachment, cream together the sugar and butter until light and fluffy. Add the eggs one at a time and mix on medium speed until incorporated. Replace the flour with 1 cup (160 g) finely milled brown rice flour, ½ cup (70 g) sweet white sorghum flour, and ½ teaspoon xanthan gum. FOR THE CRUMBLE: Replace the flour with 1 cup (160 g) finely milled brown rice flour, ¼ cup (40 g) potato starch, and ½ teaspoon xanthan gum. Increase the butter by 2 tablespoons for a total of 10 tablespoons (140 g).

HEALTHIER

FOR THE MUFFINS: Replace the sugar with ¾ cup (120 g) organic granulated palm sugar. Replace the oil with ¼ cup (60 ml) organic grapeseed oil. Replace the flour with 1 cup (100 g) whole-wheat pastry flour plus ½ cup (70 g) Sprouted Super Flour (see page 220). FOR THE CRUMBLE: Omit the crumble ingredients in the master recipe entirely and do the following instead: Stir together ½ cup (80 g) steel-cut oats (not quick cooking), ¼ cup (30 g) finely chopped lightly toasted pecans, 3 tablespoons brown sugar, 1 tablespoon honey, 1 tablespoon organic grapeseed oil, 1 tablespoon whole-wheat flour, and a pinch of salt until the mixture clumps, then proceed as directed.

These sweet and wholesome nuggets are a wonderful breakfast staple. When I'm running late or am low on energy, this is just the right pick-me-up to get my day started. They also freeze well, so you can make a large batch and have them ready to go at a moment's notice.

Hummingbird MUFFINS

{ MAKES 15 TO 18 MUFFINS }

Ingredients

FOR THE MUFFINS

1 cup (200 g) sugar
⅓ cup (75 ml) honey
2 large eggs
¼ cup (60 ml) canola oil
½ cup (120 ml) unsweetened applesauce
1 teaspoon apple cider vinegar
½ cup (120 g) drained crushed pineapple
1 large, very ripe banana, mashed with a fork
1 teaspoon vanilla extract
1½ cups (210 g) all-purpose flour
½ cup (55 g) very finely chopped pecans, lightly toasted
1 teaspoon salt
1 teaspoon baking powder
½ teaspoon baking soda
½ teaspoon ground cinnamon

FOR THE CRUMBLE

1¼ cups (175 g) all-purpose flour
¼ cup (50 g) granulated sugar
¼ cup (55 g) dark brown sugar, packed
Pinch of salt
½ cup (1 stick/115 g) unsalted butter, melted

Procedure

MAKE THE MUFFINS

- Preheat the oven to 350°F (175°C). Line a muffin tin with paper liners.
- In a large microwave-safe bowl, combine the sugar and honey. Cook it in the microwave at 50 percent power for 45 seconds to 1 minute. Remove the bowl from the microwave and stir until combined. When slightly cooled, whisk in the eggs one at a time until well combined. Add the oil, applesauce, and vinegar. Whisk until combined. Add the pineapple, banana, and vanilla. Whisk until smooth. (Alternatively, once the honey and sugar are microwaved, you can also combine all the ingredients above in a food processor and process until smooth.) Set aside.
- In a large mixing bowl, whisk together the flour, pecans, salt, baking powder, baking soda, and cinnamon. Add the flour mixture to the wet mixture and stir until the batter is well combined; do not overmix. (If you're using the food processor option, add the flour mixture to the processor and pulse until smooth).

MAKE THE CRUMBLE

- In a large mixing bowl, stir together the flour, both sugars, and salt. Pour the melted butter over the mixture and stir until the mixture forms small clumps.
- Divide the batter evenly among the muffin cavities, filling each about three quarters full. Sprinkle a light layer of the crumble on top of the batter. (If you have leftover crumble, put it in a zipper bag and freeze; it can stay frozen for up to 1 month.)
- Bake the muffins until a toothpick inserted in one comes out clean, 20 to 25 minutes.

Hummingbird
Muffins
(PAGE 69)

Berry Key Lime Angel Food Muffins

Angel food cake is light. It's fluffy. It's sweet as hell, but in the best way. It's also that cake you don't stop eating until you've scarfed the whole damn thing. That's why, if I'm going to make this addictive treat, I bake it as small muffins and divvy up the little pillows of heaven just a few at a time to keep from going into a diabetic coma.

{ MAKES 40 SMALL MUFFINS }

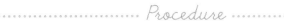

Procedure

- Preheat the oven to 350°F (175°C). Line a muffin tin with paper liners. Put a raspberry in the bottom of each muffin paper.
- In the bowl of a food processor, combine both sugars and the cornstarch and pulse until very fine. Put half of the mixture in a large mixing bowl and set the other half aside. Add the flour to the mixing bowl with the sugar-cornstarch mixture and stir to combine. Sift this mixture onto a large piece of parchment paper, then sift it again, back into the large mixing bowl; sift once more, onto the parchment.
- In the bowl of a stand mixer fitted with the whisk attachment, combine the egg whites, lime juice, lime zest, cream of tartar, and salt. Whisk on high speed until the whites become white and foamy. With the mixer on medium speed, slowly add the reserved sugar-cornstarch mixture (without the flour) to the egg whites; whisk on high speed until medium peaks form.
- Sift one quarter of the sugar-flour mixture on top of the egg whites and use a large rubber spatula to gently fold it in. In quarter portions, continue sifting the remaining sugar-flour mixture on top of the egg whites and folding it into the batter until all the sugar-flour mixture is incorporated.
- Divide the batter evenly among the muffin cavities, filling each until full. Bake until the tops of the muffins are golden brown and the cake springs back when gently poked, 10 to 15 minutes.

Ingredients

1 pint (335 g) raspberries
1¼ cups (250 g) granulated sugar
½ cup (50 g) confectioners' sugar
2 tablespoons cornstarch
1 cup (130 g) cake flour, sifted
12 large egg whites
⅓ cup (75 ml) Key lime juice
1 teaspoon grated lime zest
1 teaspoon cream of tartar
1 teaspoon salt

Check page 16 before proceeding for additional details on ensuring your recipes are gluten free and/or vegan.

VEGAN

There is no *true* vegan alternative for an angel food cake, a pastry that requires 12 damn egg whites. But this is as good a replacement as I've ever invented and I hope you agree: Omit the egg whites. In a stand mixer fitted with the whisk attachment, mix together ⅔ cup (165 ml) water, ¼ cup (60 ml) Key lime juice (this replaces the juice in the main recipe), 4 tablespoons (32 g) Ener-G egg replacer (not prepared), 1 tablespoon Versawhip 600K (not prepared), and 1 teaspoon distilled white vinegar, until light and fluffy. Add half the sugar-cornstarch mixture as you would in the master recipe and whisk to stiff peaks. Replace the cake flour with 1 cup (140 g) all-purpose flour. Add 2 tablespoons soy protein powder, ½ teaspoon baking powder, ½ teaspoon baking soda, and the salt to the flour and whisk for 30 seconds to evenly distribute the leavening, then add the remaining sugar-cornstarch mixture and sift and incorporate as per the master recipe. For best results, do not add the berry to the bottom of the cup but simply serve the cakes with berries on the side. Fill the muffin wrappers to the top and bake for 20 to 25 minutes.

GLUTEN FREE

Replace the cake flour with 1 cup (160 g) sweet white rice flour.

HEALTHIER

Replace the sugars with 1½ cups (285 g) Sucanat; pulse the Sucanat in the food processor with the cornstarch as directed above. Replace the flour with ½ cup (50 g) whole-wheat pastry flour and ½ cup (80 g) sweet white rice flour.

VEGAN

Replace the butter with ¼ cup (60 ml) organic grapeseed oil and 4 tablespoons (55 g) Earth Balance Vegan Buttery Sticks; cream together the sugar and the Buttery Sticks, then add the oil and mix to combine. Replace the eggs with 2 large eggs' worth of prepared Ener-G egg replacer (see recipe, page 12). Replace the buttermilk with ½ cup (120 ml) plain almond milk plus 1 teaspoon lemon juice, whisked together.

HEALTHIER

Replace the butter with ¼ cup (60 ml) organic grapeseed oil and ¼ cup (60 ml) unsweetened applesauce. Replace the sugar with ¾ cup (145 g) Sucanat. Use the muffin method to mix the batter: In a large bowl, stir together the grapeseed oil, applesauce, sugar, eggs, buttermilk, and lemon extract until combined. Replace the flour with 1½ cups (150 g) whole-wheat pastry flour. In a medium bowl, whisk together the flour, baking powder, salt, lemon zest, and nutmeg. Add the dry mixture to the wet mixture and fold together with a large rubber spatula until the two are combined. Fold in the blueberries.

There's nothing epically new or exciting about using lemon and blueberries together, but there's a reason for that: They are glorious together, a very happy marriage in your mouth. Adding a smidge of nutmeg to the union results in the most well adjusted nuclear family ever. We're talking "happily ever after."

(MAKES 1 DOZEN MUFFINS)

Procedure

- Preheat the oven to 325°F (165°C). Line a muffin tin with paper liners.
- In the bowl of a stand mixer fitted with the paddle attachment, combine the butter and sugar. Cream them together until light and fluffy. Add the eggs, one at a time, scraping the sides and bottom of the bowl after each addition. Add the lemon extract and mix to incorporate.
- In a small bowl, combine the flour, baking powder, salt, lemon zest, and nutmeg and whisk for 30 seconds to evenly distribute the leavening. With the mixer running on low speed, add half of the flour mixture to the butter mixture, then add the buttermilk and follow with the remaining flour mixture, mixing until just incorporated. Using a large rubber spatula, gently give the batter a few quick strokes to make sure there are no pockets of flour remaining. Fold in the blueberries.
- Fill each muffin cavity three quarters full. Bake until the muffins just spring back when gently poked, 15 to 20 minutes.

Ingredients

½ cup (1 stick/115 g) unsalted butter, at room temperature
1 cup (200 g) sugar
2 large eggs
1 teaspoon natural lemon extract
1½ cups (210 g) all-purpose flour
1½ tablespoons baking powder
1 teaspoon salt
Grated zest of 1 lemon
Pinch of freshly grated nutmeg (2 scrapes from a nutmeg)
½ cup (120 ml) low-fat buttermilk
1 cup (165 g) blueberries

OPTIONS

GLUTEN FREE

Increase the eggs by 1, for a total of 3 eggs. Replace the flour with 1 cup (160 g) finely milled brown rice flour, ½ cup (80 g) sweet white rice flour, and 1½ teaspoons xanthan gum. Reduce the buttermilk to ¼ cup (60 ml).

Lemon Blues Muffins
(PAGE 73)

Strawberry Rhubarb Crumble Muffins

When rhubarb/strawberry season rolls around, all hell breaks loose in my yard. I'm harvesting and baking. Baking and harvesting. Trying to stay ahead of hungry deer and keeping the farm animals from breaking the perimeter of the vegetable gardens and ransacking the goods (rhubarb is deadly to sheep and goats, so it really is imperative I keep them far away). But in the event I lose my crops, the early spring onslaught of the weedy scourge Japanese knotweed (which no pest or domesticated animal seems to want to disturb) can be harvested just as it's sprouting and used in lieu of rhubarb. It is, after all, widely known as wild rhubarb. It's a more delicate stalk than traditional rhubarb but it carries all the wonderful flavor of the real deal. And it's a tasty way to weed an unruly garden patch!

Strawberry Rhubarb CRUMBLE MUFFINS

{ MAKES 2 DOZEN MUFFINS }

Procedure

MAKE THE MUFFINS

- Preheat the oven to 350°F (175°C). Line a muffin tin with paper liners.
- In the bowl of a stand mixer fitted with the paddle attachment, cream together the butter and brown sugar until light and fluffy. Add the egg and mix on medium speed until incorporated. Add the vanilla and lemon zest and mix on medium speed.
- In a small bowl, combine the lemon juice and milk and stir. Let sit for 5 minutes to "sour" (after 5 minutes, it will look curdled—this is exactly as it should be).
- In a medium bowl, whisk together the flour, baking powder, and salt for 30 seconds to evenly distribute the leavening.
- Add half of the flour mixture to the butter–brown sugar mixture and mix on low speed. Add half of the soured milk mixture and continue mixing on low speed. Add the remaining flour mixture and soured milk mixture and mix on low speed until just incorporated.
- Using a large rubber spatula, fold the rhubarb and strawberries into the batter. Divide the batter evenly among the muffin cavities, filling each about three quarters full.

MAKE THE CRUMBLE

- In a large bowl, combine all the crumble ingredients using a wooden spoon or your fingers. Keep working the mixture until the butter is absorbed and the mixture starts to clump.
- Sprinkle about 1 tablespoon of the crumble on top of each muffin. Bake until the muffins spring back when gently poked, about 25 minutes.

Ingredients

FOR THE MUFFINS

½ cup (1 stick/115 g) unsalted butter, at room temperature
1 cup (220 g) light brown sugar, packed
1 large egg, at room temperature
2 teaspoons vanilla bean paste or vanilla extract
Grated zest and juice of 1 lemon
1 cup (240 ml) whole milk
2 cups (260 g) all-purpose flour
1 teaspoon baking powder
1 teaspoon salt
2 cups (245 g) diced rhubarb
1 cup (165 g) hulled and diced strawberries

FOR THE CRUMBLE

1¼ cups (175 g) all-purpose flour
½ cup (1 stick/115 g) unsalted butter, melted
¼ cup (50 g) granulated sugar
¼ cup (55 g) light brown sugar, packed
¼ teaspoon salt

Check page 16 before proceeding for additional details on ensuring your recipes are gluten free and/or vegan.

VEGAN

FOR THE MUFFINS: Replace the butter with ½ cup (120 ml) canola oil. Omit the egg. Add 1 teaspoon baking soda to the flour mixture. Replace the milk with 1 cup (240 ml) plain almond milk and add 1 tablespoon distilled white vinegar to the almond milk. (The baking soda and vinegar essentially replace the egg.) To mix, use the muffin method: Whisk together the dry ingredients (the flour, brown sugar, baking soda, baking powder, and salt) and whisk together the wet ingredients in a large mixing bowl. Fold the two together with a large rubber spatula and then stir in the strawberries and rhubarb. FOR THE CRUMBLE: Replace the butter with ½ cup (120 ml) melted virgin coconut oil.

GLUTEN FREE

FOR THE MUFFINS: Add 1 egg, for a total of 2 eggs. Reduce the milk to ½ cup (120 ml). Replace the flour, baking powder, and salt with 2 cups (240 g) King Arthur Flour Gluten-Free All-Purpose Baking Mix. FOR THE CRUMBLE: Replace the flour with 1 cup (160 g) finely milled brown rice flour, ¼ cup (40 g) potato starch, and 1 teaspoon xanthan gum. Increase the butter by 2 tablespoons for a total of 10 tablespoons (140 g).

HEALTHIER

FOR THE MUFFINS: Replace the brown sugar with 1 cup (160 g) organic granulated palm sugar. Replace the butter with ½ cup (120 ml) organic grapeseed oil. Replace the flour with 1½ cups (150 g) organic whole-wheat pastry flour and ½ cup (60 g) organic spelt flour. To mix, use the muffin method: Whisk together the dry ingredients (sugar, both flours, baking powder, and salt) in a medium bowl and whisk together the wet ingredients in a large mixing bowl. Fold the two together with a large rubber spatula and then stir in the rhubarb and strawberries. FOR THE CRUMBLE: Replace the butter with ½ cup (120 ml) organic refined virgin coconut oil, melted.

VEGAN

After mixing together the almond paste and sugar with the paddle attachment until just combined, change to the whisk attachment. Omit the butter, and replace the honey with ¼ cup (60 ml) organic agave syrup; add it to the almond paste mixture along with the vanilla and orange extract. Replace the butter with another ¼ cup (60 ml) organic grapeseed oil for a total of ¾ cup (180 ml) oil; add it next to the mixer while it's running on medium-low speed. Replace the eggs with 2 large eggs' worth of flaxseed meal mixed with water (see page 12) and ½ cup (120 ml) applesauce, mixed until combined; add it next to the mixer while it's running on medium-low speed. Increase the baking powder to 1½ teaspoons.

GLUTEN FREE

Replace the flour with ½ cup (50 g) almond flour, ½ cup (80 g) finely milled brown rice flour, and 1 teaspoon xanthan gum.

After a three-day juice cleanse, I'm craving nothing more than this moist, dense beauty of a petite cake. I won't even flinch at the sight or sound of the word *moist*. This treat also freezes incredibly well, so if you're planning on depriving yourself for any length of time, it makes life so much more pleasant with this waiting for you in the deep freeze.

Almond ORANGE MINI-LOAVES

{ MAKES 8 MINI (1.2-BY-3.1-INCH/3-BY-8-CM) LOAVES }

Procedure

- Preheat the oven to 325°F (165°C). Spray eight mini disposable loaf pans (see Resources on page 220) with nonstick cooking spray and place on a parchment-lined half sheet pan.
- In the bowl of a stand mixer fitted with the paddle attachment, combine the almond paste and sugar. Mix on medium speed until the almond paste has broken up and become somewhat smooth. Add the butter, honey, vanilla, and orange extract. Beat on high speed until light and fluffy. Scrape down the bottom and sides of the bowl. Add the eggs one at a time, scraping the bowl after each addition. Add the oil and mix until just combined.
- In a bowl, sift together the flour, baking powder, and salt. Stir in the orange zest. With the mixer running on low speed, add the flour mixture to the batter, mixing until just combined.
- Fill each of the mini loaf pans three quarters full. Bake until the cakes are golden brown and spring back when you touch them, about 45 minutes.

Ingredients

7 ounces (200 g) almond paste
1 cup (200 g) sugar
½ cup (1 stick/115 g) unsalted butter, at room temperature
¼ cup (60 ml) honey
1 teaspoon vanilla bean paste
1 teaspoon natural orange extract
6 large eggs
½ cup (120 ml) organic grapeseed oil
1 cup (130 g) cake flour
½ teaspoon baking powder
½ teaspoon salt
1 teaspoon grated orange zest

OPTIONS

HEALTHIER

Replace the sugar with ¾ cup (120 g) organic granulated palm sugar. Replace the butter with ½ cup (120 ml) applesauce and the canola oil with ½ cup (120 ml) organic grapeseed oil. Replace the flour with a ½ cup (50 g) almond flour and ½ cup (50 g) whole-wheat pastry flour.

We all know that overripe bananas left lingering on the counter mean banana bread (or fruit flies) can't be far behind. But this isn't your run-of-the-mill banana bread, because *that* has never tasted *this* good. Bake it in a Bundt pan and you've got something more extraordinary than you would expect from an ordinary banana bread.

Banana BUNDT

Procedure

FOR THE CAKE

- Preheat the oven to 350°F (175°C). Spray a 9-inch (23-cm) Bundt pan with nonstick baking spray.
- In the bowl of a food processor, combine the banana, butter, oil, both sugars, the pineapple juice, vinegar, and vanilla. Pulse until smooth.
- In a large bowl, whisk together the flour, baking soda, and salt for 30 seconds to evenly distribute the leavening. Add the flour mixture to the banana mixture and pulse until combined. Transfer to a large bowl and fold in the whipped cream. Pour the batter into the prepared pan. Bake until the quickbread springs back when gently poked, 45 to 50 minutes. Release from the pan while warmand let cool completely.

TO FINISH

- Sift confectioners' sugar over the cooled Bundt.

Ingredients

FOR THE CAKE

2 cups (460 g) food-processor-pureed banana (from about 4 large brown-ripe bananas)

1 cup (2 sticks/225 g) unsalted butter, very soft

½ cup (120 ml) canola oil

1 cup (200 g) granulated sugar

½ cup (110 g) dark brown sugar, packed

½ cup (120 ml) pineapple juice or orange juice

2 tablespoons apple cider vinegar

1 tablespoon vanilla bean paste or vanilla extract

3 cups (400 g) all-purpose flour

1½ teaspoons baking soda

1 teaspoon salt

1 cup (240 ml) heavy cream, whipped to medium peaks and refrigerated

TO FINISH

¼ cup (25 g) confectioners' sugar

Check page 16 before proceeding for additional details on ensuring your recipes are gluten free and/or vegan.

VEGAN

Replace the butter with 1 cup (240 ml) canola oil for a total of 1½ cups (360 ml) oil. Omit the cream.

GLUTEN FREE

Spray the pan with traditional nonstick cooking spray, not baking spray (which contains flour). Replace the oil with ½ cup (1 stick/115 g) unsalted butter at room temperature, for a total of 1½ cups (3 sticks/340 g) butter. Cream together the butter and both sugars until light and fluffy. Add 1 large egg to the creamed butter and sugar and mix on low speed until combined. Omit the pineapple juice. Replace the flour with 2 cups (320 g) finely milled brown rice flour, ⅔ cup (90 g) sweet white sorghum flour, 6 tablespoons (50 g) tapioca starch, and 2 teaspoons xanthan gum.

HEALTHIER

Replace the butter with 1 cup (240 ml) organic unsweetened applesauce and replace the oil with ½ cup (120 ml) organic grapeseed oil. Replace both the sugars with 1½ cups (240 g) organic granulated palm sugar. Replace the flour with 3 cups (300 g) whole-wheat pastry flour. Omit the cream.

VEGAN

Replace the flour with 1½ cups (210 g) all-purpose flour. Increase the baking soda to 1½ teaspoons. Replace the butter with 9 tablespoons (135 ml) canola oil. Heat the oil with the Guinness and cocoa and stir until smooth, as in the main recipe. Replace the buttermilk with ⅔ cup (165 ml) plain almond milk and 1 tablespoon distilled white vinegar, stirred together and allowed to sit for 5 minutes to curdle. Replace the egg with 1 large egg's worth of prepared Ener-G egg replacer see recipe, page 12).

GLUTEN FREE

Replace the flour with 1 cup (160 g) finely milled brown rice flour and 1 teaspoon xanthan gum. Replace the Guinness with a gluten-free oatmeal stout and reduce to ½ cup (120 ml). Reduce the buttermilk to ¼ cup (60 ml). Increase the eggs to 2.

HEALTHIER

Replace the flour with ½ cup (50 g) whole-wheat pastry flour and ½ cup (70 g) Sprouted Super Flour (see page 220). Replace the brown sugar with ¾ cup (120 g) organic granulated palm sugar. Add 2 tablespoons orange juice to the Guinness. Replace the butter with 5 tablespoons (75 ml) organic refined virgin coconut oil and ¼ cup (60 ml) unsweetened applesauce. Heat the coconut oil with the sugar and cocoa and stir until smooth, as in the main recipe. Whisk the applesauce with the buttermilk mixture.

This is a riff off of a Guinness bundt cake that Ray and I had on honeymoon in Ireland. Olivia was the chef onboard the Shannon Princess, a river barge that meanders down the Shannon River. Olivia presided over a tiny kitchen shoved into the hull of the ship, whipping up magic in a space that resembled nothing so much as a little cubbyhole, among them a beautiful Guinness cake. This is my homage to her.

{ MAKES ONE 9-INCH (23-CM) BUNDT CAKE }

Procedure

- Preheat the oven to 350°F (175°C). Spray a 9-inch (23-cm) Bundt pan with nonstick cooking spray.
- In a large bowl, whisk together the flour, sugar, baking soda, and salt for 30 seconds until well combined, making sure the brown sugar is well broken apart. Sift the mixture onto a large piece of parchment paper, then sift it again, back into the bowl.
- In a saucepan, melt together the Guinness, butter, and cocoa over low heat. Stir to make sure there are no cocoa lumps.
- In a large bowl, whisk together the buttermilk, egg, and vanilla. Continue whisking while adding a small amount of the Guinness mixture to temper it. Add the remaining Guinness mixture while whisking.
- Pour the wet ingredients into the dry ingredients and stir until a smooth batter forms. Pour the mixture into the prepared pan. Bake until the cake just springs back when poked, about 45 minutes. Let sit undisturbed for 30 minutes before releasing from the pan.

Ingredients

1 cup (120 g) pastry flour
1 cup (220 g) light brown sugar, packed
¾ teaspoon baking soda
½ teaspoon salt
¾ cup (180 ml) Guinness
9 tablespoons (130 g) unsalted butter, at room temperature
3 tablespoons Dutch-process cocoa powder (like Cacao Barry Extra Brute)
⅔ cup (165 ml) nonfat buttermilk
1 large egg
1 teaspoon vanilla extract

Killer COFFEE CAKE

{ MAKES ONE 9-BY-13-INCH (23-BY-33-CM) COFFEE CAKE }

Despite "coffee" getting top billing in coffee cake's name, the breakfast cake by nature contains no actual coffee. Rather, it's meant to be eaten with the hot stuff. However, I have a soft spot for java, in and out of my baked goods. I also like to take things literally. Therefore, I have included it in my recipe to bring depth to the name and the cake and to keep things honest.

Ingredients

FOR THE CAKE
3 cups (400 g) all-purpose flour
1 tablespoon baking powder
1 teaspoon salt
1 cup (220 g) light brown sugar, packed
1 cup (200 g) granulated sugar
1 cup (2 sticks/225 g) unsalted butter, at room temperature
4 large eggs
¼ cup (60 ml) canola oil
1 tablespoon vanilla bean paste
½ cup (120 ml) crème fraîche
½ cup (120 ml) whole milk
½ cup (120 ml) brewed coffee
1 cup (240 ml) heavy cream, whipped to stiff peaks and refrigerated

FOR THE FILLING
1 cup (220 g) light brown sugar, packed
1 cup (110 g) roughly chopped pecans, lightly toasted
1 tablespoon ground cinnamon

FOR THE CRUMBLE
2½ cups (330 g) all-purpose flour
½ cup (100 g) granulated sugar
½ cup (110 g) light brown sugar, packed
1 teaspoon ground cinnamon
½ teaspoon salt
1 cup (2 sticks/225 g) unsalted butter, melted

MAKE THE CAKE

- Preheat the oven to 350°F (175°C). Spray a 9-by-13-inch (23-by-33-cm) baking pan with nonstick baking spray.
- In a large bowl, whisk together the flour, baking powder, and salt.
- In the bowl of a stand mixer fitted with either the whisk or the paddle attachment, beat together both sugars and butter until light and fluffy, 4 to 5 minutes. Scrape down the bowl and mix for a second to incorporate any lingering ingredients that were stuck to the side of the bowl. Add the eggs one at a time, beating for about 1 minute between each and scraping down the sides of the bowl every now and again. Add the oil and vanilla and mix until combined. Add the crème fraîche and beat until just incorporated.
- In a small bowl, stir together the milk and the coffee.
- With the mixer running on medium-low speed, starting with the flour, alternate adding the flour mixture and the milk mixture in thirds to the mixer bowl. Scrape down the sides of the bowl again just to make sure nothing's hiding on the sides or the bottom. Using a large rubber spatula, fold the whipped cream into the batter.

MAKE THE FILLING

- Pulse all the ingredients together in a food processor until a crumbly paste forms.

MAKE THE CRUMBLE

- Put the flour, both sugars, the cinnamon, and salt in a large bowl and mix together with your hands. Pour in the melted butter and stir with a wooden spoon until the butter is fully incorporated and the mixture starts to form clumps.
- Spread three quarters of the cake batter evenly in the bottom of the prepared pan. Sprinkle the filling over the batter in an even layer, making sure to break apart any large clumps. Spread the remaining cake batter on top of the filling in an even layer. Using a long skewer or a knife, make swirling motions in the batter to incorporate some of the filling into the cake batter (do not swirl very vigorously—you still want a distinct filling layer with filling just infiltrating the top and bottom layers of the cake). Sprinkle the crumble over the top layer of batter.
- Bake until a toothpick inserted in the center comes out clean, 1 hour to 1 hour 20 minutes. About 30 minutes into the baking time, cover the top with aluminum foil to keep the crumble from burning.

Check page 16 before proceeding for additional details on ensuring your recipes are gluten free and/or vegan.

VEGAN

FOR THE CAKE: Replace the butter with ½ cup (115 g) Earth Balance Vegan Shortening and ½ cup (120 ml) organic grapeseed oil. Cream together the sugar and shortening until light and fluffy. Add the oil and mix on low speed until incorporated. Replace the eggs with 2 eggs' worth of prepared Ener-G egg replacer (see recipe, page 12), 1 egg's worth of flaxseed meal mixed with water (see page 12), and 1 tablespoon apple cider vinegar. Stir together the prepared Ener-G and flaxseed meal egg replacers and the vinegar. Add 1 extra teaspoon of baking soda to the dry ingredients. Replace the crème fraîche with vegan sour cream. Replace the milk with plain almond milk. Omit the heavy cream. **FOR THE CRUMBLE:** Replace the butter with ½ cup (120 ml) melted Earth Balance Vegan Shortening.

GLUTEN FREE

FOR THE CAKE: To prepare the pan, use traditional nonstick cooking spray, not nonstick baking spray (which contains flour). Replace the flour with 2 cups (320 g) finely milled brown rice flour, ¾ cup (100 g) sweet white sorghum flour, ¼ cup (35 g) tapioca starch, and 2 teaspoons xanthan gum. Reduce the crème fraîche to ¼ cup (60 ml), the milk to ¼ cup (60 ml), and the coffee to ¼ cup (60 ml). **FOR THE CRUMBLE:** Replace the flour with 2½ cups (400 g) finely milled brown rice flour and 1 teaspoon xanthan gum. Increase the butter by 4 tablespoons for a total of 1¼ cups (2½ sticks/280 g).

HEALTHIER

FOR THE CAKE: Replace the flour with 3 cups (300 g) whole-wheat pastry flour. Replace the sugars with 1½ cups (240 g) organic granulated palm sugar. Replace half of the butter with ½ cup (120 ml) applesauce; first cream together the remaining ½ cup (1 stick/115 g) butter with the palm sugar, then add the applesauce with the mixer on low speed. Omit the heavy cream. **FOR THE CRUMBLE:** Omit all the crumble ingredients and instead use the following: Combine 1 cup (80 g) rolled oats (not quick cooking), ½ cup (60 g) whole-wheat flour, ½ cup (80 g) organic granulated palm sugar, 2 tablespoons orange juice, ½ teaspoon ground cinnamon, and a pinch of salt in a large bowl and stir to combine. Drizzle ¼ cup (60 ml) organic grapeseed oil over the mixture and stir with a wooden spoon until the crumble starts to clump. Sprinkle over the batter and bake as directed in the main recipe.

Chocolate WHOOPIE PIES

(MAKES 1 DOZEN WHOOPIE PIES)

Ingredients

FOR THE CAKES

4 ounces (115 g) bittersweet chocolate,
    finely chopped
¼ cup (60 ml) hot brewed coffee
1½ cups (210 g) all-purpose flour
1 cup (85 g) Dutch-process cocoa powder
    (like Cacao Barry Extra Brute)
1 teaspoon instant espresso powder
1 teaspoon salt
½ teaspoon baking soda
½ teaspoon baking powder
1 cup (220 g) light brown sugar, packed
½ cup (120 ml) canola oil
1 large egg
1 cup (240 ml) buttermilk
1 tablespoon vanilla bean paste

FOR THE FILLING

2 (8-ounce/225 g) packages cream cheese,
    at room temperature
½ cup (1 stick/115 g) unsalted butter, at
    room temperature
4 cups (400 g) confectioners' sugar
Pinch of salt

Back in the day, before whoopies were available all throughout the United States, the Amish called these little treats "creamy turtles." They also called them hucklebucks, but there's just something about that name, creamy turtles, that's just so . . . so . . . ghastly. Anyway, legend has it that Amish wives placed creamy turtles in their husband's lunch pails. And when they opened them, the bearded gentlemen would yell, *"Creamy turtles!"* Just kidding. They'd yell, *"Whoopie!"* of course.

Procedure

MAKE THE CAKES

- Preheat the oven to 375°F (190°C). Line two half sheet pans with parchment paper.
- Put the chopped chocolate in a heatproof bowl. Pour the hot coffee over the chocolate and let sit undisturbed for 2 minutes to allow the chocolate to melt. Whisk to combine.
- In a bowl, whisk together the flour, cocoa powder, espresso powder, salt, baking soda, and baking powder for 30 seconds to evenly distribute the leavening.
- In the bowl of a stand mixer fitted with the whisk attachment, whisk together the brown sugar and oil until combined. Add the egg and mix.
- Add the buttermilk and vanilla to the coffee mixture and mix to combine.
- With the mixer running on medium speed, add half of the flour mixture and then add half of the buttermilk mixture to the sugar mixture, mixing after each addition until combined. Add the remaining flour and then the remaining buttermilk mixture, mixing until smooth. Using a large (3-ounce/90-ml) cookie scoop, scoop out the batter and place mounds about 3 inches (7.5 cm) apart on the prepared sheet pans. Bake until the cakes spring back when gently poked, about 15 minutes. Let cool completely.

MAKE THE FILLING

- In a stand mixer fitted with the paddle attachment, combine the cream cheese, butter, confectioners' sugar, and salt, mixing until smooth.
- Scoop ¼ cup (60 ml) of the filling onto the flat side of a cooled cake and top with another cake, flat side down; press together gently. Repeat until all the cakes are used.

OPTIONS

Check page 16 before proceeding for additional details on ensuring your recipes are gluten free and/or vegan.

VEGAN

FOR THE CAKE: Increase the baking soda to 1 teaspoon. Omit the egg. Replace the buttermilk with 1 cup (240 ml) plain almond milk and 1 tablespoon distilled white vinegar, stirred together and allowed to sit for 2 minutes undisturbed to curdle. FOR THE FILLING: Replace the cream cheese with 1 (8-ounce/225 g) package vegan cream cheese and replace the butter with 4 tablespoons (55 g) Earth Balance Vegan Buttery Sticks. Decrease the confectioners' sugar to 2 cups (200 g). As this mixture is not as stiff as the non-vegan cream cheese filling, sandwich only a few tablespoons in between the cakes.

GLUTEN FREE

FOR THE CAKE: Omit the coffee. Melt the chocolate by itself in a heatproof bowl set over a saucepan of simmering water (to make a double boiler), stirring constantly until melted. Replace the flour with 1 cup (160 g) finely milled brown rice flour, 1/3 cup (45 g) sweet white sorghum flour, 3 tablespoons tapioca starch, and 1 teaspoon xanthan gum. Replace the oil with 9 tablespoons (130 g) unsalted butter, softened. Cream together the sugar and butter until light and fluffy. Increase the eggs to 2 and add one at a time. Reduce the buttermilk to 1/2 cup (120 ml).

HEALTHIER

FOR THE CAKE: Increase the coffee by 1 tablespoon to make 1/4 cup plus 1 tablespoon (75 ml) coffee total. Replace the flour with 1/2 cup (70 g) Sprouted Super Flour (see page 220) and 1 cup (100 g) whole-wheat pastry flour. Replace the sugar with 1 cup (160 g) organic granulated palm sugar. Replace the oil with 1/4 cup (60 ml) organic grapeseed oil and 1/4 cup (60 g) pureed black beans (from a can of cooked organic black beans, pureed in a blender or food processor); first mix together the palm sugar and the oil, then add the pureed black beans, then the egg.

I sold these tea cakes at my pastry shop, Gesine Confectionary. While they were meant to be morning pastries, they were popular all day long. I kept baking these puppies from 4 a.m. until the moment we closed, at 7 p.m. Over the years, requests for this recipe outpace requests for all other Gesine Confectionary treats.

(MAKES 10 MINI-BUNDT CAKES)

Procedure

MAKE THE CAKES

- Preheat the oven to 350°F (175°C). Thoroughly spray mini-Bundt molds with nonstick baking spray.
- In the bowl of a stand mixer fitted with the paddle attachment, beat the butter on high speed until smooth. Add the sugar and continue creaming on high speed, scraping down the sides of the bowl every now and again, until the mixture is light and fluffy, 5 to 10 minutes.
- Whisk together the flour, baking powder, and salt in a large bowl. Sift the mixture onto a large piece of parchment paper. Sift the mixture again, back into the large bowl. Set aside.
- To the well-creamed butter and sugar, add the eggs one at a time, mixing on medium speed until each egg is completely incorporated, scraping down the bowl after each addition. Add the vanilla extract and paste and mix until incorporated. Add the flour mixture and mix on low speed until well incorporated. With a large rubber spatula, fold the whipped cream into the batter.
- Fill each Bundt mold half full. Bang the molds against the counter a few times to release any big air bubbles. Bake until the tops are golden brown and the cake springs back when gently poked, 20 to 25 minutes. Let cool.

MAKE THE GLAZE

- In a small bowl, combine the confectioners' sugar and milk and stir until smooth. Spoon the glaze over the cooled cakes.

Ingredients

FOR THE CAKES

8 ounces (225 g) European unsalted butter (like Plugra), slightly cooler than room temperature
1½ cups (300 g) sugar
2 cups (255 g) cake flour
1 teaspoon baking powder
½ teaspoon fine sea salt
5 large eggs
1 tablespoon vanilla extract
1 teaspoon vanilla bean paste
½ cup (120 ml) heavy cream, whipped to medium peaks and refrigerated

FOR THE GLAZE

1 cup (100 g) confectioners' sugar
2 tablespoons whole milk

Check page 16 before proceeding for additional details on ensuring your recipes are gluten free and/or vegan.

VEGAN

FOR THE CAKE: Ignore the procedure in the main recipe and do as follows: Replace the butter with ½ cup (120 ml) organic grapeseed oil and ½ cup (120 ml) plain almond milk. Replace the eggs with 10 ounces (280 g) silken tofu, drained (see page 13). Put the sugar, tofu, oil, almond milk, both vanillas, and 1 tablespoon distilled white vinegar in a food processor and pulse until smooth. Push the mixture through a sieve into a large mixing bowl. Replace the flour with 2 cups (260 g) all-purpose flour and add 1 teaspoon baking soda to the dry ingredients; whisk together in a large bowl for 30 seconds to evenly distribute the leavening. Add the dry ingredients all at once to the tofu mixture and whisk together until a smooth batter forms. Omit the heavy cream. FOR THE GLAZE: Replace the milk with 2 tablespoons plain almond milk.

GLUTEN FREE

FOR THE CAKE: To prepare the molds, use traditional nonstick cooking spray, not nonstick baking spray (which contains flour). Increase the sugar to 2 cups (400 g). Replace the flour with 2 cups (320 g) finely milled brown rice flour, ¾ cup (100 g) sweet white sorghum flour, ¼ cup (30 g) cornstarch, and 1½ teaspoons xanthan gum. Increase the baking powder to 2 teaspoons.

HEALTHIER

FOR THE CAKE: Replace half of the butter with ½ cup (120 ml) organic grapeseed oil. Replace the sugar with 1¼ cups (200 g) organic granulated palm sugar. Cream together the butter and palm sugar until light and fluffy and then add the oil, mixing until just combined. Replace the flour with 2 cups (200 g) whole-wheat pastry flour. Omit the heavy cream. FOR THE GLAZE: Leave off the glaze.

Chocolate-
ZUCCHINI
BREAD

At the end of summer in these parts, we send out email warnings: "It's that time. Lock your doors." You see, Vermont is a pretty darn safe place. It's a rare thing for anyone to lock up either house or car. But come zucchini season, the danger of someone cracking open your unbolted entry and tossing in a half dozen squash is a real risk. They grow so abundantly in our gardens that it's virtually impossible to use up the bounty. But here's a way to get rid of your zucchini and enjoy it too. With chocolate! It's fudgy, moist, and delicious; as a friend said, "It's a damn good chocolate cake." This recipe may seem like it makes an odd number (two smaller quickbread loaves), but I have good reason for writing it this way: You'll have one to freeze for later and one to eat ASAP. The other option is to give one away, but this is zucchini you'll want to keep for yourself.

(MAKES TWO 7-BY-3½-INCH (17-BY-9-CM) LOAVES)

Ingredients

2 cups (340 g) peeled and grated zucchini
    (2 to 4 zucchini)
1¼ cups (175 g) all-purpose flour
¼ cup (20 g) Dutch-process cocoa powder
    (like King Arthur Flour's Black Cocoa)
1 teaspoon baking powder
1 teaspoon baking soda
1 teaspoon instant espresso powder
1 teaspoon salt
1 large egg
½ cup (110 g) light brown sugar, packed
¼ cup (50 g) granulated sugar
4 tablespoons (55 g) unsalted butter, melted
¼ cup (60 ml) canola oil
1 tablespoon distilled white vinegar
1 teaspoon vanilla bean paste or vanilla
    extract

Procedure

- Preheat the oven to 350°F (175°C). Spray two 7-by-3½-inch (17-by-9-cm) loaf pans with nonstick cooking spray.
- Put the grated zucchini in a sieve and allow any excess moisture to drain.
- In a large mixing bowl, whisk together the flour, cocoa powder, baking powder, baking soda, espresso powder, and salt for 30 seconds to evenly distribute the leavening.
- In the bowl of a food processor, pulse together the zucchini, egg, both sugars, the melted butter, oil, vinegar, and vanilla until combined. Add the flour mixture and pulse until a homogenous batter forms. Divide the batter evenly between the prepared pans. Bake until a toothpick inserted in the center comes out mostly clean with a few moist crumbs attached, 30 to 35 minutes.

Pumpkin Gugelhupf
(PAGE 95)

Chocolate-Zucchini
Bread

Check page 16 before proceeding for additional details on ensuring your recipes are gluten free and/or vegan.

GLUTEN FREE

Reduce the zucchini to 1½ cups (255 g). Replace the flour with 1 cup (160 g) finely milled brown rice flour, ¼ cup (35 g) sweet white sorghum flour, and 1 teaspoon xanthan gum. Increase the eggs to 2. Replace the oil with 4 tablespoons (55 g) unsalted butter to make ½ cup (1 stick/ 115 g) butter total. Melt the butter and let cool slightly.

VEGAN

Replace the egg with 1 large egg's worth of flaxseed meal mixed with water (see page 12). Replace the butter with another ¼ cup (60 ml) canola oil to make ½ cup (120 ml) canola oil total.

HEALTHIER

Replace the flour with ¼ cup (40 g) Sprouted Super Flour (see page 220) and 1 cup (100 g) organic whole-wheat pastry flour. Replace both sugars with ¾ cup (120 g) organic granulated palm sugar. Replace the butter with ¼ cup (60 g) pureed black beans (from a can of cooked organic black beans, pureed in a blender or food processor). Replace the oil with ¼ cup (60 ml) organic grapeseed oil. Add 2 tablespoons orange juice to the wet ingredients.

VEGAN

FOR THE CAKE: Increase the baking soda to 3 teaspoons. Replace the eggs with 2 large eggs' worth of flaxseed meal mixed with water (see page 12). Increase the vinegar to 3 tablespoons.

GLUTEN FREE

FOR THE CAKE: Spray the gugelhupf mold with traditional non-stick cooking spray, not baking spray (which contains flour). Add 1 tablespoon brown rice flour to the sprayed mold and tap it, moving it around, so that there's a very slight film of flour attached to the cooking spray. Tap out any excess rice flour. Replace the flour with 2 cups (320 g) finely milled brown rice flour, ¾ cup (100 g) sweet white sorghum flour, ¼ cup tapioca starch (35 g), and 2 teaspoons xanthan gum. Omit the orange juice and applesauce. Add 1 cup (2 sticks/225 g) unsalted butter. Cream together the butter and sugar in a stand mixer fitted with a paddle attachment until light and fluffy. Add the eggs, one at a time, mixing until incorporated, then add 1 teaspoon natural orange extract, the pumpkin puree, vinegar, vanilla, and orange zest. Mix until just combined. Add the dry ingredients all at once and mix on low speed until a smooth batter forms. Stir in the cranberries and pecans.

HEALTHIER

FOR THE CAKE: Replace the flour with 2 cups (200 g) organic whole-wheat pastry flour and 1 cup (160 g) whole-grain teff flour. Replace the sugar with 2 cups (320 g) organic granulated palm sugar. Increase the orange juice by 2 tablespoons.

I grow sugar pumpkins on my farm, training the vines so they twist along cattle fences and dangle from trellises. When the pumpkins are ripe, all that hard work makes it look as if orange jewels are dripping from otherwise workaday structures. And once I've enjoyed their decorative effect, just around Thanksgiving, I bake and puree the flesh for the most glorious pumpkin pies and sweet breads, like this wonderful pumpkin gugelhupf. Canned pumpkin works just as well as fresh for those without a cattle fence laden with dangling orange orbs.

Procedure

MAKE THE CAKE

- Preheat the oven to 350°F (175°C). Spray a gugelhupf mold (or a Bundt pan) with nonstick baking spray.
- In a large bowl, whisk together the flour, baking soda, cinnamon, salt, ginger, and baking powder for 30 seconds to evenly distribute the leavening.
- In another large bowl, whisk together the pumpkin puree, sugar, orange juice, applesauce, eggs, vinegar, vanilla, and orange zest.
- Sift the flour mixture over the pumpkin mixture and fold together with a large rubber spatula until well incorporated. Stir in the cranberries and pecans. Pour the batter into the prepared mold and smooth with the back of a spoon. Bake until the cake springs back when gently poked it and a wooden skewer inserted into the center comes out with a few moist crumbs attached, 45 to 50 minutes. Release the cake from the pan and let cool completely.

TO FINISH

- Dust with confectioners' sugar.

Pumpkin GUGELHUPF

{ MAKES 1 GUGELHUPF OR SMALL (8 CUPS/2L) BUNDT CAKE }

Ingredients

FOR THE CAKE

3 cups (400 g) all-purpose flour
2 teaspoons baking soda
2 teaspoons ground cinnamon
1½ teaspoons salt
½ teaspoon ground ginger
½ teaspoon baking powder
2 cups (540 g) fresh roasted and pureed pumpkin or canned pumpkin puree (not pumpkin pie filling)
2 cups (400 g) sugar
⅔ cup (165 ml) orange juice
⅔ cup (165 ml) unsweetened applesauce
4 large eggs
1 tablespoon apple cider vinegar
1 teaspoon vanilla extract
Grated zest of ½ orange
1 cup (130 g) whole dried sweetened cranberries
1 cup (100 g) pecans, lightly toasted and coarsely chopped

TO FINISH

2 tablespoons confectioners' sugar

The Jasmin 5 FUDGY WUDGY BROWNIES

{ MAKES ABOUT 14 SMALL BROWNIES }

Ingredients

1 cup (85 g) unsweetened cocoa powder
     (like Ghirardelli Premium Baking Cocoa)
½ cup (70 g) all-purpose flour
1 teaspoon salt
¼ teaspoon baking powder
¾ cup (1½ sticks/170 g) unsalted butter
1 cup (200 g) granulated sugar
½ cup (110 g) dark brown sugar, packed
4 ounces (115 g) bittersweet chocolate (like
     Ghirardelli 60%), finely chopped
¼ cup (60 ml) brewed coffee
1 tablespoon vanilla bean paste or vanilla
     extract
2 large eggs, at room temperature

My favorite brownies are the ones with the glamorous, crispy sheen on top and chewy edges. I like them dense and fudgy. I like them black with chocolate. I like them all to myself. When I want to thank my neighbors, the Jasmins, for being so wonderful, I bake them a batch and run it over to them as fast as I can before I start scarfing them all up. That's why I've named these brownies after them—because they are so great to us so often that I make a lot of these brownies to thank them.

Procedure

- Preheat the oven to 325°F (165°C). Lightly spray a Baker's Edge pan (so that everyone gets a slightly chewy edge piece—my favorite) or a 9-inch (23-cm) square pan with nonstick cooking spray (too much spray will wreak havoc on the brownies but you want enough that they'll come out easily).
- In a medium bowl, whisk together the cocoa powder, flour, salt, and baking powder for 30 seconds to evenly distribute the leavening. Sift the ingredients to ensure that there are no cocoa lumps remaining.
- In a heavy-bottomed saucepan, combine the butter, both sugars, the bittersweet chocolate, coffee, and vanilla. Stir continuously over low heat until the butter, sugars, and chocolate have completely melted and slightly thickened. Remove from the heat, continuing to stir for 30 seconds to dissipate some of the heat.
- Put the eggs in the bowl of a stand mixer fitted with the whisk attachment and whisk on high speed until the eggs are completely broken up. Reduce the speed to medium and slowly pour the warm chocolate mixture into the beating eggs, pouring down the side of the bowl to allow the mixture to cool a bit so as not to scramble the eggs. Continue beating on high speed for 30 seconds.
- Turn the mixer off and add the cocoa powder mixture all at once. Mix on medium-low speed until the dry ingredients are completely incorporated and the batter is shiny and smooth. Pour the batter into the pan and, using a small offset spatula, spread the batter so it's evenly distributed.
- Bake on the top rack of the oven until the top has a light sheen and a toothpick inserted in the center comes out with moist crumbs still attached but not slick batter, 30 to 35 minutes in the Baker's Edge pan and 35 to 40 minutes in the 9-inch (23-cm) square pan. Let cool completely before cutting.

Nutella-Chèvre
Mini-Bundt
Brownies
(PAGE 99)

The Jasmin 5
Fudgy Wudgy
Brownies

Check page 16 before proceeding for additional details on ensuring your recipes are gluten free and/or vegan.

VEGAN

Increase the flour to 1¼ cups (175 g). Replace the butter with ½ cup (120 ml) organic refined virgin coconut oil and ½ cup (115 g) Earth Balance Vegan Shortening. Replace the eggs with 1 large egg's worth of prepared Ener-G egg replacer (see recipe, page 12) and 1 large egg's worth of flaxseed meal mixed with water (see page 12), whisking them together in the mixer as directed prior to adding the chocolate.

VEGAN

FOR THE BROWNIE BATTER: Increase the flour to 1¼ cups (175 g). Replace the butter with ¼ cup (55 g) Earth Balance Vegan Shortening, and melt it with the chocolate. Replace the eggs with 3 large eggs' worth of prepared Ener-G egg replacer (see recipe, page 12), and whisk together with the sugar. Continue as in the main recipe. FOR THE NUTELLA-CHÈVRE BATTER: Replace the chèvre with 8 ounces (225 g) vegan cream cheese. Replace the Nutella with 2 tablespoons vegan chocolate-hazelnut spread, such as Justin's Chocolate Hazelnut Butter.

GLUTEN FREE

FOR THE BROWNIE BATTER: To prepare the molds or pan, use traditional nonstick cooking spray, not nonstick baking spray (which contains flour). Replace the flour with ½ cup (60 g) cornstarch.

GLUTEN FREE

Replace the flour with ½ cup (60 g) cornstarch.

HEALTHIER

Use organic cocoa powder and bittersweet chocolate. Replace both sugars with 1½ cups (240 g) organic granulated palm sugar. Replace 6 tablespoons (85 g) of the butter with 6 tablespoons (90 ml) prune puree; melt the remaining 6 tablespoons (85 g) butter as indicated and add the prune puree to the eggs, whisking together well before adding the chocolate.

HEALTHIER

FOR THE BROWNIE BATTER: Replace the flour with ½ cup (45 g) hazelnut flour (hazelnuts ground very finely). Replace the chocolate with 7 ounces (200 g) 100% unsweetened baker's chocolate. Melt the chocolate alone in a double boiler. Replace the butter with 3½ ounces (100 ml) prune puree (I use organic baby food, such as Plum Organic's Just Prunes, which is exactly 3½ ounces) and ¼ cup (60 ml) organic grapeseed oil and replace the sugar with ¾ cup (120 g) organic granulated palm sugar; whisk together the sugar, oil, and prune puree until combined. Add the eggs one at a time and then slowly add the melted chocolate. FOR THE NUTELLA-CHÈVRE BATTER: Omit the Nutella. You'll get plenty of lovely hazelnut flavor with the hazelnut flour. Replace the sugar with 2 tablespoons organic granulated palm sugar.

I have a special love for goat cheese. Never has a sillier and more affection-ate creature also provided a cheese that's both tangy and creamy without being overpowering. It lends a perfect balance to desserts that might be otherwise too sweet, too rich . . . just too much. When you hide it inside a deeply chocolaty brownie batter, it manages to tame the rich cocoa while simultaneously singing chocolate's praises.

Nutella-Chèvre MINI-BUNDT BROWNIES

{ MAKES 1 DOZEN BROWNIES }

Procedure

MAKE THE BROWNIE BATTER

- Preheat the oven to 325°F (165°C). Spray mini-Bundt molds or a 9-inch (23-cm) square baking pan with nonstick baking spray.
- Whisk together the flour, cocoa powder, salt, and baking soda for 30 seconds to evenly distribute the leavening.
- In a small bowl, stir together the espresso powder and hot coffee.
- In a heatproof bowl set over a saucepan of simmering water (to make a double boiler), melt the chocolate and butter together, stirring constantly to keep the mixture from burning (or you can microwave at 50 percent power, stopping and stirring often, until melted). Add the coffee mixture and stir to combine. Set aside but keep warm.
- In the bowl of a stand mixer fitted with the whisk attachment, whisk the eggs and sugar until just combined. With the mixer running on low speed, slowly add the melted chocolate mixture until combined. Add the flour mixture all at once and mix until just incorporated; do not overmix.

MAKE THE NUTELLA-CHÈVRE BATTER

- In the bowl of a mixer fitted with the paddle attachment, mix all the ingredients until smooth. Transfer the batter to a piping bag fitted with a large plain tip.
- Fill each prepared mold half full with brownie batter (or add half of the batter to the prepared 9-inch/23-cm pan). Pipe approximately 1 teaspoon (feel free to add more or less) of the Nutella-chèvre batter onto the cen-ter of the brownie batter in each mold (or pipe dollops on top of the batter in the 9-inch/23-cm pan). Top with the remaining brownie batter. Bake until a toothpick inserted in the center comes out with moist crumbs stuck to it but not gooey batter; the Bundt molds will take about 30 minutes and the pan will take 40 to 45 minutes.

Ingredients

FOR THE BROWNIE BATTER

½ cup (70 g) all-purpose flour
2 ounces (55 g) Dutch-process cocoa powder (best to weigh this quantity; I use King Arthur Flour's Black Cocoa for the best flavor and color)
1 teaspoon salt
½ teaspoon baking soda
1 tablespoon instant espresso powder
¼ cup (60 ml) hot brewed coffee
7 ounces (200 g) semi- or bittersweet chocolate, finely chopped
½ cup (1 stick/115 g) unsalted butter
3 large eggs
¾ cup (150 g) sugar

FOR THE NUTELLA-CHÈVRE BATTER

8 ounces (225 g) chèvre cheese, at room temperature
1 large egg
2 tablespoons Nutella
1 tablespoon sugar
Pinch of salt

Linzertorte

CHERRY PIE

MEYER LEMON MOUNTAIN HIGH PIE

CHOCOLATE CARAMEL TART

Pop Tarts **MAPLE CREAM PIE**

MASCARPONE MANGO–KEY LIME PIE

PECAN **BANANA CREAM PIE**

PIE *Triple Chocolate Cream Pie*

COCONUT CREAM PIE

BLACKBERRY–LEMON
THYME CRUMBLE

Pumpkin Tart

FRUIT TART

PIES

Never underestimate the power of pie. It is magical. It brings warm comfort. The smell of a family-recipe cherry pie baking away in the oven can conjure beautiful memories of days gone by. You can arrange the parts to invoke a delicious rustic charm or sophisticated elegance. So much meaning in such a modest package, it's no wonder I want everyone to share in its joy.

I close this chapter with a few master recipes for crusts and pastry cream. This way, you can borrow, say, a vegan crust for a filling recipe that's been in the family for years and just happens to be animal-product free but needs a correspondingly vegan crust. Or you have a pie filling you think is the tops but you need a gluten-free pastry crust to go along with it. Rest assured, there are plenty of combinations to tempt you, so feel free to venture out into the world of pie, explore, and get inspired.

PECAN PIE

{ MAKES ONE 9-INCH (23-CM) PIE }

FOR THE CRUST
½ batch Flaky Pie Crust Dough (page 137)

FOR THE FILLING
½ cup (1 stick/115 g) unsalted butter, cut
　　into small pieces
½ cup (110 g) dark brown sugar, packed
¼ cup (60 ml) maple syrup
2 tablespoons bourbon
1 tablespoons vanilla bean paste
1 teaspoon salt
3 large eggs
2 cups (200 g) pecan halves, lightly toasted

When I take a bite of pecan pie, I'm always left with the impression that I've stolen someone's candy bar. This pie is illicit in its tender sweetness. It refuses to behave like any other pie—maybe it just didn't get the memo. Because even though it reads like pie on paper, with that flaky crust and the sweet filling, once it's in your pie hole it breaks all the rules. And thank goodness it does.

Procedure

MAKE THE CRUST

- Preheat the oven to 350°F (175°C). Line a sheet pan with parchment paper.
- On a lightly floured work surface, roll the dough out into a 12-inch (30.5-cm) round and transfer to a 9-inch (23-cm) pie pan. Crimp the edges and dock the bottom of the dough. Freeze for 20 minutes.
- Line the dough-lined pie pan with parchment paper and fill to the rim with dried beans or pie weights. Bake for 15 minutes. Remove the weights and parchment and bake until the crust no longer has a raw dough sheen, about 5 minutes more. Set aside.

MAKE THE FILLING

- In a large saucepan, combine the butter, brown sugar, maple syrup, bourbon, vanilla, and salt. Stir over low heat until the butter is completely melted. Whisk the eggs in a small bowl, then add them to the mixture in the saucepan, stirring constantly. Continue stirring until the mixture has thickened slightly, about 5 minutes. Remove from the heat.
- Set aside at least 20 whole pecans and chop the remaining into small pieces. Add the chopped pecans to the hot butter mixture and stir to coat.
- Place the prepared pie crust on the prepared sheet pan. Pour the chopped pecan mixture into the crust. Place whole pecans decoratively atop the filling, pushing each one down just enough to barely submerge it, so that the liquid filling coats the pecan without it sinking to the bottom.
- Reduce the oven temperature to 300°F (150°C) just before putting the pie in the oven. Bake until the filling is set, 55 to 60 minutes.

Check page 16 before proceeding for additional details on ensuring your recipes are gluten free and/or vegan.

VEGAN

FOR THE CRUST: Use the vegan version of the Flaky Pie Crust Dough on page 137. FOR THE FILLING: Replace the butter with ¼ cup (60 ml) organic refined virgin coconut oil. Combine only the brown sugar, maple syrup, bourbon, and salt in a saucepan over medium heat and stir until the sugar has completely melted. Attach a candy thermometer to the pan and bring the mixture to 245°F (120°C; the firm ball stage). Remove from the heat and set aside. Replace the eggs with 4 ounces (115 g) firm silken tofu that's been drained (see page 13). In the bowl of a food processor, combine the drained tofu, the sugar mixture, coconut oil, and 2 tablespoons tapioca starch; blend until smooth. Unlike the master recipe, chop all of the pecans. Pour the tofu mixture into a bowl and stir in the pecans and vanilla. Spread the filling in the prepared pie crust and bake until the filling is just set, 45 to 50 minutes.

GLUTEN FREE

FOR THE CRUST: Use the gluten-free version of the Flaky Pie Crust Dough on page 137.

HEALTHIER

FOR THE CRUST: Use the healthier version of the Flaky Pie Crust Dough on page 137. FOR THE FILLING: Replace the brown sugar with ½ cup (80 g) organic granulated palm sugar.

VEGAN

FOR THE CRUST: Use the vegan version of the Pâte Brisée on page 138. FOR THE FILLING: Replace the evaporated milk with 1½ cups (360 ml) full-fat coconut milk. Replace the eggs with 2 large eggs' worth of prepared Ener-G egg replacer (see recipe, page 12) and add 2 tablespoons melted organic refined virgin coconut oil. Omit the crème fraîche. Increase the cornstarch to ¼ cup (30 g). TO FINISH: Use the vegan version of the Maple Cookies on page 58.

GLUTEN FREE

FOR THE CRUST: Use the gluten-free version of the Pâte Brisée on page 138. TO FINISH: Use the gluten-free version of the Maple Cookies on page 58.

HEALTHIER

FOR THE CRUST: Use the healthier version of the Pâte Brisée on page 138. FOR THE FILLING: Use organic evaporated milk. Replace the sugar with ½ cup (80 g) organic granulated palm sugar. Reduce the eggs to 2 and increase the cornstarch (use organic) to ¼ cup (30 g). TO FINISH: Use the healthier version of the Maple Cookies on page 58.

Just as the spring brings a thaw, I plant my sugar pumpkin seeds at the base of our arched cattle fence. At the first sight of a shoot, I train the emerging vine so that it spins its tendrils round and round, up and over the fence. By fall, the fence and arch have become a living, breathing pumpkin extravaganza. As they ripen completely, I roast the pumpkins and scoop out the sweet yumminess inside. It's this that I turn into pumpkin filling for the best damn pumpkin pie you've ever tasted. You can roast some sugar pumpkins of your own or you can get a good-quality pumpkin puree at your grocery store.

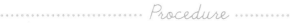

Procedure

MAKE THE CRUST

- Preheat the oven to 350°F (175°C). Line a sheet pan with parchment paper.
- Roll the dough out to a 12-inch (30.5-cm) round and line a 9-inch (23-cm) round or square fluted tart pan with the dough. Dock the bottom of the dough and freeze for 20 minutes.
- Line the tart pan with parchment paper and fill to the rim with dried beans or pie weights. Bake for 15 minutes. Remove the weights and parchment and bake until the crust loses its raw dough sheen, about 5 minutes more. Set aside.

MAKE THE FILLING

- In a large bowl, whisk together the pumpkin puree, evaporated milk, brown sugar, eggs, crème fraîche, cornstarch, cinnamon, vanilla, salt, ginger, nutmeg, cloves, and allspice until smooth. Transfer to a large pitcher or a vessel large enough to hold the filling and that has a spout for pouring.
- Place the prepared tart crust on the prepared sheet pan. Pull the rack of the oven out about halfway, then place the sheet pan on it. Pour the filling into the tart pan; make sure the filling doesn't slop over the edges of the crust. (You may have excess filling; you can bake it off without crust in small muffin cups to make little baked pumpkin custards.) Carefully push the rack back in and bake until the pie is set at the edges but gives a slight shimmy at the very center, 55 to 60 minutes. Let cool completely.

TO FINISH

- Garnish each slice with a cookie, if you like.

PUMPKIN TART

{ MAKES ONE 9-INCH (23-CM) TART }

Ingredients

FOR THE CRUST
½ batch Pâte Brisée (page 138)

FOR THE FILLING
1 (15-ounce/425-g) can pumpkin puree (not pumpkin pie filling; about 1¾ cups fresh roasted and pureed pumpkin)
1 (12-ounce/354-ml) can evaporated milk
¾ cup (165 g) dark brown sugar, packed
4 large eggs
¼ cup (60 ml) crème fraîche
2 tablespoons cornstarch
1 teaspoon ground cinnamon
1 teaspoon vanilla bean paste
½ teaspoon salt
½ teaspoon ground ginger
¼ teaspoon freshly grated nutmeg
¼ teaspoon ground cloves
¼ teaspoon ground allspice

TO FINISH
12 Maple Cookies (page 58; optional)

Blackberry-Lemon Thyme Crumble
(PAGE 109)

Cherry Pie

We have cherry trees on our property. They sit among our plums, peaches, and apples. All these trees produce gloriously. We look forward to each and every one of them bearing fruit. But it's the cherries, those red orbs of juiciness, that have us beside ourselves with anticipation. The problem is, the birds share our enthusiasm. The second the cherries come to peak ripeness, we enter a battle of wits. It's cause for great celebration when we manage to harvest enough for a single pie, and once we do I take pains to let the cherries sing without adding a slew of competing flavors.

{ MAKES ONE 9-INCH (23-CM) PIE }

Procedure

MAKE THE BOTTOM CRUST

- Preheat the oven to 350°F (175°C).
- On a lightly floured work surface, roll the larger disk of pie dough into a 12-inch (30.5-cm) round. Line a 9-inch (23-cm) pie pan with the dough and dock the bottom with a fork. Crimp the edges. Refrigerate for 20 minutes. Keep the second disk of dough tightly wrapped in plastic wrap and refrigerated.

MAKE THE FILLING

- Pit the cherries and put them in a large bowl.
- In a small bowl, whisk together the orange juice and vanilla bean paste. Pour the mixture over the cherries and stir to coat evenly.
- In another bowl, stir together the sugar, ClearJel, nutmeg, salt, and orange zest. Pour over the cherries and stir to evenly coat.

ASSEMBLE THE PIE

- On a lightly floured work surface, roll out the remaining disk of dough into a 12-inch (30.5-cm) round. Cut the round into twelve ½-inch (12-mm) strips (or whatever suits your fancy). Cover with plastic wrap and set aside in a cool area of your kitchen (refrigerating will make the lattice process tough, but too warm will make the strips mushy).
- Fill the prepared bottom crust with the cherry mixture. Using a cheese grater, grate the frozen butter over the top of the cherries.
- Form a lattice with the dough strips, weaving the strips to form a basket weave. Trim the extra dough and reroll. Using a ¼-inch (6-mm) round cookie cutter, cut circles from the dough and place around the edge of the pie. Using a pastry brush, brush the entire top crust with the egg wash and sprinkle with Sugar in the Raw. Bake until the top crust is deeply golden brown and the filling is bubbling, 45 minutes to 1 hour.

Ingredients

1 batch Flaky Pie Crust Dough (page 137)

FOR THE FILLING

2 pounds (910 g) dark sweet cherries
2 tablespoons orange juice
1 teaspoon vanilla bean paste
1 cup (200 g) sugar
¼ cup (40g) ClearJel
Pinch of freshly grated nutmeg (2 scrapes from a nutmeg)
Pinch of salt
Grated zest of 1 orange

TO ASSEMBLE

2 tablespoons unsalted butter, frozen
1 large egg whisked together with 1 tablespoon water to make an egg wash
3 tablespoons Sugar in the Raw or sparkling sugar

Check page 16 before proceeding for additional details on ensuring your recipes are gluten free and/or vegan.

VEGAN

FOR THE CRUST: Use the vegan version of the Flaky Pie Crust Dough on page 137. FOR THE FILLING: Omit the butter. TO ASSEMBLE: Brush the top crust with 3 tablespoons plain soy milk instead of the egg wash.

GLUTEN FREE

FOR THE CRUST: Use the gluten-free version of the Flaky Pie Crust Dough on page 137. FOR THE FILLING: Replace the ClearJel with ¼ cup (40 g) minus 1 table-spoon tapioca starch. Whisk the tapioca starch together with the sugar and coat the cherries as you do in the master recipe.

HEALTHIER

FOR THE CRUST: Use the healthier version of the Flaky Pie Crust Dough on page 137. FOR THE FILLING: Omit the butter. Replace the sugar with ½ cup (80 g) organic granulated palm sugar.

VEGAN

FOR THE CRUST: Use the vegan version of the Flaky Pie Crust Dough on page 137. FOR THE CRUMBLE: Replace the butter with 1 cup (240 ml) melted organic refined virgin coconut oil. Serve with vegan vanilla ice cream (optional, page 194).

GLUTEN FREE

FOR THE CRUST: Use the gluten-free version of the Flaky Pie Crust Dough on page 137. FOR THE FILLING: Replace the ClearJel with 2 tablespoons tapi-oca starch and whisk together with the sugar. FOR THE CRUMBLE: Replace the flour with 2½ cups (400 g) finely milled brown rice flour. Increase the butter by 4 tablespoons for a total of 1¼ cups (2½ sticks/280 g).

HEALTHIER

FOR THE CRUST: Use the healthier version of the Flaky Pie Crust Dough on page 137. FOR THE FILLING: Replace the sugar with ¼ cup (40) organic granulated palm sugar. FOR THE CRUMBLE: Omit the crumble ingredients entirely and do the following instead: Combine 1 cup (80 g) rolled oats (not quick cooking), ½ cup (50 g) whole-wheat pastry flour, ½ cup (80 g) organic granulated palm sugar, 2 tablespoons orange juice, ½ teaspoon ground cinnamon, and a pinch of salt in a large bowl. Stir to combine. Drizzle ¼ cup (60 ml) organic grapeseed oil over the mixture and stir with a wooden spoon until the crumble starts to clump. Put the crumble mixture on top of the blackberry mix-ture and proceed as directed in the main recipe. Serve with healthier vanilla ice cream (optional, page 194).

It's so simple, just blackberries and a sweet crumble topping, served with a scoop of vanilla ice cream. Yet this is a dessert that tugs at my sweet tooth like no other. Even as a kid, when high-octane, fluorescently hued treats ruled the day, this fruity delight held sway. Add a hint of lemon thyme and you've brought an added dimension of sophistication and flavor to the works. (If you can't find fresh lemon thyme, leave it out—it will be delicious as is.)

Blackberry- LEMON THYME CRUMBLE

(MAKES ONE 9-INCH (23-CM) PIE)

Procedure

MAKE THE CRUST

- Preheat the oven to 350°F (175°C). Line a sheet pan with parchment paper.
- On a lightly floured work surface, roll the dough out to a 12-inch (30.5-cm) round and transfer it to a 9-inch (23-cm) pie pan, or break the dough into small pieces and press the dough into the pan, in the bottom and up the sides, with your fingers. Crimp the edges. Freeze for 20 minutes.
- Line the dough-lined pie pan with parchment paper and fill to the rim with dried beans or pie weights. Bake for 15 minutes. Remove the weights and parchment and bake until the crust has lost its raw dough sheen, about 5 minutes more. Set aside to cool completely.

MAKE THE FILLING

- Whisk together the sugar, ClearJel, lemon zest, thyme, and salt. Pour over the blackberries and toss to coat.

MAKE THE CRUMBLE

- In a large bowl, combine the flour, butter, both sugars, and the salt. Stir together, working the crumbs with a spoon or your fingers until the butter is absorbed and forms clumps.

ASSEMBLE THE PIE

- Fill the prepared pie crust with the blackberry mixture. Top the blackberries with the crumble. Gently press down on the crumble to make sure it doesn't roll off the pie. Place the assembled pie on the prepared sheet pan and bake until the crumble is golden brown and the filling starts to bubble, 35 to 45 minutes. Serve warm with a scoop of vanilla ice cream, if you like.

Ingredients

FOR THE CRUST
½ batch Flaky Pie Crust Dough (page 137)

FOR THE FILLING
¼ cup (50 g) sugar
2 tablespoons ClearJel
1 teaspoon grated lemon zest
¼ teaspoon finely chopped fresh lemon thyme
Pinch of salt
4 pints (1.4 kg) blackberries

FOR THE CRUMBLE
2½ cups (330 g) all-purpose flour
1 cup (2 sticks/225 g) unsalted butter, melted
½ cup (100 g) granulated sugar
½ cup (110 g) light brown sugar, packed
½ teaspoon salt

Vanilla ice cream, for serving (optional; see Vanilla Bean Ice Cream, page 195)

This pie is everything a tropical summer pie should be, lush and zesty. An added bump of zest ups the citrus ante. Adding mascarpone to this zingy pie brings a little creamy tang to the party. When you serve this pie, get ready for some faces to light up with joy.

Procedure

MAKE THE CRUST

- Preheat the oven to 350°F (175°C).
- Line a 9-inch (23-cm) round tart pan with dough by breaking up the dough into small pieces and using your fingers to press it into an even layer in the bottom and up the sides of the pan. Freeze for 20 minutes.
- Line the dough-lined pan with parchment paper and fill with dried beans or pie weights. Bake for 15 minutes. Remove the weights and parchment and bake until the crust loses its raw dough sheen, about 5 minutes more. Set aside.

MAKE THE FILLING

- In a large bowl, whisk together the condensed milk, mango juice, Key lime juice, egg yolks, mascarpone, maple syrup, lime zest, and salt. Pour into the pie crust and bake until the center of the filling just barely shimmies and is set, 25 to 30 minutes. Let cool completely at room temperature, then refrigerate.

TO FINISH

- In the bowl of a stand mixer fitted with the whisk attachment, whisk together the cream, mascarpone, and confectioners' sugar to stiff peaks. Transfer the whipped cream to a pastry bag fitted with a St. Honoré tip. Pipe "commas" all along the perimeter of the cooled pie and then continue piping them in the center until the whipped cream fills the entire surface.
- Peel the mango. Cut ¼-inch-thick (6-mm-thick) slices and, using a small heart cookie cutter, stamp out heart shapes from the slices. Place the hearts on top of the whipped topping or just place a solitary heart in the center.

Ingredients

FOR THE CRUST
½ batch Sweet Tart Dough (page 139)

FOR THE FILLING
1 (14-ounce/396-g) can sweetened condensed milk
½ cup (120 ml) mango juice
¼ cup (60 ml) Key lime juice
2 large egg yolks
2 tablespoons mascarpone cheese
2 tablespoons maple syrup
1 teaspoon grated lime zest
Pinch of salt

TO FINISH
2 cups (480 ml) cold heavy cream
1 cup (240 ml) mascarpone cheese
½ cup (50 g) confectioners' sugar
1 mango

OPTIONS

Check page 16 before proceeding for additional details on ensuring your recipes are gluten free and/or vegan.

VEGAN

FOR THE CRUST: Use the vegan version of the Sweet Tart Dough on page 139 and bake through completely. Let the crust cool completely after baking. FOR THE FILLING: Omit the filling ingredients entirely and do the following instead: In a small bowl, whisk together ½ cup (100 g) vegan sugar, ¼ cup (30 g) cornstarch, 2 tablespoons Genutine vegetarian gelatin, and ¼ teaspoon salt. In a large saucepan, combine 1 (13½-ounce/400-ml) can full-fat coconut milk, 1¼ cups (300 ml) vanilla soy milk, ¾ cup (180 ml) mango juice, and ¼ cup (60 ml) Key lime juice and simmer over low heat. Add the sugar mixture to the saucepan and whisk until the sugar and gelatin have dissolved and the mixture is smooth. Increase the heat to medium-high and continue whisking until the mixture thickens to the consistency of ketchup. Transfer the mixture to the cooled prepared pie crust. Refrigerate to set, at least 2 hours to overnight. FOR THE TOPPING: Replace the cream and mascarpone with 1¼ cups (300 ml) full-fat coconut cream. Whisk the coconut cream to stiff peaks with the confectioners' sugar.

GLUTEN FREE

FOR THE CRUST: Use the gluten-free version of the Sweet Tart Dough on page 139.

HEALTHIER

FOR THE CRUST: Use the healthier version of the Sweet Tart Dough on page 139. Let the crust cool completely after baking. FOR THE FILLING: Omit the filling ingredients entirely and do the following instead: In a small bowl, whisk together ½ cup (80 g) organic granulated palm sugar, ¼ cup (30 g) cornstarch, 2 tablespoons Genutine vegetarian gelatin, and ¼ teaspoon salt. In a large saucepan, combine 1 (13½-ounce/400-ml) can full-fat coconut milk, 1½ cups (360 ml) plain soy milk, ½ cup (120 ml) mango juice, and ¼ cup (60 ml) Key lime juice and simmer over low heat. Add the dry ingredients to the saucepan and whisk until the sugar and gelatin have dissolved and the mixture is smooth. Transfer the mixture to the cooled prepared pie crust. Refrigerate to set, at least 2 hours to overnight. FOR THE TOPPING: Replace the cream and mascarpone with 1¼ cups (300 ml) full-fat coconut cream. Replace the confectioners' sugar with 3 tablespoons organic granulated palm sugar.

This is the best "bang for your buck" tart out there. For just a little work, you get a work of art. This is my favorite summer tart, and I trot it out whenever I want to impress but have very little time. That it's delectable is almost beside the point.

Procedure

MAKE THE CRUST

- Preheat the oven to 350°F (175°C).
- On a lightly floured work surface, roll the dough out to a 12-inch (30.5-cm) round and line a 9-inch (23-cm) pie pan with the dough. Crimp the edges and dock the bottom of the dough. Freeze for 20 minutes.
- Line the dough-lined pie pan with parchment paper and fill with dried beans or pie weights. Bake for 15 minutes. Remove the weights and parchment and bake until the crust is golden brown and baked through, 15 to 20 minutes more. Set aside to cool completely.

MAKE THE FILLING

- Transfer the hot pastry cream directly to the prepared cooled pie shell. Refrigerate, covering the pie with a piece of plastic wrap directly touching the cream to prevent a skin from forming, until completely cool, about 1 hour.

TO FINISH

- Arrange the fruit on top of the chilled pastry cream in a decorative manner.
- Put the preserves in a small saucepan with 2 tablespoons water. Stir over low heat until the preserves melt into the water, creating a smooth glaze. Set aside to cool slightly.
- Using a pastry brush, paint the cooled glaze over the arranged fruit to create a lasting sweet sheen over the tart.

Ingredients

FOR THE CRUST
½ batch Flaky Pie Crust Dough (page 137)

FOR THE FILLING
1 batch still-hot Pastry Cream (page 141)

TO FINISH
2 pints (670 g) mixed berries and/or cherries
2 kiwi, peeled and thinly sliced
¼ cup (60 ml) seedless red berry preserves (any flavor, as long as it's seedless, will work)

Check page 16 before proceeding for additional details on ensuring your recipes are gluten free and/or vegan.

VEGAN

FOR THE CRUST: Use the vegan version of the Flaky Pie Crust Dough on page 137. FOR THE FILLING: Use the vegan version of the Pastry Cream on page 141.

VEGAN

FOR THE CRUST: Replace the butter with 1 cup (225 g) room-temperature organic palm oil shortening. Replace the eggs with 1 large egg's worth prepared of Ener-G egg replacer (see recipe, page 12) and 1 large egg's worth of flaxseed meal mixed with water (see page 12).

GLUTEN FREE

FOR THE CRUST: Use the gluten-free version of the Flaky Pie Crust Dough on page 137.

GLUTEN FREE

FOR THE CRUST: Replace the flour with 1¼ cups (200 g) finely milled brown rice flour, ½ cup (70 g) sweet white sorghum flour, ¼ cup (35 g) tapioca starch, and 1 teaspoon xanthan gum.

HEALTHIER

FOR THE CRUST: Use the healthier version of the Flaky Pie Crust Dough on page 137. FOR THE FILLING: Use the healthier version of the Pastry Cream on page 141. TO FINISH: Choose a sugar-free preserve.

HEALTHIER

FOR THE CRUST: Replace both sugars with 1½ cups (240 g) organic granulated palm sugar. Replace the butter with 1 cup (240 ml) organic refined virgin coconut oil (melted to measure, then resolidified to room temperature). Replace the flour with 1 cup (100 g) whole-wheat pastry flour and 1 cup (160 g) finely milled brown rice flour. FOR THE FILLING: Use sugar-free raspberry preserves.

LINZERTORTE

{ MAKES ONE 9-INCH (23-CM) TORTE }

Ingredients

FOR THE CRUST

1 cup (200 g) granulated sugar
1 cup (220 g) light brown sugar, packed
12 ounces (340 g) pecans, roughly chopped
1 cup (2 sticks/225 g) unsalted butter, at
    room temperature
2 large eggs
2 cups (260 g) all-purpose flour
1 teaspoon grated orange zest
1 teaspoon ground cinnamon
½ teaspoon salt
Pinch of freshly grated nutmeg (2 scrapes
    from a nutmeg)

FOR THE FILLING

1 cup (240 ml) raspberry preserves

1 pint (335 g) berries, for serving

Alongside pumpkin pie, my mother would always bake a linzertorte for Thanksgiving dessert. Up until her very last Thanksgiving with us, she gifted us with her sublime baking talents and her abiding love through pie. This traditional European staple ever reminds me of my mother, with its complex flavors and its beautiful design. Mom would be so thrilled that I found a way to bring this gem of hers to everyone's table.

Procedure

MAKE THE CRUST

- Preheat the oven to 325°F (165°F). Lightly spray a 9-inch (23-cm) square or round tart pan with a removable bottom with nonstick cooking spray.
- In the bowl of a food processor, combine both sugars and the pecans and pulse until a smooth paste forms. Add the butter and pulse until smooth. Add the eggs and pulse until smooth. In a bowl, whisk together the flour, orange zest, cinnamon, salt, and nutmeg until combined. Add the flour mixture, all at once, to the food processor and pulse until well incorporated and smooth.
- Transfer a little over half the dough to a large pastry bag fitted with a large plain tip. Cover the bowl with the remaining dough with plastic wrap and refrigerate.
- In the prepared pan, pipe the dough in touching, concentric squares or circles, from the outside in, so that they form an even base. Smooth with an offset spatula. Don't worry about creating sides to the crust. Bake the crust until it just begins to brown, about 20 minutes. Let cool slightly.

MAKE THE FILLING

- Spread the raspberry preserves in an even layer over the slightly cooled crust, leaving a ½-inch (12-mm) edge free around the perimeter. Transfer the remaining dough to the pastry bag with the large open tip and pipe dots around the edge and parallel lines 1 inch (2.5 cm) apart across the surface of the tart. Pipe another set of parallel lines perpendicular to the first set, creating a lattice pattern. Bake for 30 minutes, or just until the pastry begins to brown. Let cool completely.
- Serve with berries.

Meyer Lemon

MOUNTAIN HIGH

PIE

{ MAKES ONE 9-INCH (23-CM) PIE }

Ingredients

FOR THE CRUST

½ cup (1 stick/115 g) unsalted butter, slightly
    cooler than room temperature
½ cup (100 g) sugar
1 large egg
½ teaspoon vanilla extract
Grated zest of ½ Meyer lemon
1½ cups (210 g) all-purpose flour
½ teaspoon salt

FOR THE FILLING

1½ cups (3 sticks/340 g) unsalted butter
1¼ cups (300 ml) Meyer lemon juice (from
    about 10 lemons)
1 cup (200 g) plus 2 tablespoons sugar
Grated zest of 1 Meyer lemon
Pinch of salt
8 large eggs
5 large egg yolks
1 teaspoon unflavored gelatin (optional)

FOR THE MERINGUE

10 large egg whites
2 cups (400 g) sugar
2 tablespoons corn syrup
Generous pinch of salt

More isn't necessarily better. But in this case, it is. More meringue on top of an extra-zippy and tart filling makes for a decadent pie-eating experience. But not only does this stuff taste fantastic, it looks absolutely transcendent. At first, in the pie pan, you see a vision of a snow-capped mound of sweetness. Once you slice into the confectionary Rockies, flaky crust gives way to lush yellow lemony happiness, and up rises that meringue. Oh lordy.

Procedure

MAKE THE CRUST

- In the bowl of a stand mixer fitted with the paddle attachment, cream together the butter and sugar until light and fluffy. Add the egg and mix until well combined. Scrape down the sides and bottom of the bowl. Add the vanilla and lemon zest and mix again to combine. Add the flour and salt. Mix until the dough starts to come together in small chunks.
- Transfer the dough to a large piece of plastic wrap. Knead it gently to incorporate any errant flour blobs. Press the dough into a disk and wrap in plastic wrap. Refrigerate for at least 20 minutes.
- Spray a 9-inch (23-cm) pie pan with nonstick cooking spray. Crumble half the dough onto the bottom of the pan and pat it down to cover the bottom. Take small pieces of the remaining dough and press them against the sides of the pan. (Tightly wrap the remaining dough and refrigerate for another use—this stuff makes the best cookies.) Dock the dough with a fork and freeze for 20 minutes.
- Preheat the oven to 350°F (175°C).
- Line the dough-lined pan with parchment paper and fill with dried beans or pie weights. Bake the crust until completely baked through, about 20 to 25 minutes. Remove the weights and parchment. Let cool completely.

MAKE THE FILLING

- Put the butter in a very large saucepan and melt it over low heat. Add the lemon juice, sugar, lemon zest, and salt and stir until the sugar is completely dissolved.

continued

- In a bowl, whisk together the eggs and egg yolks. Continue whisking and add a cupful of the warm butter-juice mixture to temper them. Add the tempered mixture to the saucepan, whisking all the while. Continue whisking the mixture over medium-low heat until the filling thickens to the consistency of ketchup. (This can take a very long time—I'm not going to lie. Give yourself a good 30 minutes to slave away whisking. It's worth it.) Remove from the heat and sprinkle the gelatin over the top of the hot filling (it really helps set the mixture). Let sit for a minute, then whisk the gelatin into the filling until completely melted.
- Pour the hot filling into the cooled pie crust. Refrigerate uncovered until set, about 2 hours. (At this point, you have a beautiful Tarte au Citron. You can serve it just like this, without the meringue, and you'll be a star.)

MAKE THE MERINGUE

- Once the filling is cool and set, in the bowl of a stand mixer fitted with the whisk attachment, combine the egg whites, sugar, corn syrup, and salt.
- Place the bowl over a large saucepan of simmering water (to make a double boiler) and whisk until the sugar is completely melted and a candy thermometer reads 160°F (71°C).
- Transfer the bowl back to the stand mixer and whisk on high speed until stiff peaks form and the bowl is cool to the touch. Dollop the meringue on top of the filling. Using a kitchen torch, gently brown the exterior of the meringue. Do not place under the broiler; otherwise you'll melt your filling.

OPTIONS

GLUTEN FREE

FOR THE CRUST: Use the gluten-free version of the Sweet Tart Dough on page 139, adding 1 teaspoon grated Meyer lemon zest with the flour mixture.

Check page 16 before proceeding for additional details on ensuring your recipes are gluten free and/or vegan.

VEGAN

FOR THE CRUST: Use the vegan version of the Sweet Tart Dough on page 139, adding 1 teaspoon grated Meyer lemon zest with the flour mixture. FOR THE FILLING: Omit the filling ingredients entirely and do the following instead: In a small bowl, whisk together ½ cup (100 g) vegan sugar, ¼ cup (30 g) cornstarch, 2 tablespoons Genutine vegetarian gelatin, and ¼ teaspoon salt. In a large saucepan, combine 1 (13½-ounce/400-ml) can full-fat coconut milk, 1¼ cup (300 ml) Meyer lemon juice, and 1 cup (240 ml) vanilla soy milk and simmer over low heat. Add the sugar mixture to the saucepan and whisk until the sugar and gelatin have dissolved and the mixture is smooth. Increase the heat to medium-high and continue whisking until the mixture thickens to the consistency of ketchup. Transfer the mixture to the cooled prepared pie crust. Refrigerate to set, at least 2 hours to overnight. FOR THE MERINGUE: Omit the meringue ingredients entirely and do the following instead:

3 tablespoons Versawhip 600K (not prepared)
2 teaspoons Ener-G egg replacer (not prepared)
1 teaspoon baking powder
1 cup (200 g) sugar
⅓ cup (75 ml) corn syrup

1 tablespoon vanilla bean paste
1 tablespoon Genutine vegetarian gelatin
½ teaspoon salt
¼ teaspoon lemon juice

- In the bowl of a stand mixer fitted with the whisk attachment, combine the Versawhip, egg replacer, and baking powder. Add ½ cup (120 ml) water and whisk to combine. Let sit for 3 minutes to saturate. Whip on high speed until light and fluffy. In the meantime, combine the sugar, corn syrup, ¼ cup (60 ml) water, the vanilla, vegetarian gelatin, salt, and lemon juice in a large saucepan. Stir over medium heat until the sugar is completely dissolved. Attach a candy thermometer and cook, undisturbed, until the mixture reaches 243°F (120°C).
- With the mixer running on medium-high speed, carefully pour the hot sugar mixture into the whisking mixture, making sure to pour down the side of the bowl to prevent the hot sugar from splashing. The mixture will deflate—this is normal. Continue whisking on high speed until the mixture is very fluffy and holds stiff peaks and the mixing bowl is cool to the touch, 15 to 20 minutes. Dollop on top of the cooled filling and serve immediately.

HEALTHIER

FOR THE CRUST: Use the healthier version of the Sweet Tart Dough on page 139, adding the grated zest of 1 Meyer lemon to the flour mixture. FOR THE FILLING: Reduce the butter to ½ cup (1 stick/115 g). Add a ¼ cup (30 g) cornstarch to the Meyer lemon juice to create a slurry first, then add to the melted butter. Replace the sugar with 1 cup (160 g) organic granulated palm sugar. Reduce the eggs to 4 and the egg yolks to 1. Add the palm sugar, eggs, egg yolk, zest, and salt. Whisk over medium heat until the mixture thickens to the consistency of mayonnaise. Make sure to use the gelatin as indicated in the main recipe to ensure that the mixture sets. FOR THE MERINGUE: Replace the sugar with 2 cups (320 g) organic granulated palm sugar.

Chocolate CARAMEL TART

{ MAKES ONE 13¾-BY-4½-INCH (35-BY-11-CM) RECTANGULAR TART }

Ingredients

FOR THE CRUST
½ batch Chocolate Tart Dough (page 140)

FOR THE CARAMEL FILLING
2 cups (400 g) sugar
⅓ cup (75 ml) corn syrup
¼ teaspoon lemon juice
1 teaspoon salt
½ cup (120 ml) heavy cream
½ cup (1 stick/115 g) unsalted butter
1 teaspoon vanilla bean paste

FOR THE GANACHE
4 ounces (115 g) bittersweet chocolate, finely
    chopped
⅓ cup (75 ml) heavy cream
2 tablespoons unsalted butter
½ teaspoon vanilla bean paste
Pinch of salt

Cut into this tart. Pull out a slice. Be quick about it. The caramel nestled within the confines of the cocoa walls of this beauty will start to slowly ooze from its pastry vessel. It's a glorious sight and cause for great celebration. But like I said, serve up this treat with haste so that everyone gets a slice with caramel. If you plan on keeping this tart around for a few days in the fridge, I'd suggest you buy a pie dam that will keep the caramel in place between servings. Another option is to firm up the caramel more on the stovetop before ladling into the tart shell, making the caramel the consistency of that in a candy bar. The choice is yours, a soft scrumptious ooze or a chewy gooey caramel dream.

Procedure

MAKE THE CRUST
- Preheat the oven to 350°F (175°C).
- Spray a 13¾-by-4½-inch (35-by-11-cm) rectangular tart pan with a removable bottom (or one 9-inch/23-cm round tart pan with a removable bottom) with nonstick baking spray and line with the dough by pressing the dough into an even layer in the bottom and up the sides of the tart pan with your fingers. Freeze for 20 minutes.
- Line the pan with parchment paper and fill to the rim with dried beans or pie weights. Bake for 15 minutes. Remove the weights and parchment and bake until the crust looks dry and baked through, 10 to 15 minutes. Set aside to cool completely.

MAKE THE CARAMEL FILLING
- In a large, heavy saucepan, combine the sugar, ½ cup (120 ml) water, the corn syrup, lemon juice, and salt. Stir over medium heat until the sugar is completely dissolved. While stirring, take a damp pastry brush and wipe down any sugar granules that are clinging to the sides of the pan.
- Once the sugar has completely melted, stop stirring and allow the sugar syrup to continue cooking until it turns a medium amber color (a bit lighter than the color of a penny). Remove from the heat and immediately add the cream, butter, and vanilla; the mixture will bubble vigorously, so stand back and allow it to calm. Stir the mixture until the butter is completely melted and the ingredients are completely incorporated. Set aside to thicken slightly, about 20 minutes. This caramel will be soft and just a tad thicker than a traditional sundae caramel sauce. To make firmer candy-bar-consistency caramel, once you've added the butter and cream, return

continued

the caramel to the stovetop and attach a candy thermometer. Stir the caramel over medium-low heat until the thermometer reads 243°F (120°C; the firm ball stage).

- Carefully remove the sides of the tart pan from around the tart dough. (Because this dough is fragile, I keep the removable bottom attached to stabilize the tart and transfer it to a serving plate.)
- Pour the thickened caramel into the prepared tart shell. Refrigerate to set, about 20 minutes.

MAKE THE GANACHE

- Put the chocolate in a heatproof bowl. Set aside.
- In a heavy saucepan, combine the cream, butter, vanilla, and salt. Bring to a simmer, making sure the butter is completely melted.
- Pour the cream mixture over the chopped chocolate and let sit undisturbed for 2 minutes to allow the chocolate to melt. Whisk the chocolate until the ganache is shiny and smooth. Carefully pour the ganache over the set caramel and gently tip the tart from side to side to allow the ganache to cover the top of the tart completely. Allow the ganache to set, about 30 minutes, before cutting and serving.

CHOCOLATE CARAMEL TART

OPTIONS

Check page 16 before proceeding for additional details on ensuring your recipes are gluten free and/or vegan.

VEGAN

FOR THE CRUST: Use the vegan version of the Chocolate Tart Dough on page 140. FOR THE CARAMEL FILLING: Replace the cream with ½ cup (120 ml) well-shaken full-fat coconut milk. Replace the butter with 4 tablespoons organic palm oil shortening. FOR THE GANACHE: Replace the cream with ⅓ cup (75 ml) well-shaken full-fat coconut milk. Replace the butter with 2 tablespoons organic palm oil shortening.

GLUTEN FREE

FOR THE CRUST: Use the gluten-free version of the Chocolate Tart Dough on page 140. Spray the tart pan with traditional nonstick cooking spray, not baking spray (which contains flour).

HEALTHIER

FOR THE CRUST: Use the healthier version of the Chocolate Tart Dough on page 140. FOR THE CARAMEL FILLING: Replace the sugar with 2 cups (320 g) organic granulated palm sugar. Replace the corn syrup with ⅓ cup (75 ml) organic agave syrup. Because palm sugar is very dark, it's impossible to gauge when it's become "medium amber," so it's best to attach a candy thermometer after the sugar has melted to gauge when the syrup has reached 305°F (150°C). At that point, remove it from the heat. Replace the cream with ½ cup (120 ml) well-shaken full-fat coconut milk.

You like chocolate? I'll give you chocolate. Three distinct layers of it, in fact. There's so much decadence in one slice, you'll likely go into a chocolate coma. But who said that's a bad thing?

Procedure

MAKE THE CRUST

- Preheat the oven to 350°F (175°C).
- Spray a 9-inch (23-cm) round fluted tart pan or pie pan with nonstick baking spray and line with the dough by pressing the dough into an even layer in the bottom and up the sides of the tart pan with your fingers. Freeze for 20 minutes.
- Line the pan with parchment paper and fill to the rim with dried beans or pie weights. Bake for 20 minutes. Remove the weights and parchment and bake until the crust looks dry and baked through, 10 to 15 minutes. Set aside to cool completely.

MAKE THE FILLING

- To the hot pastry cream, add the butter (as called for in the Pastry Cream recipe on page 141) and the chocolate and let sit undisturbed for 5 minutes. Whisk until both the butter and chocolate are completely melted into the pastry cream. Transfer all but 1 cup (240 ml) of the warm pastry cream to the cooled prepared tart shell and smooth into an even layer with a small offset spatula. Cover the pie with plastic wrap, making sure the plastic wrap touches the pastry cream to prevent a skin from forming, and refrigerate until set and cooled, about 1 hour. Put the reserved pastry cream in a bowl and cover with plastic wrap, making sure the plastic wrap touches the pastry cream. Refrigerate until completely cool and set, about 1 hour.
- Once the reserved pastry cream has cooled, place the heavy cream in the bowl of a stand mixer fitted with the whisk attachment. Whisk the cream to stiff peaks. Briefly stir the reserved pastry cream with a spoon to loosen. Using a large rubber spatula, carefully fold the whipped cream into the pastry cream and then carefully spread atop the pastry cream in the tart shell.

TO FINISH

- In the bowl of a stand mixer fitted with the whisk attachment, whisk the heavy cream with the confectioners' sugar until you achieve stiff peaks. Spoon the whipped cream atop the tart. Serve immediately.

Triple Chocolate CREAM PIE

{ MAKES ONE 9-INCH (23-CM) PIE }

Ingredients

FOR THE CRUST
½ batch Chocolate Tart Dough (page 140)

FOR THE FILLING
1 batch Pastry Cream (page 141), prepared up until the point the butter is to be added
8 ounces (225 g) bittersweet chocolate, finely chopped
1 cup (240 ml) cold heavy cream

TO FINISH
2 cups (480 ml) cold heavy cream
¼ cup (25 g) confectioners' sugar

Check page 16 before proceeding for additional details on ensuring your recipes are gluten free and/or vegan.

VEGAN

FOR THE CRUST: Use the vegan version of the Chocolate Tart Dough on page 140. FOR THE FILLING: Base your pastry cream on the vegan version on page 141, adding the chocolate with the Buttery Sticks. Replace the heavy cream with 1 cup (240 ml) ice-cold full-fat coconut cream. FOR FINISH: Replace the heavy cream with 2 cups (480 ml) ice-cold full-fat coconut cream.

GLUTEN FREE

FOR THE CRUST: Use the gluten-free version of the Chocolate Tart Dough on page 140. Spray the tart pan with traditional nonstick cooking spray, not baking spray (which contains flour).

HEALTHIER

FOR THE CRUST: Use the healthier version of the Chocolate Tart Dough on page 140. FOR THE FILLING: Use the healthier of the Pastry Cream version on page 141, adding organic bittersweet chocolate just as you add the butter.

a note from my sweet tooth

If you've ever opened a typical can of coconut milk, you'll notice that often there's a thick layer of coconut cream hovering above a thin watery substance. When I add coconut milk in lieu of plain milk, I just shake everything together. However, when I want to use the stuff to whip, like a whipped topping, I only want the thick stuff on top, not the watery stuff. This is how you ensure optimal whipping: (1) Don't shake the can. (2) Store your coconut milk in the fridge to keep the cream layer firm. (3) Carefully turn the can upside down, open it from the bottom, and gently pour off the thin coconut water. Scoop out the thick cream for whipping. Different brands provide varying degrees of cream; I like to use the Thai brand Chaokoh, which is available at Asian food markets.

But you'll be saying to yourself, "This is a very uncertain way of gathering an essential ingredient." Well, a way of guaranteeing you'll have the amount of coconut cream you'll need in a recipe is by buying "coconut cream" (not cream of coconut, which is something else entirely) at some Asian markets and at Trader Joe's and high-end markets.

Bananas are already creamy, aren't they? Of all the fruits, it's the only one that I'd describe as "creamy." (Other than the paw paw, of course, also known as the custard apple. I grow them here on the farm, but when I mention to people that I have paw paws in season, no one knows what the hell I'm talking about.) And what could be better for a cream pie than an already creamy fruit?

Banana
CREAM
PIE

{ MAKES ONE 9-INCH (23-CM) PIE }

Procedure

MAKE THE CRUST

- Preheat the oven to 350°F (175°C).
- On a lightly floured work surface, roll the disk of pie dough into a 12-inch (30.5-cm) round. Line a 9-inch (23-cm) pie pan with the dough and dock the bottom with a fork. Crimp the edges. Freeze for 20 minutes.
- Line the dough-lined pie pan with parchment paper and fill to the rim with dried beans or pie weights. Bake for 15 to 20 minutes. Remove the weights and parchment. Bake for 10 to 15 minutes more, until the dough is baked through. Set aside to cool completely.

MAKE THE FILLING

- In a small bowl, mash 4 of the bananas. Put the cream and milk as called for in the pastry cream recipe on page 141 in a saucepan along with the mashed bananas. Bring the mixture to a simmer, then remove from the heat and set aside to cool completely. Pour the mixture into a sieve set over a bowl, using a rubber spatula to gently press out any liquid caught in the bananas (but don't press so hard that you mush the bananas through the sieve—if a bit comes through, that's okay). Discard the solids.
- Transfer the liquid to a saucepan and make the pastry cream as in the recipe on page 141, using the banana-infused liquid for the milk and cream. Transfer 1 cup (240 ml) of the finished pastry cream to a small bowl and cover with plastic wrap, making sure the plastic wrap touches the surface of the pastry cream to prevent a skin from forming. Refriger-ate until completely cool, about 30 minutes.
- Slice the remaining 4 bananas into ¼-inch (6-mm) rounds and line the bottom of the prepared pie crust with them, overlapping the pieces. Pour the remaining still-warm pastry cream on top of the bananas. Cover with plastic wrap, making sure the wrap touches the surface of the cream. Refrigerate until completely cool, about 1 hour.

continued

Ingredients

FOR THE CRUST
½ batch Flaky Pie Crust Dough (page 137)

FOR THE FILLING
8 bananas
1 batch Pastry Cream (page 141), prepared up until the point the cream and milk are to be added

FOR THE TOPPING
2 cups (480 ml) heavy cream
¼ cup (25 g) confectioners' sugar

MAKE THE TOPPING

- In the bowl of a stand mixer fitted with the whisk attachment, whisk the heavy cream and confectioners' sugar to stiff peaks.

- Stir the remaining 1 cup (240 ml) pastry cream to loosen. Gently fold ½ cup (120 ml) of the whipped heavy cream into the pastry cream to lighten it. Spread the lightened pastry cream over the cooled pastry cream in the pie pan. Dollop the remaining whipped cream on top of the lightened pastry cream and swirl decoratively with the back of a spoon.

BANANA CREAM PIE

OPTIONS

Check page 16 before proceeding for additional details on ensuring your recipes are gluten free and/or vegan.

VEGAN

FOR THE CRUST: Use the vegan version of the Flaky Pie Crust Dough on page 137. FOR THE FILLING: Use the vegan version of the Pastry Cream on page 141, infusing the alternative milk with bananas as in the main recipe. FOR THE TOPPING: Replace the heavy cream with full-fat coconut cream, whipped to stiff peaks with the confectioners' sugar.

GLUTEN FREE

FOR THE CRUST: Use the gluten-free version of the Flaky Pie Crust Dough on page 137.

HEALTHIER

FOR THE CRUST: Use the healthier version of the Flaky Pie Crust Dough on page 137. FOR THE FILLING: Use the healthier version of the Pastry Cream on page 141, infusing the milks with bananas as in the main recipe. FOR THE TOPPING: Replace 1 cup (240 ml) of the heavy cream with full-fat coconut cream. Replace the confectioners' sugar with 2 tablespoons organic granulated palm sugar. Whisk the heavy cream and coconut cream with the palm sugar to stiff peaks.

Coconut Cream Pie
(PAGE 130)

Banana Cream Pie
(PAGE 127)

Coconut CREAM PIE

{ MAKES ONE 9-INCH (23-CM) PIE }

Ingredients

FOR THE CRUST
½ batch Flaky Pie Crust Dough (page 137)

FOR THE FILLING
1 batch Pastry Cream (page 141), prepared
    with 2 cups (480 ml) full-fat coconut
    milk instead of the cream and milk

FOR THE TOPPING
2 cups (180 g) sweetened shredded coconut
2 cups (480 ml) heavy cream
¼ cup (25 g) confectioners' sugar

For all my complaining through the years about my hatred of coconut, I certainly have changed my tune. Now I love the stuff. Can't get enough of it. This pie layers coconut upon coconut, from a thick custard, to a creamy light topping, to a sweet and crunchy flurry of shredded coconut. If this pie doesn't convert you to the coconut cause, I don't know what will.

Procedure

MAKE THE CRUST

- Preheat the oven to 350°F (175°C).
- On a lightly floured work surface, roll the disk of pie dough into a 12-inch (30.5-cm) round. Line a 9-inch (23-cm) pie pan with the dough and dock the bottom with a fork. Crimp the edges. Freeze for 20 minutes.
- Line the dough-lined pie pan with parchment paper and fill to the rim with dried beans or pie weights. Bake for 15 to 20 minutes. Remove the weights and parchment. Bake for 10 to 15 minutes more, until the dough is baked through. Set aside to cool completely.

MAKE THE FILLING

- Put 1 cup (240 ml) of the pastry cream in a small bowl and cover with plastic wrap, making sure the plastic wrap touches the surface of the pastry cream to prevent a skin from forming. Refrigerate until completely cool, about 30 minutes.
- Pour the remaining still-warm pastry cream into the prepared pie crust. Cover with plastic wrap, making sure the plastic wrap touches the surface of the pastry cream. Refrigerate until completely cool, about 1 hour.

MAKE THE TOPPING

- Preheat the oven to 225°F (110°C). Line a half sheet pan with parchment paper.
- Spread the coconut in an even layer on the prepared pan. Bake until golden brown, checking it every 2 minutes and stirring with a wooden spoon so that it browns evenly, about 10 minutes. Let cool completely.
- In the bowl of a stand mixer fitted with the whisk attachment, whisk the heavy cream and confectioners' sugar to stiff peaks.
- Stir the chilled reserved pastry cream to loosen. With a large rubber spatula, gently fold ½ cup (120 ml) of the whipped heavy cream into the pastry cream to lighten it. Spread the lightened pastry cream over the cooled pastry cream in the pie pan. Dollop the remaining whipped cream on top of the lightened pastry cream and swirl decoratively with the back of a spoon. Sprinkle with the coconut.

Check page 16 before proceeding for additional details on ensuring your recipes are gluten free and/or vegan.

VEGAN

FOR THE CRUST: Use the vegan version of the Flaky Pie Crust Dough on page 137. FOR THE FILLING: Use the vegan version of the Pastry Cream on page 141. FOR THE TOPPING: Replace the heavy cream with 2 cups (480 ml) full-fat coconut cream, whipped to stiff peaks with the confectioners' sugar.

GLUTEN FREE

FOR THE CRUST: Use the gluten-free version of the Flaky Pie Crust Dough on page 137.

HEALTHIER

FOR THE CRUST: Use the healthier version of the Flaky Pie Crust Dough on page 137. FOR THE FILLING: Use the healthier version of the Pastry Cream on page 141. FOR THE TOPPING: Replace 1 cup (240 ml) of the heavy cream with coconut cream. Replace the confectioners' sugar with 2 tablespoons organic granulated palm sugar. Whisk the remaining heavy cream and coconut cream with the palm sugar to stiff peaks.

Maple CREAM PIE

{ MAKES ONE 9-INCH (23-CM) PIE }

Ingredients

FOR THE CRUST

½ batch Flaky Pie Crust Dough (page 137)
    or ½ batch Pâte Brisée (page 138), cold
    (see headnote)

FOR THE FILLING

1 batch still-warm Pastry Cream (page 141),
    made with ½ cup (120 ml) maple syrup
    instead of sugar

TO FINISH

2 cups (480 ml) cold heavy cream
½ cup (120 ml) cold mascarpone cheese
¼ cup (60 ml) maple syrup or ¼ cup (40 g)
    maple sugar
12 Maple Cookies (page 58; optional)

I'm a Vermonter. Therefore, I could live on maple syrup. So much so that I'm often inclined to use maple to replace sugar in a recipe when only a little is called for. But if you've ever had a maple candy, you know that when concentrated, maple sugar can be wicked sweet. I've found that this is the case with most maple pies I've run across. So in this recipe, I've made sure that there's just enough sweetness without overwhelming the pie, while still keeping this luscious treat full of maple flavor.

You'll see I've given you two options for the crust. Both are delicious. If you'd like a more rustic pie, use the flaky pie crust in a traditional pie pan. If you'd like a more elegant presentation, use the pâte brisée in a fluted tart pan.

Procedure

MAKE THE CRUST

- Preheat the oven to 350°F (175°C).
- For a flaky crust, on a lightly floured work surface, roll the flaky pie crust dough out to a 12-inch (30.5-cm) round. Line a 9-inch (23-cm) pie pan with the dough. Crimp the edges and dock the bottom of the dough with a fork. For a pâte brisée crust, line a tart pan with the pâte brisée by gently pressing the dough into the bottom and sides of a fluted 9-inch (23-cm) round tart pan so that it's ⅛ to ¼ inch (3 to 6 mm) thick. For either option, freeze the dough in the pan for 20 minutes.
- Line the dough-lined pan with parchment paper and fill to the rim with dried beans or pie weights. Bake for 20 minutes. Remove the weights and parchment. Continue baking until the crust is baked through, 15 to 20 more minutes. Let cool completely.

MAKE THE FILLING

- Instead of transferring the warm pastry cream to a bowl to cool, pour it directly into the cooled prepared crust. Cover the tart with plastic wrap and refrigerate until cool.

TO FINISH

- In the bowl of a stand mixer fitted with the whisk attachment, whisk the heavy cream, mascarpone, and maple syrup to stiff peaks. Using a small offset spatula, spread the topping across the surface of the pie.
- Garnish each slice with a cookie, if you like.

Check page 16 before proceeding for additional details on ensuring your recipes are gluten free and/or vegan.

VEGAN

FOR THE CRUST: Use the vegan version of the Flaky Pie Crust Dough on page 137 or Pâte Brisée on page 138. FOR THE FILLING: Use the vegan version of the Pastry Cream on page 141, replacing the sugar with ½ cup (120 ml) maple syrup. TO FINISH: Replace the cream and mascarpone with 2 cups (480 ml) full-fat coconut cream. In a stand mixer fitted with the whisk attachment, whip the coconut cream with the maple syrup until stiff. Use the vegan version of the Maple Cookies on page 58, if using.

GLUTEN FREE

FOR THE CRUST: Use the gluten-free version of the Flaky Pie Crust Dough on page 137 or Pâte Brisée on page 138. TO FINISH: Use the gluten-free version of the Maple Cookies on page 58, if using.

HEALTHIER

FOR THE CRUST: Use the healthier version of the Flaky Pie Crust Dough on page 137 or Pâte Brisée on page 138. FOR THE FILLING: Use the healthier version of the Pastry Cream on page 141, replacing the sugar with ½ cup (120 ml) maple syrup. TO FINISH: Replace the cream and mascarpone with 1 cup (240 ml) nonfat Greek yogurt, making sure to drain off any visible whey. Stir in only 3 tablespoons maple syrup. In lieu of slathering the entire pie with the cream, add a small dollop to each individual slice. Use the healthier version of the Maple Cookies on page 58, if using.

POP TARTS

{ MAKES ABOUT 2 DOZEN TARTS }

Ingredients

FOR THE CRUST
½ batch Pâte Brisée (page 138)

TO ASSEMBLE
1 large egg whisked together with 1
    tablespoon water to make an egg wash
Lollipop sticks
1 cup (240 ml) strawberry (or other berry)
    jam or Nutella or other hazelnut-
    chocolate spread

TO FINISH
1 cup (100 g) confectioners' sugar
1 to 2 tablespoons whole milk
Multicolored sprinkles

For my birthday, my mother would make a cake. Every year, weeks before the day, she'd ask, "Sina, what kind of cake this year?" Any manner of dream confection I concocted in my sweets-addicted brain, she'd conjure for my special day. And while the cakes changed each year due to my unabashed appreciation and curiosity for all things pastry, my mother always made one thing consistently: Little flower-shaped cookies she'd bake on sticks and then arrange in vases lining the table, the original (and much tastier) edible arrangement. Do I really need to say that I had the best mom ever? I have taken her beautiful idea and translated it to buttery pastry.

Procedure

MAKE THE CRUST
- Preheat the oven to 350°F (175°C). Line two sheet pans with parchment paper.
- Roll the dough to ⅛ inch (3 mm) thick. Cut 1-by-2-inch (2.5-by-5-cm) rectangles from the dough or use a 2-inch (5-cm) flower cookie cutter. Gently smoosh together the scraps, reroll, and continue cutting, but limit the number of times you reuse so that you don't overwork the dough. Place half of the rectangles or flowers of dough on the prepared pans (set the others aside to use as the tops), leaving about 3 inches (7.5-cm) of space between them and keeping in mind that you'll need space for the lollipop stick.

ASSEMBLE THE POP TARTS
- Brush the edges of a rectangle or flower on the pan with the egg wash. Place a lollipop stick on the dough and gently press. Place a scant 1 teaspoon jam in the center of the dough and place a second piece of dough on top. Gently press the edges of the dough to seal. You can decorate the edges by pressing another lollipop stick along the edges of the dough to create a scalloped edge. Brush the top of the dough with egg wash. Repeat with the remaining dough shapes and jam. Bake until the dough is golden brown, 10 to 15 minutes. Let cool completely.

TO FINISH
- Make a glaze by stirring the confectioners' sugar with 1 tablespoon of the milk until the mixture is smooth. If the mixture is too thick, add a bit more milk and continue stirring.
- Spoon a scant 1 teaspoon glaze over the top of each pop tart. Scatter a few sprinkles over the glaze when it's still tacky so that they stick. Allow the glaze to set before serving.

OPTIONS

Check page 16 before proceeding for additional details on ensuring your recipes are gluten free and/or vegan.

VEGAN

FOR THE CRUST: Use the vegan version of the Pâte Brisée on page 138. TO ASSEMBLE: Replace the egg wash with 3 tablespoons plain soy milk. TO FINISH: Replace the milk with full-fat coconut milk.

GLUTEN FREE

FOR THE CRUST: Use the gluten-free version of the Pâte Brisée on page 138.

HEALTHIER

FOR THE CRUST: Use the healthier version of the Pâte Brisée on page 138. TO ASSEMBLE: Use a sugar-free preserve to fill the pop tarts. TO FINISH: Use less glaze or eliminate it altogether.

---

a note from my sweet tooth

A common mistake in pie dough making is to add too much moisture and to overwork the dough, making for a tough pie crust. In this dough, you'll notice that it may look a bit "shaggy" after adding the water and you'll feel inclined to either add more water or process it more. Refrain! Do the "pinch" test indicated in the instructions; if the dough holds together, you're good. Simply press the dough into a disk and let it rest in the fridge. The dough will continue to hydrate as it rests and will bake up flaky and delicious.

Procedure

- In the bowl of a food processor, pulse together the flour, sugar, and salt until combined. Add the butter and pulse until the mixture resembles coarse cornmeal.
- While continuing to pulse, slowly add the water and lemon juice until the dough just comes together. Squeeze a small amount of dough between your thumb and index finger to make sure it holds its shape. If it doesn't, add cold water 1 tablespoon at a time while still pulsing, but make sure that the dough doesn't form into a wet ball.
- Remove the dough from the food processor. Divide the dough in half (if making a double-crusted pie, make one half slightly heavier than the other). Press each half of dough into a disk and wrap with plastic wrap. Refrigerate the dough for 20 minutes. The dough will keep for up to 1 month, wrapped well, in the freezer.

OPTIONS

Check page 16 before proceeding for additional details on ensuring your recipes are gluten free and/or vegan.

VEGAN

Replace the butter with well-chilled Earth Balance Vegan Buttery Sticks, 1 cup (225 g) Earth Balance Vegan Shortening, or 1 cup (240 ml) refined virgin coconut oil. If using coconut oil, make sure that the bits of fat and flour, when processed, resemble fine cornmeal not coarse cornmeal.

GLUTEN FREE

Replace the flour with 1 cup (160 g) finely milled brown rice flour, ½ cup (80 g) potato starch, ¼ cup (35 g) sweet white sorghum flour, ¼ cup (35 g) tapioca starch, and 2 teaspoons xanthan gum. This dough does well with 10 minutes more baking time than the traditional dough in order to keep its crispness, as the xanthan gum retains moisture and the longer baking time helps evaporate any excess. This dough is more delicate when rolled out as well. Use a large cake spatula to transfer the dough to the pie pan so that it keeps its shape.

HEALTHIER

Replace the flour with 2 cups (200 g) organic whole-wheat pastry flour. Replace half of the butter with ½ cup (120 ml) very cold organic refined virgin coconut oil. Process the coconut oil with the flour mixture first, until the mixture resembles fine cornmeal. Add the butter and pulse until the mixture resembles coarse cornmeal. Increase the water to ½ cup plus 2 tablespoons (150 ml).

{ MAKES ENOUGH FOR 1 DOUBLE OR 2 SINGLE 9-INCH (23-CM) PIE CRUSTS, OR 12 INDIVIDUAL HAND PIES }

This is my go-to flaky, quick, and delicious pie crust that works beautifully with both sweet and savory fillings. It makes just enough dough for a double-crusted pie (or two single crusts), or you can divide the dough into 12 pieces and make adorable individual hand pies.

Ingredients

2 cups (260 g) all-purpose flour
1 tablespoon sugar
1 teaspoon salt
1 cup (2 sticks/225 g) unsalted butter, cut into small pieces and chilled in the freezer for 10 minutes
½ cup (120 ml) ice-cold water
1 teaspoon lemon juice

Pâte

BRISÉE

{ MAKES ENOUGH FOR
TWO 9-INCH (23-CM) TART SHELLS }

Pâte brisée is a buttery, tender crust that holds its shape beautifully when baked. It's flaky but has a glorious texture that's perfect for using in tart molds (unlike my pie crust). My brisée is a bit different from most in that I use sweetened condensed milk and vanilla. The condensed milk helps hold the dough together, and the two give the whole affair a lovely caramel flavor without adding undue sweetness. This dough works equally well with sweet and savory tarts and it comes together in just a few minutes.

Ingredients

2 cups (260 g) all-purpose flour
½ teaspoon salt
1 cup (2 sticks/225 g) cold
    unsalted butter, cut into
    small pieces
1 large egg yolk
2½ tablespoons sweetened
    condensed milk
½ teaspoon vanilla extract

Procedure

- In the bowl of a food processor, pulse together the flour and salt until combined. Add the cold butter and pulse until the mixture resembles very coarse cornmeal.
- In a small bowl, whisk together the egg yolk, condensed milk, and vanilla. While continuing to pulse, slowly add the egg yolk mixture to the food processor. Continue pulsing until the mixture is almost together but not smooth (you'll still see chunks of flour and butter).
- Turn the dough out onto a lightly floured work surface. Fold the dough over a few times, just until it is smooth and all the flour is combined; don't overwork the dough. Shape the dough into two disks, wrap them in plastic wrap, and refrigerate for 20 minutes. The dough will keep for up to 1 month, wrapped well, in the freezer.
- Once baked per the particular recipe, allow the crust to cool completely before unmolding.

OPTIONS

Check page 16 before proceeding for additional details on ensuring your recipes are gluten free and/or vegan.

VEGAN

Replace the butter with 1 cup (2 sticks/ 225 g) cold Earth Balance Vegan Buttery Sticks or 1 cup (240 ml) organic refined virgin coconut oil (melted to measure and resolidified in the fridge). Replace the egg yolk with 1 teaspoon flaxseed meal mixed with 1 tablespoon warm water; allow the mixture to sit until it gels before using. Replace the condensed milk with 2½ tablespoons full-fat coconut milk. Mix together the flaxseed mixture, coconut milk, and vanilla before adding to the food processor.

GLUTEN FREE

Replace the flour with 1 cup (160 g) finely milled brown rice flour, ½ cup (80 g) potato starch, ¼ cup (35 g) sweet white sorghum flour, ¼ cup (35 g) tapioca starch, and 2 teaspoons xanthan gum. This dough is delicate to work with. Be sure to allow the baked crust to cool completely before removing from its pan.

HEALTHIER

Replace the flour with 2 cups (200 g) organic whole-wheat pastry flour. Replace half of the butter with ½ cup (120 ml) organic refined virgin coconut oil (melted to measure and resolidifed in the fridge). Replace the condensed milk with 2½ tablespoons full-fat coconut milk. Mix the egg yolk, coconut milk, and vanilla together with 2 tablespoons ice-cold water before adding to the food processor.

- In the bowl of a food processor, pulse together the flour, cornstarch, both sugars, and the salt until combined. Add the butter and pulse until the mixture resembles coarse cornmeal.
- In a small bowl, whisk together the egg, condensed milk, and vanilla. While continuing to pulse, slowly add the egg mixture to the food processor. Continue pulsing until the dough just begins to come together.
- Turn the dough out onto a lightly floured work surface. Gently knead it until smooth. Divide the dough in half. Shape into two compact disks, wrap them in plastic wrap, and refrigerate for at least 20 minutes before using. The dough will keep for up to 1 week, wrapped, in the fridge.
- Once baked per the particular recipe, allow the crust to cool completely before unmolding.

OPTIONS

Check page 16 before proceeding for additional details on ensuring your recipes are gluten free and/or vegan.

VEGAN

Replace the butter with 1¼ cups (2½ sticks/ 280 g) Earth Balance Vegan Buttery Sticks, cut into small pieces and frozen for at least 30 minutes; or with 1¼ cups (300 ml) organic refined virgin coconut oil, gently melted to measure, cooled in a shallow pan in the refrigerator, and then broken into small pieces. Replace the egg with 1 large egg's worth of flaxseed meal mixed with water (see page 12). Replace the condensed milk with 3 tablespoons full-fat coconut milk.

GLUTEN FREE

Replace the flour with 1 cup (160 g) sweet white rice flour, ½ cup (80 g) finely milled brown rice flour, ½ cup (70 g) tapioca starch, and 1 teaspoon xanthan gum. Keep the 1 cup (120 g) cornstarch. This is a delicate dough. Be sure to allow the baked crust to cool completely before removing from its pan.

HEALTHIER

Replace the confectioners' sugar with ½ cup (95 g) Sucanat. Replace the sugar with ¼ cup (40 g) organic granulated palm sugar. Replace the butter with Earth Balance Vegan Buttery Sticks or 1¼ cups (300 ml) organic refined virgin coconut oil; prior to using, cut the buttery sticks into small pieces and freeze for at least 30 minutes; or, if using coconut oil, gently heat it until liquid to measure, then pour into a shallow pan, chill in the fridge until solid, and break into small pieces.

Sweet Tart
DOUGH

{ MAKES ENOUGH FOR TWO 9-INCH (23-CM) TART SHELLS }

Sweet dough, also known as short crust, is a delicate gem of a dough. Many bakers know it as pâte sucré, a sweet dough common in French pastry. I grew up with the German version, *Mürbeteig*. Whether you speak of this delectable shortbreadlike dough in English, French, or German, you'll be speechless once you get a bite of any tart made with the stuff.

····· *Ingredients* ·····

2 cups (260 g) all-purpose flour
1 cup (120 g) cornstarch
½ cup (50 g) confectioners' sugar
¼ cup (50 g) granulated sugar
1 teaspoon salt
1¼ cups (2½ sticks/280 g) cold unsalted butter, cut into small pieces
1 large egg
3 tablespoons sweetened condensed milk
1 teaspoon vanilla bean paste

Chocolate Tart
DOUGH

{ MAKES ENOUGH FOR
TWO 9-INCH (23-CM) TARTS }

Sometimes all it takes to put a tart over the top (in the best way) is to add a crisp chocolate crust. This dough is challenging to work with; it's soft and not conducive to traditional rolling out. But once you resolve to simply use your fingers to pat it into place, you'll have no trouble working with this sumptuous dough.

Ingredients

1 cup (2 sticks/225 g) unsalted butter, at room temperature
1 cup (200 g) sugar
2 cups (260 g) all-purpose flour
¾ cup (60 g) Dutch-process cocoa powder (like Cacao Barry Extra Brute)
1 teaspoon instant espresso powder
1 teaspoon salt

Procedure

- In the bowl of a stand mixer fitted with the paddle attachment, cream together the butter and sugar until light and fluffy.
- In a large bowl, whisk together the flour, cocoa powder, espresso powder, and salt.
- With the mixer running on low speed, add the flour mixture to the creamed butter mixture and mix until the dough comes together.
- Turn the dough out onto a lightly floured work surface and gently knead until smooth. Return to the bowl, cover with plastic wrap, and refrigerate for at least 20 minutes before using. The dough will keep for up to 1 week, wrapped, in the fridge.
- Once baked per the particular recipe, allow the crust to cool completely before unmolding.

OPTIONS

Check page 16 before proceeding for additional details on ensuring your recipes are gluten free and/or vegan.

VEGAN

Replace the butter with 1 cup (225 g) organic palm oil shortening.

GLUTEN FREE

Replace the flour with 2 cups (320 g) finely milled brown rice flour and 1 teaspoon xanthan gum. This dough is very delicate. Be sure to allow the baked crust to cool completely before removing from its pan.

HEALTHIER

Replace the sugar with 1 cup (160 g) organic granulated palm sugar. Replace half of the butter with ½ cup (120 ml) organic grapeseed oil, adding it after creaming the butter and palm sugar. Replace the flour with 1 cup (160 g) finely milled brown rice flour and 1 cup (100 g) whole-wheat pastry flour. Refrigerate the dough in the bowl, covered with plastic wrap, for at least 30 minutes before using.

- In the bowl of a stand mixer fitted with the whisk attachment, combine the egg yolks, sugar, cornstarch, and salt, whisking until smooth and pale.
- In a large, heavy saucepan, combine the cream, milk, and vanilla and bring to a simmer. With the mixer running on medium speed, slowly and carefully pour the hot milk mixture into the mixer and whisk until combined.
- Transfer the mixture back to the saucepan and whisk constantly over medium-low heat until the mixture thickens to the consistency of mayonnaise. Remove the pastry cream from the heat and add the butter, whisking until incorporated.
- Transfer the pastry cream to a large bowl and cover with plastic wrap, making sure that the plastic wrap touches the surface of the pastry cream to prevent a skin from forming. Refrigerate until cool, about 2 hours. (Once cool, pastry cream will "set" and become a very thick consistency, often quite firm, even firm enough to cut. This is normal. Before using, simply whisk the mixture until smooth.)

Check page 16 before proceeding for additional details on ensuring your recipes are gluten free and/or vegan.

Pastry CREAM

{ MAKES 3 CUPS }

Pastry cream is a go-to filling for many pies, primarily cream pies. It's best used the day it's made. However, as it often happens, we tend to use just as much as we need, say a cup or two, and then leave the rest in the fridge to be forgotten until it's too late. In the case of pastry cream, if you've realized a few days after making it that it's languishing in the back of the icebox, use the creamy stuff to add to apple pie filling or other baked fillings or in lieu of frangipane. Luckily, my master recipe for pastry cream is already gluten free.

Ingredients

6 large egg yolks
½ cup (100 g) sugar
¼ cup (30 g) cornstarch
Pinch of salt
1 cup (240 ml) heavy cream
1 cup (240 ml) whole milk
1 tablespoon vanilla bean paste
    or vanilla extract
2 tablespoons unsalted butter, at
    room temperature

VEGAN

Omit all of the pastry cream ingredients and instead use the following: In a small bowl, whisk together ½ cup (100 g) sugar, ½ cup (60 g) cornstarch, 1 teaspoon Versawhip 600K, 1 teaspoon vegetarian gelatin, and ¼ teaspoon salt until combined. In a large saucepan, bring 2½ cups (600 ml) plain soy milk, full-fat coconut milk, or plain almond milk to a simmer over low heat. Add the sugar mixture and whisk constantly over medium-low heat until the mixture thickens to the consistency of mayonnaise. Remove from the heat and whisk in 2 tablespoons Earth Balance Vegan Buttery Sticks until incorporated. Transfer to a bowl, cover with plastic wrap touching the surface to prevent a skin from forming, and refrigerate until cool, about 2 hours.

GLUTEN FREE

This recipe is already gluten free.

HEALTHIER

Reduce the egg yolks to 3. Replace the sugar with ½ cup (80 g) organic granulated palm sugar or ⅓ cup (75 ml) maple syrup or raw honey. Increase the cornstarch by 3 tablespoons. Replace the cream with 1 cup (240 ml) additional organic whole milk or 1 cup (240 ml) plain almond milk or full-fat coconut milk.

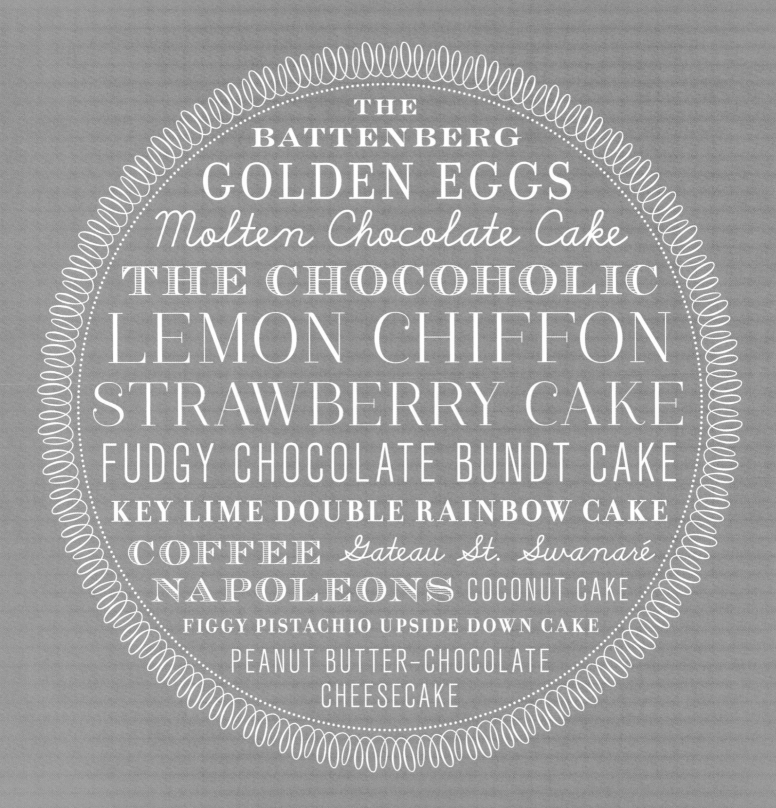

THE
BATTENBERG
GOLDEN EGGS
Molten Chocolate Cake
THE CHOCOHOLIC
LEMON CHIFFON
STRAWBERRY CAKE
FUDGY CHOCOLATE BUNDT CAKE
KEY LIME DOUBLE RAINBOW CAKE
COFFEE *Gateau St. Swanaré*
NAPOLEONS COCONUT CAKE
FIGGY PISTACHIO UPSIDE DOWN CAKE
PEANUT BUTTER–CHOCOLATE
CHEESECAKE

CAKES

Cakes make the celebratory world go round. If there's an event that's intended to bring joy, cake will likely be an integral part of it. I should know, I'm a pastry chef and was owner of a popular small-town pastry shop in Vermont. For every birthday, Passover, wedding, anniversary, bon voyage, christening, and holiday party, there'd be a cake for me to bake. Often, there would be special requests accompanying the order. And I'm not talking about just flavor or decoration (although the kinky nun cake was a pretty special request).

More and more often, I'd get a note on the order slip to make it gluten free or egg free. Or egg and dairy free. Or soy free. There was one little boy that was so beset with allergies that I called his birthday cakes "no-ingredient conundrums." No flour, no dairy, no eggs. For a baker, that's as no-ingredient as you can get. But when you get to know your customers, you end up baking for people you care for, and there's no way that kid you've got a soft spot for is not going to get a birthday cake he or she can gorge on. And so it happened that I became quite adept at adapting my recipes in such a way that every parishioner in my little chapel of pastry could enjoy these treats.

LEMON CHIFFON *Strawberry* CAKE

{ MAKES ONE 12-INCH-LONG (30.5-CM-LONG) RECTANGULAR CAKE }

This cake is springtime in your mouth. The combination of strawberries and lemon is sweet and bright, and there's just enough mint in the pastry cream to refresh without overwhelming the fruit. The almond paste that drapes over this cake adds a richness and balance with every bite. Everything in this cake works in symmetry, so why not build the cake to look symmetrical? I did and it's gorgeous.

Ingredients

FOR THE MINT AND ALMOND PASTRY CREAM
¾ cup (180 ml) whole milk
¾ cup (180 ml) heavy cream
3 large fresh mint leaves, cut into thin strips
4 large egg yolks
⅓ cup (65 g) sugar
¼ cup (30 g) cornstarch
Pinch of salt
1 tablespoon unsalted butter
½ teaspoon almond extract

FOR THE STRAWBERRY COULIS
¼ cup (50 g) finely chopped strawberries
3 tablespoons sugar
1 tablespoon lemon juice

FOR THE LEMON CHIFFON CAKE
4 large eggs, at room temperature, separated
½ cup (120 ml) lemon juice
¼ cup (60 ml) plus 2 tablespoons organic
    grapeseed oil
Grated zest of 2 lemons
1 cup (120 g) pastry flour
1 cup (200 g) sugar
1 teaspoon baking powder
½ teaspoon salt
½ teaspoon cream of tartar

TO FINISH
3 cups (720 ml) cold heavy cream
1 pound (455 g) small strawberries, hulled
    (about 30)
7 ounces (200 g) almond paste
A few fresh mint leaves

MAKE THE MINT AND ALMOND PASTRY CREAM

- Combine the milk, cream, and mint in a large saucepan and bring to a simmer.
- In a large bowl, combine the egg yolks, sugar, cornstarch, and salt. Whisk until the mixture ribbons thickly. Slowly add the hot milk mixture to the egg yolk mixture, whisking all the while so that the eggs don't curdle. Continue whisking until smooth.
- Transfer the mixture back to the saucepan and whisk over medium heat until the mixture thickens to the consistency of mayonnaise. Remove from the heat and add the butter and almond extract, whisking until combined. Pour the pastry cream through a fine sieve into a large bowl. Cover the pastry cream with plastic wrap, making sure to press the plastic wrap onto the surface of the cream to prevent a skin from forming. Refrigerate until completely cool, about 2 hours.

MAKE THE STRAWBERRY COULIS

- In a small saucepan, combine the strawberries, sugar, and lemon juice and simmer over low heat until the strawberries are very soft and all the sugar has dissolved, about 10 minutes.
- Transfer the coulis to a blender and process until smooth. Pour through a sieve into a small bowl. Cover with plastic wrap and chill in the fridge until cool, about 30 minutes.

MAKE THE LEMON CHIFFON CAKE

- Preheat the oven to 325°F (165°C). Line a sheet pan with parchment paper and spray lightly with nonstick cooking spray.
- In a large bowl, whisk together the egg yolks, lemon juice, oil, and lemon zest. Sift the flour, ½ cup (100 g) of the sugar, the baking powder, and salt over the egg yolk mixture and whisk until very smooth.
- In the bowl of a stand mixer fitted with the whisk attachment, combine the egg whites and cream of tartar. Whisk on high until the egg whites turn white and increase slightly in volume. With the mixer still running, slowly add the remaining ½ cup (100 g) sugar and continue whisking on high speed

until you achieve smooth, stiff peaks (don't whisk so much that they become dry and chunky). Gently fold the egg whites into the egg yolk mixture until a smooth batter forms and no white streaks remain.
- Transfer the batter to the prepared sheet pan and gently spread it into an even layer with a large offset spatula. Bake until the cake gently springs back when gently poked and just begins to pull away from the sides of the pan, about 25 minutes. Let cool completely.
- Run a sharp knife along the edge of the cake to fully release it. Place a piece of parchment on top of the cake and place a second sheet pan on top of that parchment. Flip the cake and turn the cake out onto the second sheet pan. Cut the cake into three long, even strips, 5⅓ by 12 inches (13.5 by 30.5 cm).

TO FINISH

- In the bowl of a stand mixer fitted with the whisk attachment, whip the heavy cream to stiff peaks. Whisk one third of the whipped cream into the pastry cream. With a large rubber spatula, gently fold the remaining whipped cream into the pastry cream. Transfer the lightened pastry cream to a large pastry bag fitted with a large plain tip.
- Place a strip of cake on a cake platter. Place 15 strawberries hulled side down onto the cake. Pipe half of the lightened pastry cream in between and over the strawberries, using a small offset to smooth the cream over the strawberries. Place a second layer of cake atop the cream-laced strawberries and arrange the remaining 15 strawberries atop the second layer. Pipe the remaining pastry cream among the strawberries and smooth the top with an offset spatula. Place the final layer of cake on top and place in the freezer to set, about 2 hours.
- Meanwhile, roll out the almond paste to measure slightly larger than 5⅓ by 12 inches (13.5 by 30.5 cm) and punch a random pattern of hearts into the almond paste using a 2-inch (5-cm) heart cookie cutter.

continued

- Once the cake has set (test the cream to see if it feels very firm; it should not be fully frozen), remove from the freezer. Place the almond paste sheet on top of the cake. Dip a very sharp serrated knife into hot water and wipe dry. Trim the sides of the cake, gently sawing to keep the cream from spurting out the sides of the cake. The firmer the cake is, the cleaner the trimmed sides will be, but it will be much harder to cut. So take your time in your gentle sawing and keep the knife hot and clean throughout the process.

- Gently spoon the coulis into the holes in the almond paste. Serve immediately or cover the sides of the cake with parchment, cover with plastic wrap to keep the cake moist, and keep refrigerated.

OPTIONS

LEMON CHIFFON STRAWBERRY CAKE

Check page 16 before proceeding for additional details on ensuring your recipes are gluten free and/or vegan.

VEGAN

FOR THE PASTRY CREAM: Use the vegan version of the Pastry Cream on page 141, but first simmer together the coconut milk of that version with 3 large fresh mint leaves cut into strips, let steep for 20 minutes, and then strain out the mint before proceeding. FOR THE CAKE: Omit the cake ingredients entirely and do the following instead: In a large mixing bowl, combine 1½ cups (195 g) cake flour, 1 teaspoon baking powder, 1 teaspoon baking soda, and ½ teaspoon salt. Whisk for 30 seconds until well distributed. Add 1 cup (200 g) sugar and whisk to combine. Make a well in the middle of the flour mixture. In a liquid measuring cup, combine ¾ cup (180 ml) vanilla soy milk, ¼ cup plus 2 tablespoons (90 ml) canola oil, ¼ cup (60 ml) lemon juice, 1 teaspoon distilled white vinegar, and 2 drops lemon oil. Stir to combine. Add the liquid to the well in the dry ingredients and stir with a wooden spoon until smooth and no lumps of dry ingredients remain. Bake as in the main recipe. TO FINISH: Replace the heavy cream with 3 cups (720 ml) coconut cream and whip as directed.

GLUTEN FREE

FOR THE CAKE: Replace the flour with ¾ cup (120 g) finely milled brown rice flour, ¼ cup (35 g) sweet white sorghum flour, and 1 teaspoon xanthan gum. Replace the lemon juice with 2 teaspoons natural lemon extract.

HEALTHIER

FOR THE PASTRY CREAM: Make the healthier version of the Pastry Cream on page 141, but first simmer together the coconut milk of that version with 3 large fresh mint leaves cut into strips, let steep for 20 minutes, and then strain out the mint before proceeding. FOR THE CAKE: Replace the sugar with 1 cup (160 g) organic granulated palm sugar.

I don't know if you love figs as much as I do. I don't know if that's even possible. But assuming you possess a smidge of my devotion, you'll appreciate this elegant yet straightforward use of the fruit. In the event you have no love in your heart for the wondrous things, you can substitute most any fruit in place of them, including pineapple, apples, mango, pears . . . you get the idea.

Procedure

MAKE THE FIG LAYER

- Preheat the oven to 350°F (175°C). Line the bottom of a 9-inch (23-cm) round cake pan with a round of parchment paper and spray the parchment and sides liberally with nonstick cooking spray.
- Pour the melted butter into the prepared pan. Evenly sprinkle the brown sugar over the butter and place the figs cut side down in concentric circles on top of the brown sugar.

MAKE THE CAKE

- In a small bowl, combine the all-purpose flour, pistachio flour, baking powder, and salt. Whisk for 30 seconds to evenly distribute the leavening.
- In the bowl of a stand mixer fitted with the paddle attachment, combine the butter and sugar. Mix on high speed until light and fluffy. Add the eggs one at a time, scraping down the sides and bottom of the bowl after each addition. Add the vanilla and orange zest and mix until just combined. With the mixer running on low speed, add half of the flour mixture, then the milk, then the remaining flour. Mix until well combined. Gently spoon the batter over the figs and carefully spread the batter evenly with a small offset spatula. Bake until the cake is golden brown and springs back when gently poked, 45 to 50 minutes.

TO FINISH

- While the cake is still warm, turn the cake out upside down onto a platter. Sprinkle with the chopped pistachios.

Ingredients

FOR THE FIG LAYER

2 tablespoons unsalted butter, melted
¼ cup (55 g) dark brown sugar, packed
13 small fresh Mission or Calmyrna figs, stems removed, cut in half

FOR THE CAKE

1 cup (140 g) all-purpose flour
¼ cup (20 g) pistachio flour (finely ground pistachios)
1 teaspoon baking powder
1 teaspoon salt
¾ cup (1½ sticks/170 g) unsalted butter, at room temperature
½ cup (100 g) plus 2 tablespoons sugar
2 large eggs, at room temperature
1 tablespoon vanilla bean paste
1 teaspoon grated orange zest
⅓ cup (75 ml) whole milk

TO FINISH

¼ cup (30 g) roughly chopped salted pistachios

Check page 16 before proceeding for additional details on ensuring your recipes are gluten free and/or vegan.

VEGAN

FOR THE FIG LAYER: Replace the butter with 2 tablespoons Earth Balance Vegan Buttery Sticks, melted. FOR THE CAKE: Reduce the baking powder to ¼ teaspoon and combine it with 1 teaspoon baking soda. Replace the butter with ½ cup (120 ml) olive oil. Replace the eggs with 2 large eggs' worth of prepared Ener-G egg replacer (see recipe, page 12). Replace the milk with ½ cup (120 ml) orange juice and 1 tablespoon apple cider vinegar. In a large mixing bowl, whisk together the flour, pistachio flour, sugar, baking powder, baking soda, and salt. In the bowl of a stand mixer fitted with the whisk attachment, combine the prepared egg replacer, orange juice, oil, orange zest, vanilla, and vinegar. Whisk until combined. Add the dry ingredients and whisk until the batter is smooth. Gently smooth the batter over the figs and bake for 40 to 45 minutes, until the cake springs back when gently poked.

GLUTEN FREE

FOR THE CAKE: Replace the flour with ¾ cup (120 g) sweet white rice flour and 1 teaspoon xanthan gum; increase the pistachio flour to ½ cup (40 g). Reduce the milk to ¼ cup (60 ml). Bake for 40 to 45 minutes.

HEALTHIER

FOR THE CAKE: Replace the all-purpose flour with 1 cup (120 g) white whole-wheat flour. Replace the butter with 6 tablespoons (90 ml) organic grapeseed oil and 6 tablespoons (90 ml) prune puree (I use organic baby food, such as Plum Organics Just Prunes). Replace the sugar with ½ cup (80 g) organic granulated palm sugar. Mix together the sugar, oil, and prune puree until well combined. Add ¼ cup (60 ml) orange juice to the milk.

I've already waxed poetic about my conversion from coconut loather to coconut's number-twenty fan. One thing I have to say about this cake, though, is that it's so damn good and coconutty that devout coconut haters . . . well, they'll hate it. It's really full of all that tropical creamy goodness that you can't mistake it for anything else.

COCONUT CAKE

{ MAKES ONE 8-INCH (20-CM) TRIPLE-LAYER CAKE }

Ingredients

FOR THE CAKE
2 cups (400 g) sugar
1 cup (240 ml) unrefined coconut oil (melt to measure then resolidify at room temperature)
5 large eggs, at room temperature
2 teaspoons vanilla bean paste
1½ cups (195 g) cake flour
1 cup (110 g) coconut flour
1 teaspoon baking powder
1 teaspoon salt
1 cup (240 ml) sweetened cream of coconut (like Coco Lopez)

FOR THE FROSTING
10 large egg whites
2 cups (400 g) sugar
Pinch of salt
1 cup (240 ml) full-fat coconut cream (not cream of coconut)
2 cups (4 sticks/450 g) unsalted butter, slightly cooler than room temperature
2 drops blue gel food coloring

TO ASSEMBLE
4 ounces (115 g) bittersweet chocolate, finely chopped
½ teaspoon vegetable shortening
Blue gel food coloring (optional)
2 tablespoons fondant (optional)
¼ cup (20 g) sweetened shredded coconut (optional)

MAKE THE CAKE

- Preheat the oven to 325°F (165°C). Spray three 8-inch (20-cm) cake pans with nonstick cooking spray. Line the bottom of each pan with a round of parchment paper.
- In the bowl of a stand mixer fitted with the paddle attachment, combine the sugar and coconut oil and whisk on high speed until light and fluffy. Scrape down the sides of the bowl. Add the eggs one at a time, mixing well after each addition. Add the vanilla.
- In a medium bowl, whisk together the cake flour, coconut flour, baking powder, and salt. Whisk for 30 seconds to evenly distribute the leavening.
- Add half the flour mixture to the sugar mixture and mix briefly. Add the coconut cream and mix briefly again. Add the rest of the flour and continue mixing on low speed until a smooth batter forms.
- Divide the batter equally among the three prepared pans. Bake until the tops of the cakes just begin to become golden brown and the cake springs back when gently poked, 35 to 40 minutes. Let cool completely.

MAKE THE FROSTING

- In the bowl of a stand mixer fitted with the whisk attachment, combine the egg whites, sugar, and salt. Place the mixing bowl with the egg whites and sugar over a saucepan of simmering water (to make a double boiler) and whisk constantly until the sugar has completely dissolved and the temperature reads 160°F (71°C) on a candy thermometer. Immediately place the bowl back on the stand mixer and whisk on high speed until the bowl is cool to the touch and the meringue is shiny, white, and very stiff.
- With the mixer running on medium-low speed, add the coconut cream and whisk to combine. The egg whites will deflate. Add the butter, a few tablespoons at a time (you may not need to add it all), and continue whisking. Once the buttercream appears as if it's starting to curdle a bit, add just 2 more tablespoons butter and whisk on high speed until the buttercream comes together into a smooth, spreadable

frosting. Add the food coloring and whisk on high until the frosting is uniformly blue.

ASSEMBLE THE CAKE

- Place a cake layer on a serving platter. Using an offset spatula, spread 1½ cups (360 ml) of the frosting evenly over the layer. Place a second cake layer on top and spread another 1½ cups (360 ml) frosting in an even layer over the cake. Top with the final layer. Cover the cake with plastic wrap and refrigerate for 20 minutes.
- Using an offset spatula, cover the chilled cake in a smooth layer of frosting. Refrigerate to set the frosting, about 20 minutes.
- Put the chocolate and shortening in a heatproof bowl and set it over a saucepan of simmering water (to make a double boiler); stir until melted.
- Cover a work surface with parchment. Remove the cake from the refrigerator and place the cake in the middle of the parchment. Dip the tines of a fork in the melted chocolate. From about 1 foot (30.5 cm) away, flick the chocolate-coated fork toward the cake so that little brown flecks attach to the cake. Turn the cake and continue dipping and flicking until there's a smattering of chocolate speckles over the entire cake. Refrigerate the cake to set, about 20 minutes.
- Dip a toothpick into the blue food coloring and transfer a small dot to the fondant, if using. Knead the fondant to evenly distribute the color.
- Divide the fondant into 3 or 4 small pieces. Roll each piece into an egg shape. Place the eggs on a piece of parchment and speckle with chocolate as you did with the sides and top of the cake.
- Place a mound of the shredded coconut, if using onto the top of the cake and press gently at the center of the mound to create a nest. Place the eggs in the nest and serve.

Check page 16 before proceeding for additional details on ensuring your recipes are gluten free and/or vegan.

VEGAN

FOR THE CAKE: Replace the eggs with 2 large eggs' worth of flaxseed meal mixed with water (see page 12), 2 teaspoons baking soda, and 2 tablespoons distilled white vinegar. FOR THE FROSTING: Omit all the ingredients and do the following instead:

1 cup (225 g) organic palm oil shortening, at room temperature
1 cup (2 sticks/225 g) Earth Balance Vegan Buttery Sticks, at room temperature
7 cups (700 g) confectioners' sugar
Pinch of salt
½ cup (120 ml) full-fat coconut cream (not cream of coconut)
1 teaspoon vanilla bean paste
Vegan blue food coloring (like Select 100% Natural Food Coloring), optional

In the bowl of a stand mixer fitted with the paddle attachment, combine the shortening and Vegan Buttery Sticks with 1 cup (100 g) of the confectioners' sugar and the salt. Cream on high speed until light and fluffy. Add the remaining confectioners' sugar and mix on low speed until incorporated. Add the coconut cream, vanilla, and 1 scant teaspoon food coloring (if using) and beat on high speed until smooth and light, about 5 minutes. TO ASSEMBLE: Replace the sweetened shredded coconut with unsweetened shredded coconut. Omit the fondant and food coloring and replace with a few vegan jelly beans, such as Surf Sweets Organic Jelly Beans.

GLUTEN FREE

FOR THE CAKE: Increase the eggs by 1, for a total of 6 eggs. Replace the cake flour and coconut flour with 1½ cups (165 g) coconut flour, ¾ cup (120 g) sweet white rice flour, ¼ cup (35 g) sweet white sorghum flour, and 2 teaspoons xanthan gum. Reduce the cream of coconut to ½ cup (120 ml).

HEALTHIER

FOR THE CAKE: Replace the sugar with 2 cups (320 g) organic granulated palm sugar. FOR THE FROSTING: Omit all the ingredients and do the following instead:

6 cups (960 g) organic granulated palm sugar
Pinch of salt
1 cup (225 g) organic palm oil shortening, at room temperature
1 cup (2 sticks/225 g) Earth Balance Vegan Buttery Sticks, at room temperature
½ cup (120 ml) full-fat coconut cream (not cream of coconut)
1 teaspoon vanilla bean paste
Vegan blue food coloring (like Select 100% Natural Food Coloring), optional

In a food processor, pulse the palm sugar and salt until it becomes a fine powder. In the bowl of a stand mixer fitted with the paddle attachment, combine the shortening and Vegan Buttery Sticks with 1 cup (160 g) of the processed palm sugar. Cream on high speed until light and fluffy. Add the remaining palm sugar and mix on low speed until incorporated. Add the coconut cream, vanilla, and 1 scant teaspoon food coloring and beat on high speed until smooth and light, about 5 minutes. TO ASSEMBLE: Omit the fondant and food coloring and replace with a few vegan jelly beans, such as Surf Sweets Organic Jelly Beans.

Your chocolate's in my peanut butter! Your peanut butter's in my chocolate! Hey! Hold on a minute, they're both in my cheesecake! And you know what, the combination is epic. As long as you're going to be indulging in some creamy and dreamy cheesecake, why not bring my favorite flavor combination along for the ride?

PEANUT BUTTER- CHOCOLATE Cheesecake

{ MAKES ONE 9-INCH (23-CM) CHEESECAKE }

Procedure

MAKE THE CRUST

- Preheat the oven to 325°F (165°C). Spray a 9-inch (23-cm) springform pan with nonstick baking spray.
- Press the dough into an even layer in the bottom of the pan. Bake for 15 minutes. Set aside to cool completely.

MAKE THE FILLING

- In the bowl of a stand mixer fitted with the paddle attachment, combine the cream cheese and sugar and beat on high speed until smooth. Add the crème fraîche and mix until incorporated. Scrape down the bottom and sides of the bowl and mix again. Add the eggs one at a time, mixing well after each addition. Add the vanilla and salt and mix. Sift the cornstarch over the batter and mix until incorporated.
- Put 1 cup (240 ml) of the batter in a small bowl and stir in the peanut butter. Stir in the cream. Set aside.
- Add 2 heaping spoonfuls of the plain batter to the melted chocolate and stir to combine. Transfer the chocolate mixture to the remaining plain batter and mix on low speed until the batter is smooth and the chocolate is evenly distributed.
- Transfer the chocolate batter to the prepared crust. Spoon dollops of the peanut butter batter on top of the chocolate batter and swirl into the chocolate batter with a knife. Bake until the edges of the filling are set but the center still faintly shimmies, 1 hour 45 minutes to 2 hours. Turn off the oven. Run a thin paring knife around the edge of the pan to release the cheesecake, then return the pan to the oven and keep the door propped open. Let cool slowly in the cooling oven for about 2 hours.
- Refrigerate the cheesecake until cool before serving.

Ingredients

FOR THE CRUST
¼ batch Chocolate Tart Dough (page 140)

FOR THE FILLING
2 (8-ounce/225-g) packages cream cheese, at room temperature
1 cup (200 g) sugar
1 cup (240 ml) crème fraîche
3 large eggs, at room temperature
1 tablespoon vanilla bean paste
¼ teaspoon salt
¼ cup (30 g) cornstarch
½ cup (130 g) smooth peanut butter
2 tablespoons heavy cream
8 ounces (225 g) bittersweet chocolate, melted and slightly cooled

Check page 16 before proceeding for additional details on ensuring your recipes are gluten free and/or vegan.

VEGAN

FOR THE CRUST: Use the vegan version of the Chocolate Tart Dough on page 140. FOR THE FILLING: Omit all of the filling ingredients and do the following instead: Preheat oven to 350°F (175°C). Combine 1 cup (200 g) of vegan sugar and ⅓ cup (75 ml) brewed coffee in a large saucepan and stir over medium heat until the sugar has completely melted. Stop stirring, clip on a candy thermometer and continue heating until the temperature of the sugar reaches 250°F (120°C). Remove the pan from the heat and add ¼ cup (60 ml) almond milk; be careful, as the mixture will bubble rapidly. Once the mixture has calmed, stir in 1 tablespoon of vanilla bean paste and 8 ounces (225 g) roughly chopped vegan bittersweet chocolate and stir until the chocolate has completely melted. Set aside. Place 2 pounds (910 g) firm silken tofu that's been drained (see page 13), another 1 cup (200 g) vegan sugar, and ¼ cup (20 g) unsweetened Dutch-process cocoa powder to a food processor and puree until smooth. Add two (8-ounce/225-g) packages vegan cream cheese to the processor and pulse until smooth. Add the chocolate mixture to the batter ingredients in the processor and pulse until smooth. Transfer 1 cup of the chocolate batter to a small bowl and stir in ½ cup (130 g) peanut butter. Pour the chocolate batter into the prepared crust. Spoon dollops of the peanut butter batter on top of the chocolate batter and swirl into the chocolate batter with a knife. Bake until the edges of the filling are set but the center still faintly shimmies, 1 to 1½ hours. Turn off the oven. Run a thin paring knife around the edge of the pan to release the cheesecake, then return the pan to the oven and keep the door propped open. Let cool slowly in the cooling oven for about 2 hours.

GLUTEN FREE

FOR THE CRUST: Use traditional nonstick cooking spray instead of baking spray (which contains flour). Use the gluten-free version of the Chocolate Tart Dough on page 140.

HEALTHIER

FOR THE CRUST: Use the healthier version of the Chocolate Tart Dough on page 140. FOR THE FILLING: Replace the cream cheese with Neufchâtel cheese. Replace the sugar with 1 cup (160 g) organic granulated palm sugar. Replace the crème fraîche with nonfat Greek yogurt. Use organic, unsweetened peanut butter.

FUDGY CHOCOLATE Bundt Cake

{ MAKES ONE 10-INCH (25-CM) BUNDT CAKE }

Ingredients

8 ounces (225 g) bittersweet chocolate (like Ghirardelli 60% baking chocolate), very finely chopped
1 teaspoon vanilla extract
1 cup (240 ml) very hot brewed coffee
½ cup (120 ml) buttermilk
1½ cups (3 sticks/340 g) unsalted butter, at room temperature
3 cups (600 g) sugar
¾ cup (180 ml) canola oil
6 large eggs, at room temperature
4 cups (520 g) all-purpose flour
¼ cup (20 g) Dutch-process cocoa powder (like Cacao Barry Extra Brute) plus ¼ cup (20 g) regular cocoa powder; or ½ cup (40 g) regular cocoa powder total
¾ teaspoon baking powder
1 teaspoon salt

You may pause and wonder why there's no glaze, no adornment, no filling with this cake. Quite simply, it doesn't need it. This cake does just fine on its own, thank you very much. You may feel the need to serve it with fruit, with whipped cream, with ice cream, despite my recommendation. Go right on ahead. But once you start eating this cake straight, you'll get my drift and dump the dead weight.

Procedure

- Preheat the oven to 350°F (175°C). Spray a 10-inch (25-cm) Bundt pan with nonstick baking spray.
- Put the chocolate and vanilla in a heatproof bowl and pour the hot coffee over them. Let sit undisturbed for 2 minutes, then whisk to incorporate the chocolate. If there are still large unmelted chunks of chocolate, place the bowl over a saucepan of simmering water (to make a double boiler), stirring all the while, until the chocolate is completely melted. Set aside to cool completely. Once cool, stir in the buttermilk.
- In the bowl of a stand mixer fitted with the paddle attachment, combine the butter and sugar. Beat on high speed until light and fluffy. Scrape down the sides and bottom of the bowl and add the oil. Mix until just combined. Add the eggs one at a time, scraping down the sides and bottom of the bowl after each addition.
- In a large bowl, whisk together the flour, cocoa powder, baking powder, and salt for 30 seconds to evenly distribute the leavening.
- With the mixer running on medium-low speed, alternate adding the flour mixture and the coffee mixture, mixing until all is fully incorporated. Pour the batter into the prepared pan and smooth with the back of a spoon. Bake until the cake springs back when gently poked, at least 1 hour and up to 1 hour 30 minutes. Let the cake cool in the pan for about 15 minutes, then release the cake onto a cooling rack and let cool completely.

Check page 16 before proceeding for additional details on ensuring your recipes are gluten free and/or vegan.

VEGAN

Replace the buttermilk with ½ cup (120 ml) plain almond milk. Replace the butter with 1½ cups (3 sticks/340 g) Earth Balance Vegan Shortening and cream together with the sugar. Replace the eggs with 2 large eggs' worth of prepared Ener-G egg replacer (see recipe, page 12), 2 large eggs' worth of flaxseed meal mixed with water (see page 12), 2 teaspoons baking soda, and 2 tablespoons distilled white vinegar, adding the prepared Ener-G and flax egg replacements as you would add the eggs in the master recipe. Whisk the extra baking soda into the dry ingredients and add the vinegar to the coffee mixture.

GLUTEN FREE

Use traditional nonstick cooking spray instead of baking spray (which contains flour). Reduce the coffee to 2 tablespoons and reduce the buttermilk to ¼ cup (60 ml). Put the chocolate in a microwave-safe bowl, pour the coffee over the chocolate, and stir. Microwave in 30-second intervals, stirring between blasts, until completely melted. Alternatively, place the chocolate and coffee in a large heatproof bowl and set it over a saucepan of simmering water (to make a double boiler), stirring until the chocolate is melted. Mix the vanilla into the melted chocolate mixture. Replace the flour with 2½ cups (400 g) finely milled brown rice flour, ¾ cup (100 g) sweet white sorghum flour, ¾ cup (105 g) tapioca starch, and 3 teaspoons xanthan gum.

HEALTHIER

Reduce the butter to ½ cup (1 stick/115 g). Replace the sugar with 2½ cups (400 g) organic granulated palm sugar. After creaming the butter and palm sugar together, mix in 4 ounces (115 g) pureed black beans (from a can of cooked organic black beans, pureed in a blender or food processor) and 4 ounces (120 ml) unsweetened applesauce (these replace the additional butter in the main recipe). Replace the oil with ¾ cup (180 ml) organic grapeseed oil. Replace the flour with 3 cups (300 g) whole-wheat pastry flour, and ½ cup (70 g) Sprouted Super Flour (see page 220), ½ cup (50 g) almond flour.

This cake was a big deal in the '80s. When I was a kid, my mother took my friend Mecki and me to the World Trade Center's four-star restaurant, Windows on the World. As usual, I remember only the dessert, and what a dessert it was: a chocolate lava cake, the center oozing with chocolate magma. Despite its being a bit old-fashioned these days, I can't help but include it here in memory of my wonderful mother and her insistence that her children experience wondrous things like sitting atop the most glorious building in all the world while eating gooey chocolate cake.

······ *Procedure* ······

MAKE THE CAKE

- Preheat the oven to 350°F (175°C). Spray 4-ounce (120-ml) ramekins or ovenproof coffee cups with nonstick baking spray.
- In a small bowl, whisk together the coffee, crème fraîche, vinegar, and vanilla.
- In large bowl, whisk together the flour, cocoa powder, baking soda, and salt for 30 seconds to evenly distribute the leavening.
- In the bowl of stand mixer fitted with the paddle attachment, beat together the brown sugar and butter until light and fluffy. Add the eggs one at a time, then add the oil. Mix until just combined. Add the flour mixture and mix until just combined. Add the coffee mixture and mix until combined. Using a large rubber spatula, scrape the sides and bottom of the bowl and gently fold the batter to ensure that the ingredients are well distributed.
- Place 3 tablespoons batter in the bottom of each prepared ramekin. Divide the chocolate chips among the ramekins, placing them in the center of the batter, then spoon ¼ cup (60 ml) batter on top of the chips in each. Bake until the cakes barely start to puff and a nickel-sized sheen remains at the center of the cake. Let the cakes sit for 5 minutes before carefully turning them out onto individual plates.

TO FINISH

- Sift confectioners' sugar over the cakes. Serve while still warm.

{ MAKES EIGHT 4-OUNCE (120-ML) MOLTEN CAKES }

······ *Ingredients* ······

FOR THE CAKE
½ cup (120 ml) hot brewed coffee
¼ cup (60 ml) crème fraîche or plain whole-fat Greek yogurt
1 tablespoon white wine vinegar
1 tablespoon vanilla bean paste
1¼ cups (175 g) all-purpose flour
½ cup (40 g) unsweetened cocoa powder
1 teaspoon baking soda
½ teaspoon salt
1 cup (220 g) dark brown sugar, packed
6 tablespoons (85 g) unsalted butter, at room temperature
2 large eggs, at room temperature
¼ cup (60 ml) canola oil
8 ounces (225 g) bittersweet chocolate chips

TO FINISH
¼ cup (25 g) confectioners' sugar

Check page 16 before proceeding for additional details on ensuring your recipes are gluten free and/or vegan.

VEGAN

FOR THE CAKE: Replace the crème fraîche with ¼ cup (60 ml) vegan sour cream. Replace the butter with Earth Balance Vegan Shortening or 6 tablespoons (90 ml) organic refined virgin coconut oil. Omit the eggs. Beat together the sugar and shortening, then add the oil and mix until just combined. Increase the baking soda to 2 teaspoons and whisk it to the flour mixture; add to the sugar mixture. Mix until just combined. Increase the vinegar to 2 tablespoons and add it to the vegan sour cream mixture; quickly stir into the batter by hand until a smooth batter forms.

GLUTEN FREE

FOR THE CAKE: Use traditional nonstick cooking spray instead of baking spray (which contains flour) and, after spraying, add 1 teaspoon cocoa powder to each ramekin and gently turn the ramekin so the cocoa powder coats the sides and bottom. Replace the flour with 1 cup (160 g) sweet white rice flour, ¼ cup (40 g) potato starch, and 1 teaspoon xanthan gum.

HEALTHIER

FOR THE CAKE: Use nonfat plain Greek yogurt. Replace the flour with 1¼ cups (125 g) whole-wheat pastry flour. Replace the brown sugar with ¾ cup (120 g) organic granulated palm sugar. Reduce the butter to 3 tablespoons and add 3 tablespoons prune puree (I use organic baby food, such as Plum Organic's Just Prunes) to the coffee mixture. Replace the canola oil with ¼ cup (60 ml) organic grapeseed oil.

The CHOCOHOLIC

Chocolate cake layers, chocolate mousse filling, and a fluffy chocolate ganache coating make for the most decadent of cakes. No matter the version you choose, the chocoholic in you will be deeply satisfied.

{ MAKES ONE 8-INCH (20-CM) LAYER CAKE }

········· Ingredients ·········

FOR THE CAKE
2 cups (260 g) all-purpose flour
½ cup (40 g) Dutch-process cocoa powder
    (like Cacao Barry Extra Brute)
1 teaspoon baking powder
1 teaspoon baking soda
1 teaspoon salt
¼ cup (60 ml) hot brewed coffee
4 ounces (115 g) bittersweet chocolate (like
    Lindt 70%), finely chopped
1 cup (240 ml) buttermilk
1 cup (220 g) light brown sugar, packed
1 cup (200 g) granulated sugar
1 cup (240 ml) canola oil
3 large eggs
1 teaspoon vanilla bean paste

FOR THE CHOCOLATE MOUSSE FILLING
2 cups (480 ml) cold heavy cream
4 large eggs, separated
2 tablespoons plus ¼ cup (50 g) sugar
1 tablespoon vanilla bean paste
8 ounces (225 g) bittersweet chocolate
    (at least 70%), finely chopped
Pinch of salt

FOR THE GANACHE
1 pound (455 g) bittersweet chocolate,
    finely chopped
2 tablespoons unsalted butter
1½ cups (360 ml) heavy cream
Pinch of salt

MAKE THE CAKE

- Preheat the oven to 325°F (165°C). Spray three 8-inch (20-cm) round cake pans with nonstick cooking spray and line the bottoms with a round of parchment paper.
- In a large bowl, whisk together the flour, cocoa powder, baking powder, baking soda, and salt for 30 seconds to evenly distribute the leavening.
- In a heat proof bowl, pour the hot coffee over the chopped chocolate and let sit undisturbed for 3 minutes to allow the chocolate to melt. Whisk to combine. Add the buttermilk and stir.
- In the bowl of a stand mixer fitted with the whisk attachment, beat both sugars and the oil together until well combined. Add the eggs one at a time, mixing well after each addition. Add the vanilla and mix.
- With the mixer running on low speed, add half of the flour mixture, then add half of the buttermilk mixture. Add the remaining flour mixture, then the remaining buttermilk mixture, and mix until smooth and well combined. Divide the batter evenly among the prepared pans and bake until the cake springs back when gently poked, 30 to 40 minutes. Let cool completely.

MAKE THE CHOCOLATE MOUSSE FILLING

- Combine 1 cup (240 ml) of the cream, the egg yolks, the 2 tablespoons sugar, and the vanilla in a heatproof bowl and whisk to combine. Place the bowl over a saucepan of simmering water (to make a double boiler) and whisk constantly until the mixture thickens and coats the back of a spoon. Add the chocolate and continue whisking until the chocolate melts into the mixture. Set aside and let cool to room temperature.

- In the clean bowl of a stand mixer fitted with the whisk attachment, combine the egg whites, the remaining ¼ cup (50 g) sugar, and the salt. Place the bowl over a saucepan of simmering water (to make a double boiler) and whisk constantly until the sugar dissolves and the temperature of the mixture reaches 160°F (71°C) on a candy thermometer. Transfer the bowl to the stand mixer and whisk until the meringue forms stiff, very smooth white peaks (don't whisk so much that they become dry and chunky).
- Using a large rubber spatula, carefully fold the egg whites into the room-temperature chocolate mixture until smooth.
- In the same bowl you whipped the egg whites, whip the remaining 1 cup (240 ml) cream to stiff peaks. Gently fold the whipped cream into the chocolate mixture with the large rubber spatula. Cover the bowl with plastic wrap and refrigerate until the mousse has set, about 1 hour.
- Using an offset spatula, spread half the mousse onto a chocolate cake layer. Place a second cake layer atop the mousse filling and spread the remaining mousse over the second cake layer. Place the final layer of cake on top of the mousse filling and cover the cake tightly with plastic wrap. Refrigerate until the mousse has set, at least 2 hours.

MAKE THE GANACHE

- Put the chocolate and butter in a large heatproof bowl.
- In a large saucepan, bring the cream and salt to a simmer, but do not boil. Pour the cream over the chocolate, making sure that the chocolate is completely covered. Let sit undisturbed for 3 minutes, then whisk the mixture until smooth. Cover the bowl with plastic wrap and set aside until the ganache has cooled to room temperature but is still spreadable, about 45 minutes.
- Place the ganache in the bowl of a stand mixer fitted with the whisk attachment and whisk until it lightens and becomes fluffy. Spread the ganache over the top and sides of the assembled cake.

Check page 16 before proceeding for additional details on ensuring your recipes are gluten free and/or vegan.

VEGAN

FOR THE CAKE: Increase the baking soda to 2 teaspoons. Increase the coffee to 2 cups (480 ml). Replace the buttermilk with 1 cup (240 ml) plain almond milk and 2 tablespoons distilled white vinegar, and add to the melted chocolate–coffee mixture. Omit the eggs. FOR THE FILLING: Omit the filling ingredients entirely and do the following instead: In a heatproof metal bowl, combine 1 pound (455 g) finely chopped solid chocolate (at least 70% cocoa), ¾ cup (180 ml) brewed coffee, and a pinch of salt. Place the bowl over a saucepan of simmering water (to make a double boiler) and stir until melted. Place the melted chocolate mixture over a large bowl filled with ice and whisk the mixture constantly until it thickens to the consistency of ketchup. (If the mixture starts to form granules and get gritty, you've whisked too much. Simply re-melt the mixture and start again.) Refrigerate until set, about 1 hour, then spread over the cake layers as in the main recipe. FOR THE GANACHE: Replace the butter with organic refined virgin coconut oil and replace the cream with 1½ cups (360 ml) full-fat coconut milk.

GLUTEN FREE

FOR THE CAKE: Replace the flour with 1¼ cups (200 g) finely milled brown rice flour, ½ cup (50 g) almond flour, ¼ cup (35 g) sweet white sorghum flour, and 2 teaspoons xanthan gum. Reduce the buttermilk to ½ cup (120 ml). Replace the oil with 1 cup (2 sticks/225 g) unsalted butter. Cream together the sugar and butter until light and fluffy. Increase the eggs to 4 and add them to the creamed sugar and butter mixture, one at a time, scraping the bottom and sides of the bowl after each addition.

HEALTHIER

FOR THE CAKE: Replace the flour with ½ cup (70 g) Sprouted Super Flour (see page 220) and 1½ cups (150 g) whole-wheat pastry flour. Replace the sugars with 2 cups (320 g) organic granulated palm sugar. Replace the oil with ½ cup (120 g) pureed black beans (from a can of cooked organic black beans, pureed in a blender or food processor) and ½ cup (120 ml) organic grapeseed oil or organic unrefined virgin coconut oil. FOR THE FILLING: Omit the filling ingredients entirely and do the following instead: In a heatproof metal bowl, combine 1 pound (455 g) finely chopped bittersweet chocolate, ¾ cup (180 ml) brewed coffee, and a pinch of salt. Place the bowl over a saucepan of simmering water (to make a double boiler) and stir until melted. Place the melted chocolate mixture over a large bowl filled with ice and whisk the mixture constantly until it thickens to the consistency of ketchup. (If the mixture starts to form granules and get gritty, you've whisked too much. Simply re-melt the mixture and start again.) Refrigerate until set, about 1 hour, then spread over the cake layers as in the main recipe. FOR THE GANACHE: Replace the butter with 2 tablespoons organic refined virgin coconut oil and replace the cream with 1½ cups (360 ml) full-fat coconut milk.

Key Lime DOUBLE RAINBOW CAKE

{ MAKES TWO 6-INCH-LONG (15-CM-LONG) TRIANGULAR CAKES }

Ingredients

FOR THE CAKE
2 cups (4 sticks/450 g) unsalted butter, at
    room temperature
4 cups (800 g) sugar
10 large eggs
2 teaspoons lemon extract
6 cups (780 g) all-purpose flour
2 tablespoons baking powder
2 teaspoons salt
1½ cups (360 ml) buttermilk
1 cup (240 ml) Key lime juice
Orange, yellow, and red gel food coloring

FOR THE BUTTERCREAM FROSTING
5 large egg whites
1 cup (200 g) sugar
Pinch of salt
2 cups (4 sticks/450 g) unsalted butter,
    slightly cooler than room temperature

TO FINISH
Candy-coated sunflower seeds

This is one of those cakes that packs a wallop visually. It's also scrumptious. It's also amenable to any color scheme you can dream up. So while I've decided upon a sunshiny version, you might go for a rainbow! Or lovely pastels! Or oceanic blues! With that in mind, you could make it for a kid's birthday to much "squee"ing or present it at a very adult dinner party to many "ooh"s and "aaah"s. The world is your oyster with this one. Just keep a steady hand.

Procedure

MAKE THE CAKE

- Preheat the oven to 350°F (175°C). Line two half sheet pans with parchment paper. Using a ruler and a Sharpie marker, divide and mark each pan into three long sections. Turn the parchment over (you do not want the batter to touch the ink directly, but you do want to see the dividing lines).
- In the bowl of a stand mixer fitted with the paddle attachment, cream together the butter and sugar until light and fluffy. Add the eggs one at a time and beat for a few seconds after each addition. Add the lemon extract.
- Sift together the flour, baking powder, and salt into a large bowl. Whisk for 30 seconds to evenly distribute the leavening.
- In a medium bowl, combine the buttermilk and lime juice. Add one quarter of the buttermilk mixture to the butter mixture and mix until just combined, then add one third of the flour mixture and mix until combined. Continue alternating between the buttermilk and flour mixtures until both are completely incorporated; do not overmix.
- Divide the batter equally among six bowls (about 1⅓ cups/315 ml batter in each bowl). Add food coloring to the batters as needed to create six different colors. To create sunshine-colored cake layers: Leave the first bowl of batter plain. Mix in 2 healthy drops yellow to the second bowl, 4 drops yellow to the third bowl, 4 drops yellow and 2 drops orange to the fourth bowl, 4 drops orange and 4 drops yellow to the fifth bowl, and 4 drops orange, 4 drops yellow, and 1 drop red to the sixth bowl. Play with the colors until you get them just as you like them.

continued

- Fill a pastry bag fitted with a large open tip with the plain batter. Pipe the batter onto the first marked-off third of the first prepared pan; use all the batter. Clean the tip and bag (unless you use disposable bags). Fill the clean bag with the next lightest color of batter. Pipe the batter onto the middle third of the pan (starting the batter immediately next to the plain batter). Clean and refill the bag with the next lightest color, then pipe it onto the last third of the prepared pan. Pipe the remaining three colored batters in the same manner onto the second prepared pan.
- Bake until the cake springs back when gently poked, 25 to 30 minutes. Let cool completely.

MAKE THE BUTTERCREAM FROSTING

- In the bowl of a stand mixer fitted with the whisk attachment, combine the egg whites, sugar, and salt. Place the bowl over a saucepan of simmering water (to make a double boiler) and whisk constantly until the sugar has completely dissolved and the temperature of the mixture reaches 160°F (71°C).
- Immediately transfer the bowl to the stand mixer and whisk on high speed until the bowl is cool to the touch and the egg whites are shiny, white, and stiff.
- Add the butter in small pieces, a little at a time, until the mixture thickens and becomes smooth and spreadable. (You may not need all the butter.) As you're adding butter, the buttercream may appear as if it's curdling—this is fine and means you're very close to the buttercream coming together. Add only 2 more tablespoons butter and keep whisking until the buttercream becomes smooth and spreadable.

- Once the cakes have cooled, trim each cake into separate strips by color. Transfer the darkest layer to a clean sheet pan lined with parchment. Apply a very thin and even layer of buttercream over the layer and then carefully transfer the next darkest layer on top of the frosted layer. Continue frosting and layering the cakes from darkest to lightest. Freeze the assembled cake for 30 minutes to stabilize it. Cover the frosting with plastic wrap and leave at room temperature.
- Remove the cake from the freezer and trim the sides with a very sharp serrated knife; the sides need to be perfectly straight, so be slow and steady. Cut the cake in half so you have two shorter identical pieces (see photo 1). Wrap both cakes in plastic wrap and freeze to set, 20 to 30 minutes.
- Turn the cakes on their ends, so the layers are standing vertically. From the top to the bottom, cut each cake in half diagonally (see photo 2) so that you end up with four triangles of cake. Match up the corresponding halves into two pyramid cakes with layers parallel to the counter: one made out of two triangles with dark bottom layers, and the other made out of two triangles with light bottom layers (see photo 3 and 4). (On your first go around you may be flipping pieces around quite a bit, but you'll eventually find each piece's soul mate.) Once you've found the right pairings, spread a small amount of filling between the matching pieces and seal them together. Trim the ends of both cakes.
- Cover the outside of the cakes with icing. (If you like, instead of two separate cakes, you can stick them together with frosting into one long pyramid.)

TO FINISH

- Sprinkle the candy-coated sunflower seeds decoratively on the cake.

Check page 16 before proceeding for additional details on ensuring your recipes are gluten free and/or vegan.

VEGAN

FOR THE CAKE: Replace the butter with 2 cups (450 g) Earth Balance Vegan Shortening. Replace the eggs with 3 large eggs' worth of prepared Ener-G egg replacer (see recipe, page 12) and 4 large eggs' worth of golden flax meal mixed with water (see page 12). Replace the buttermilk with plain almond milk whisked together with 1 tablespoon lemon juice. Use vegan food coloring, such as Seelect 100% Natural Food Color. FOR THE FROSTING: Omit all the frosting ingredients and do this instead:

> ½ cup (1 stick/ 115 g) Earth Balance Vegan Buttery Sticks
> ½ cup (115 g) Earth Balance Vegan Shortening
> ¼ cup (60 ml) full-fat coconut cream
> 4 cups (400 g) confectioners' sugar
> 1 teaspoon vanilla bean paste
> Pinch of salt

In the bowl of a stand mixer fitted with the whisk attachment, combine all the ingredients and whisk until light and fluffy, about 5 minutes. TO FINISH: Omit the candied sunflower seeds.

GLUTEN FREE

FOR THE CAKE: Replace the flour with 4 cups (640 g) finely milled brown rice flour, 1½ cups (205 g) sweet white sorghum flour, ½ cup (70 g) tapioca starch, and 2 tablespoons xanthan gum. Reduce the buttermilk to ¾ cup (180 ml) and the Key lime juice to ½ cup (120 ml). Use all-natural candied sunflower seeds that are made in a gluten-free facility, like Kimmie Candy Sunbursts.

HEALTHIER

FOR THE CAKE: Replace half of the butter with 1 cup (240 ml) organic grapeseed oil. Replace the sugar with 4 cups (760 g) Sucanat (keep in mind that Sucanat will make your batter slightly darker than traditional granulated sugar). Cream together the remaining 1 cup (2 sticks/225 g) butter and the Sucanat first, then incorporate the oil. Replace the flour with 6 cups (720 g) white whole-wheat flour. Use nonfat buttermilk. FOR THE FROSTING: Replace the sugar with 1 cup (190 g) Sucanat.

These were some of the most popular little morning treats at my pastry shop, Gesine Confectionary. They are so sweet to behold, with their shiny exterior, looking to all the world like they're a pile of those wondrous golden goose eggs. And that's not the only trick of this cake: They also taste ever so slightly like a donut, even though they're not fried.

GOLDEN EGGS

{ MAKES ABOUT 2 DOZEN 3-INCH (7.5-CM) EGG-SHAPED CAKES }

·········· Procedure ··········

MAKE THE CAKE

- Preheat the oven to 325°F (165°C). Spray a plain egg mold with nonstick baking spray.
- In a large mixing bowl, combine the flour, baking powder, salt, and nutmeg. Whisk for 30 seconds to evenly distribute the leavening.
- In the bowl of a stand mixer fitted with the paddle attachment, combine the sugar and butter. Mix on high speed until light and fluffy, 3 to 5 minutes. Scrape down the bottom and sides of the bowl. Add the eggs one at a time, mixing well after each addition. Add the vanilla.
- Add half of the flour mixture, mix briefly, then add half of the buttermilk. Alternate between the flour mixture and buttermilk until both are completely incorporated and a smooth batter is formed; do not overmix.
- Using a large rubber spatula, scrape the sides and bottom of the bowl and gently fold the batter to ensure there are no clumps of butter remaining.
- Fold the whipped cream into the batter until no white streaks remain. Fill the egg mold cavities three quarters full with the batter. (You may need to bake in batches; if so, refrigerate the batter between bakes.) Bake until the batter pulls away from the sides of the molds, is golden brown, and springs back when gently poked, 15 to 20 minutes.

TO FINISH

- In a small saucepan, melt the clarified butter over low heat.
- In a small bowl, whisk together the sugar and cinnamon.
- Using a pastry brush, brush the still-warm cakes with a light coating of butter. Sprinkle with the cinnamon-sugar mixture.

·········· Ingredients ··········

FOR THE CAKE

3 cups (400 g) all-purpose flour
1 tablespoon baking powder
1 teaspoon salt
¼ teaspoon freshly grated nutmeg
2 cups (400 g) sugar
1 cup (2 sticks/225 g) unsalted butter, at room temperature
5 large eggs, at room temperature
1 teaspoon vanilla bean paste
1¼ cups (300 ml) buttermilk
½ cup (120 ml) heavy cream, whipped to medium peaks and refrigerated

TO FINISH

½ cup (120 ml) clarified butter or ghee
1 cup (200 g) sugar
¼ teaspoon ground cinnamon

Check page 16 before proceeding for additional details on ensuring your recipes are gluten free and/or vegan.

VEGAN

FOR THE CAKE: Replace the butter with Earth Balance Vegan Shortening. Replace the eggs with 2 large eggs' worth of prepared Ener-G egg replacer (see recipe, page 12) and 2 large eggs' worth of flaxseed meal mixed with water (see page 12). Replace the buttermilk with 1¼ cups (300 ml) plain almond milk whisked together with 1 tablespoon lemon juice. Omit the cream. TO FINISH: Replace the butter with ½ cup (115 g) Earth Balance Vegan Shortening.

GLUTEN FREE

FOR THE CAKE: Use traditional nonstick cooking spray instead of baking spray (which contains flour). Replace the flour with 2 cups (320 g) finely milled brown rice flour, ¾ cup (100 g) sweet white sorghum flour, ¼ cup (35 g) tapioca starch, and 3 teaspoons xanthan gum. Reduce the buttermilk to ¾ cup (180 ml). Omit the cream.

HEALTHIER

FOR THE CAKE: Replace the flour with 3 cups (300 g) whole-wheat pastry flour. Replace half of the butter with ½ cup (120 ml) organic grapeseed oil. Replace the sugar with 2 cups (320 g) organic granulated palm sugar. Whip together the ½ cup (1 stick/115 g) butter and the palm sugar until light and fluffy and then add the oil. Use nonfat buttermilk and increase to 1½ cups (360 ml). Omit the cream. TO FINISH: Omit the butter. When the cakes are still very hot, sprinkle very lightly with the cinnamon-sugar mixture or simply omit it.

A Battenberg cake is a marzipan-covered almond sponge. You slice it open to reveal four squares of alternating pink and yellow cake blocks. It's named in commemoration of the marriage between Prince Louis of Battenberg (who later changed his family name to Mountbatten, for those keeping score) and Queen Victoria's granddaughter, Princess Victoria of Hesse and by Rhine. Germans might not have been well liked in England at the time, but their artistry with pastry was very well appreciated. The German prince's court pastry chefs brought their marzipan and brightly colored sponge batters and made plenty of friends at the nuptials with their sweet magic.

The
BATTENBERG

{ MAKES ONE 12-BY-4-INCH (30.5-BY-10-CM) RECTANGULAR CAKE }

Ingredients

FOR THE CAKE
1½ cups (125 g) sifted cake flour
½ cup (50 g) almond flour
1 teaspoon baking powder
1 teaspoon salt
1 cup (2 sticks/225 g) unsalted butter, at
    room temperature
1 cup (200 g) sugar
4 large eggs, at room temperature
½ teaspoon almond extract
½ teaspoon vanilla bean paste or vanilla
    extract
2 drops red gel food coloring

TO ASSEMBLE
½ cup (120 ml) smooth apricot or
    lingonberry jam
2 (7-ounce/200 g) tubes Odense marzipan

Procedure

MAKE THE CAKE
- Preheat the oven to 350°F (175°C).
- Line an 8-by-12-inch (20-by-30.5-cm) baking pan (I use a hotel pan) with parchment paper. Fold the parchment in half lengthwise to create a separator in the pan for the batters that's at least 2 inches (5 cm) high in the middle (see photo 1). Spray the parchment with nonstick cooking spray.

- Sift together the cake flour, almond flour, baking powder, and salt. Whisk together for 30 seconds to evenly distribute the leavening.
- In the bowl of a stand mixer fitted with the paddle attachment, cream together the butter and sugar until light and fluffy, scraping down the sides of the bowl every few minutes. This takes a while, up to 7 minutes, so take your time. Add the eggs one at a time, making sure each egg is completely incorporated into the batter and scraping down the bottom and sides of the bowl before adding the next. Add the almond extract and vanilla and mix until just combined. Add the dry ingredients all at once and mix on low speed until incorporated.
- Divide the batter equally between two bowls (about 15½ ounces/445 ml in each) and add 2 drops of red food coloring to one of the batters, stirring until the color is even.
- Spread the plain batter on one side of the divide in the prepared baking pan and the colored batter on the other side, using a small offset spatula to smooth the batters. Bake until the cake gently springs back when poked, 30 to 35 minutes. Let cool completely.

continued

ASSEMBLE THE CAKE

- Trim the top of each cake to make sure it is level. Measure the height of the trimmed cakes (each should be about 1½ inches/4 cm thick) and using that measurement, mark and cut each of the two cakes into two long equal pieces (about 2 by 2 by 12 inches/5 by 5 by 30.5 cm, depending on how deep your cake layer is).

- Place two strips of cake (one of each color) on a work surface. Spread a layer of jam on one long side of one plain piece and press a pink piece onto the jam, forging them into a rectangle. Spread a layer of jam on one long side of another plain piece and press a pink piece onto the jam, forging them into a rectangle (see photo 1). Trim the ends of the cakes so that the two forged rectangles are the same length (see photo 2). Spread the top of one of the forged rectangles with jam (see photo 3) and put the other rectangle on top of it (see photo 4); the short ends of the assembled cake should now form a checkerboard pattern (see photo on page 176). Tightly wrap the assembled cake with plastic wrap and freeze for 20 minutes to 1 hour.

- Knead the two marzipan blocks together until smooth. Roll the marzipan between two sheets of parchment into an even 8-by-12-inch (20-by-30.5-cm) rectangle. Spread the entire outside of the assembled cake with a thin layer of jam. Place the cake on the edge of the marzipan and carefully lift the other end of the marzipan to wrap around and cover the rest of the cake, gently pressing at the seam and then trimming with a sharp knife. Place the cake seam side down on a serving platter.

3

4

Check page 16 before proceeding for additional details on ensuring your recipes are gluten free and/or vegan.

VEGAN

FOR THE CAKE: Reduce the baking powder to ½ teaspoon. Stir 2 teaspoons baking soda into the flour mixture until combined. Replace the butter with 1 cup (240 ml) canola oil. In the bowl of a stand mixer fitted with the whisk attachment, combine the oil and sugar and whisk together until combined. Replace the eggs with 2 large eggs' worth of prepared Ener-G egg replacer (see recipe on page 12), then add 2 tablespoons distilled white vinegar and add to the sugar and oil mixture. Replace the red food coloring with 1 tablespoon concentrated cherry juice.

GLUTEN FREE

FOR THE CAKE: Replace the cake flour with ¾ cup (120 g) finely milled brown rice flour, ½ cup (70 g) sweet white sorghum flour, ¼ cup (35 g) tapioca starch, and 2 teaspoons xanthan gum. Increase the almond flour to 1 cup (100 g).

HEALTHIER

FOR THE CAKE: Replace the cake flour with 1 cup (110 g) coconut flour and ½ cup (50 g) whole-wheat pastry flour. Increase the almond flour to 1 cup (100 g). Replace the butter with ½ cup (120 ml) organic grapeseed oil and ½ cup (120 ml) organic unsweetened applesauce and replace the sugar with 1 cup (160 g) organic granulated palm sugar; whisk the oil, applesauce, and palm sugar in the stand mixer until combined. Add the flour mixture and mix until combined.

We call them Napoleons. The French, those gorgeous pastry geniuses who invented them, call them mille-feuille. Napoleon seems like an odd choice after whom to name such a delicate, long, French pastry, as he was gruff, squat, and Corsican. I think a finer choice would have been to name them after his wife, Empress Josephine, an elegant woman by all accounts. Better yet, we should have translated directly from the French and called them "a thousand leaves" because that really does describe the glory of this pastry best. A thousand leaves of buttery, crunchy puff pastry cradling luscious pastry cream.

COFFEE NAPOLEONS

{ MAKES 12 NAPOLEONS }

Ingredients

FOR THE PUFF PASTRY DOUGH
2 pounds (910 g) all-purpose flour
1 tablespoon salt
2 pounds (8 sticks/910 g) cold unsalted butter
1¼ cups (300 ml) ice-cold water

FOR THE COFFEE PASTRY CREAM
1 batch Pastry Cream (page 141), prepared up
   until the point the cream and milk are to
   be added
¼ cup (60 ml) brewed espresso

TO LIGHTEN THE PASTRY CREAM
1 cup (240 ml) cold heavy cream

FOR THE GLAZE
2 cups (200 g) confectioners' sugar, plus ¼ cup
   (25 g) extra if needed
1 to 2 tablespoons lemon juice
½ teaspoon instant espresso powder

FOR THE ROYAL ICING
1 cup (100 g) confectioners' sugar, plus ½ cup
   (50 g) extra, if needed
1 teaspoon egg white powder
1 to 2 tablespoons lukewarm water
¼ teaspoon instant espresso powder
Purple and green gel food coloring

.... Procedure ....

MAKE THE PUFF PASTRY DOUGH
- In a large bowl, combine the flour and salt. Stir well.
- Chop the butter into large cubes and add to the flour mixture; toss to coat. Massage the butter into the flour with the tips of your fingers until the butter pieces are a bit smaller, about the size of dimes. Add the cold water and stir with a wooden spoon to coat as much of the mixture with moisture as you can. Using your hands, gently massage the dough just enough to evenly distribute the flour and water so that no large dry or wet patches remain. Press down on the dough to create a compact mass in the bowl and cover with plastic wrap. Let rest for 10 to 15 minutes.
- Turn the dough out onto a lightly floured surface. Roll the dough out to a rough 12-by-20-inch (30.5-by-50-cm) rectangle. Make a letter fold: Bring one short edge of the dough to the middle of the rectangle, then fold the other short side over on top of the first fold, like folding a letter.
- Turn the dough 90 degrees and roll out into a rough 12-by-20-inch (30.5-by-50-cm) rectangle again. Perform another letter fold. Do this two more times (turning the dough block 90 degrees, rolling into a rectangle, and folding), for a total of 4 letter folds. Wrap tightly with plastic wrap and let rest in the fridge for at least 20 minutes before using.

MAKE THE COFFEE PASTRY CREAM
- Make the pastry cream as directed in the main recipe on page 141, with this change: Simmer the espresso with the milk and cream mixture before adding it to the egg and sugar mixture. Cover with plastic wrap, making sure the plastic wrap touches the pastry cream to prevent a skin from forming, and refrigerate until completely cool, about 2 hours.

continued

LIGHTEN THE PASTRY CREAM

- Once the pastry cream is cool, whip the heavy cream to stiff peaks in the bowl of a stand mixer fitted with the whisk attachment.
- Stir the cooled pastry cream until loosened and smooth. Fold in the whipped cream with a large rubber spatula. Refrigerate until needed.

BAKE THE PUFF PASTRY

- Preheat the oven to 375°F (190°C). Line a half sheet pan with parchment paper.
- Cut the puff pastry dough in half. Wrap one half in plastic wrap and refrigerate or freeze for a future use. Roll the second piece of dough into a rough 19-by-14-inch (48-by-35.5-cm) rectangle. (Be sure that you are rolling the dough out in the right direction—that is, with the layers stacked—so you get the full effect of the "puffed" layers as it bakes.) Trim the sides with a very sharp knife so that the dough fits snugly in the prepared pan; they usually measure a scant 18 by 13 inches (46 by 33 cm). Transfer the dough to the pan. Place a piece of parchment on top of the dough and place another sheet pan on top of that (which will weigh down the dough while baking). Bake for 15 minutes. Remove the top sheet pan and parchment and continue baking until the pastry is baked through and deep golden brown, about 20 minutes. Set aside to cool completely.
- With a very sharp knife, cut the pastry into three even, short strips, so that each measures about 6 by 13 inches (15 by 33 cm).

MAKE THE GLAZE

- In a small bowl, stir together the confectioners' sugar and 1 tablespoon lemon juice until smooth. Dip a clean spoon into the glaze, then remove it. The glaze should coat the spoon so well that it's almost opaque. If it's too translucent, add 1 tablespoon more confectioners' sugar at a time until thick enough. If too thick, add a few more drops of lemon juice at a time to thin.
- Stir in the espresso powder. The mixture should be slightly thicker than the plain glaze but should not be a paste. Add another 1 or 2 drops of lemon juice to the mixture to thin, if needed. Make sure it's completely smooth with no lumps.
- Line a sheet pan with parchment paper and place a cooling rack on top of it. Place the best and most intact piece of puff pastry on the rack. Spoon the glaze over it and spread evenly using a small offset spatula to coat the entire piece. Allow the glaze to set until very firm.
- Once firm, using a very sharp knife, cut the pastry into twelve 1-inch (2.5-cm) pieces. (Why, you ask, would you cut the top by itself and not when it's atop the assembled pastry? Well, this makes the pastry easier to cut: Create a clean first cut that acts as a guide and the rest will follow.)
- Set a layer of unglazed puff pastry on a serving platter. Fill a large pastry bag fitted with a large plain tip with half of the lightened pastry cream. Pipe the pastry cream evenly onto the first layer. Place the second unglazed puff pastry layer atop the pastry cream and press down only so much that the layer fits snugly. If the pastry cream between the puff pastry layers feels as if it may not keep its shape, place in the freezer to set for 20 to 30 minutes. Place the remaining lightened pastry cream in the pastry bag and pipe it evenly onto the second layer of puff pastry. Using a small offset spatula, place the twelve glazed and cut pieces of puff on top of the pastry cream, setting them very close together. Freeze to set, at least 1 hour and up to 2.

MAKE THE ROYAL ICING

- In a small bowl, combine the confectioners' sugar and egg white powder. Stir until the egg white powder is evenly distributed. Add lukewarm water, 1 tablespoon at a time, and stir until smooth. Keep adding water until a smooth, pipeable paste forms. When piped, the royal icing should keep its shape and not spread. If the icing is too loose, add confectioners' sugar 1 tablespoon at a time until you've reached the correct consistency.
- Divide the royal icing evenly among three small bowls. Add ¼ teaspoon espresso powder to one and stir to distribute. Cover with plastic wrap so that the plastic wrap touches the surface of the icing. Add a drop of purple food coloring to

another bowl, stir to distribute the coloring, and cover with plastic wrap so that the plastic wrap touches the surface of the icing. Add a drop of green food coloring to the third bowl, stir to distribute the coloring, and cover with plastic wrap so that the plastic wrap touches the surface of the icing.

- Transfer the espresso icing to a pastry bag fitted with a small plain tip. Outline each glazed piece of puff with a thin thread of icing.

- Transfer the green icing to a pastry bag fitted with a small plain tip and pipe a wavy line down the center of the pastry to create a stem.
- Transfer the purple icing to a pastry bag fitted with a small plain tip and pipe small petals along the sides of the green stem.
- Allow the royal icing décor to set completely in the refrigerator, about 20 minutes. Once set, serve immediately.

OPTIONS

COFFEE NAPOLEONS

Check page 16 before proceeding for additional details on ensuring your recipes are gluten free and/or vegan.

VEGAN

FOR THE PUFF PASTRY: Replace the butter with 2 pounds (8 sticks/910 g) Earth Balance Vegan Shortening. FOR THE COFFEE PASTRY CREAM: Use the vegan version of the Pastry Cream on page 141, adding the espresso during the simmering stage. TO LIGHTEN THE PASTRY CREAM: Replace the heavy cream with cold full-fat coconut cream, whipped to stiff peaks. FOR THE ROYAL ICING: Omit the icing ingredients entirely and do the following instead: Stir together 1 cup (100 g) confectioners' sugar, 2 teaspoons almond milk, and 2 teaspoons corn syrup until smooth. Add more confectioners' sugar as needed to create a pipable icing. Use vegan food coloring.

GLUTEN FREE

FOR THE PUFF PASTRY: Replace the flour with 2 pounds (910 g) gluten-free flour blend (great types include King Arthur Flour's Gluten-Free All-Purpose Baking Mix, Bob's Red Mill Gluten-Free All-Purpose Baking Flour, and Thomas Keller's Cup 4 Cup blend) and 2 tablespoons xanthan gum. Proceed as per the master recipe.

HEALTHIER

FOR THE PUFF PASTRY: Replace the flour with 2 pounds (910 g) whole-wheat pastry flour. Replace half of the butter with 1 cup (240 ml) organic refined virgin coconut oil that's been melted to measure and resolidified. Massage the coconut oil into the flour first until it resembles fine cornmeal and then add the remaining butter as in the main recipe. FOR THE COFFEE PASTRY CREAM: Use the healthier version of the Pastry Cream on page 141 and add the espresso powder at the simmering stage. TO LIGHTEN THE PASTRY CREAM: Replace the heavy cream with full-fat coconut cream, whipped to stiff peaks.

GATEAU *St.* SWANARÉ

{ MAKES ONE 12-INCH (30.5-CM) DESSERT }

The patron saint of pastry is St. Honoré, for whom the famous dessert made of puff pastry, cream puffs, and pastry cream is named. It's a simple affair. A round of puff, with a ring of small cream puffs lining the perimeter, pastry cream pooled in the middle. I've always wondered why it is that I couldn't dress up the thing, add a little whimsy to the delicious pastry. And then I realized that there's nothing—and no one—stopping me from doing just that! So I've transformed the simple cream puffs into swans with little to no effort, upping the whimsy quotient by a factor of 100. I think St. Honoré would approve.

This recipe makes far more puff pastry than you'll need for this dessert. Due to the process of making it, though, it's imperative that you make it in quantity. But it's also the most delicious stuff ever and is perfect for turnovers, appetizers, pie crusts . . . so many things. And it freezes well, so you'll have this wonderful time-saver on hand in the event of a pastry emergency.

Ingredients

FOR THE PUFF PASTRY DOUGH
2 pounds (910 g) all-purpose flour
1 tablespoon salt
2 pounds (8 sticks/910 g) cold unsalted butter
1¼ cups (300 ml) ice-cold water

FOR THE PASTRY CREAM
1 cup (200 g) sugar
¼ teaspoon lemon juice
1 cup (240 ml) heavy cream
1 cup (240 ml) whole milk
6 large egg yolks
¼ cup (30 g) cornstarch
1 teaspoon vanilla bean paste
¼ teaspoon salt

FOR THE CHOUX SWANS
¾ cup (1½ sticks/170 g) unsalted butter, cut into small pieces
1 cup (140 g) plus 2 tablespoons all-purpose flour
2 teaspoons sugar
½ teaspoon salt
6 large eggs

TO LIGHTEN THE PASTRY CREAM
1 cup (240 ml) cold heavy cream

TO FINISH
½ cup (100 g) granulated sugar
¼ teaspoon lemon juice
Gold dust (optional)
2 cups (480 ml) cold heavy cream
¼ cup (25 g) confectioners' sugar
½ teaspoon vanilla bean paste

MAKE THE PUFF PASTRY DOUGH

- In a large bowl, combine the flour and salt. Stir well.
- Chop the butter into large cubes and add to the flour mixture; toss to coat. Massage the butter into the flour with the tips of your fingers until the butter pieces are a bit smaller, about the size of dimes. Add the cold water and stir with a wooden spoon to coat as much of the mixture with moisture as you can. Using your hands, gently massage the dough just enough to evenly distribute the flour and water so that no large dry or wet patches remain. Press down on the dough to create a compact mass and cover with plastic wrap. Let rest for 10 to 15 minutes.
- Turn the dough out onto a lightly floured surface. Roll the dough out to a rough 12-by-20-inch (30.5-by-50-cm) rectangle. Make a letter fold: Bring one short edge of the dough to the middle of the rectangle, then fold the other short side over on top of the first fold, like folding a letter.
- Turn the dough 90 degrees and roll out into a rough 12-by-20-inch (30.5-by-50-cm) rectangle again. Perform another letter fold. Do this two more times (turning the dough block 90 degrees, rolling into a rectangle, and folding). Wrap tightly with plastic wrap and let rest in the fridge for at least 20 minutes before using. (You can wrap leftover puff pastry tightly and keep in the freezer for up to 1 month. Let defrost in the refrigerator overnight before using.)

MAKE THE PASTRY CREAM

- Combine the sugar with ⅓ cup (75 ml) water and the lemon juice in a large heavy saucepan. Stir together over medium heat until the sugar is dissolved. Once the sugar has dissolved, stop stirring and continue cooking the sugar until it turns a medium amber.
- Remove from the heat and immediately pour in the cream; the mixture will bubble vigorously, so stand back until it calms. Stir until the mixture is homogenous. Set aside.

- In the bowl of a stand mixer fitted with the whisk attachment, whisk the milk, egg yolks, cornstarch, vanilla, and salt to combine. Continue whisking on medium speed and slowly pour the hot sugar-cream mixture down the side of the mixing bowl into the egg yolk mixture. Continue mixing until smooth.
- Transfer the mixture back to the saucepan and whisk constantly over medium-low heat until the mixture thickens to the consistency of mayonnaise. Transfer the pastry cream to a bowl and cover with plastic wrap, making sure the plastic wrap touches the pastry cream to prevent a skin from forming. Refrigerate until cool, about 2 hours.

MAKE THE CHOUX SWANS

- Preheat the oven to 400°F (205°C). Line three half sheet pans with parchment paper.
- In a saucepan, bring 1¼ cups (300 ml) water and the butter to a boil. Add the flour, sugar, and salt to the boiling mixture all at once and stir immediately and briskly with a wooden spoon until a paste forms and it starts to pull away from the sides of the pan. Continue stirring for 2 to 3 minutes to allow more water to evaporate.
- Transfer the choux paste to the bowl of a stand mixer fitted with the paddle attachment and mix on low speed. Add the eggs one at a time, mixing thoroughly after each addition. You may not need all of them. The finished mixture should be a soft paste but still stiff enough that it holds its shape when piped.
- Transfer ¼ cup (60 ml) of the paste to a pastry bag fitted with a medium-small plain tip (the opening about the size of a pea). On the first sheet pan, pipe the batter into the shape of the number "2," about 2½ inches (6 cm) tall and ½ inch (12 mm) wide; this will be the swan head and neck. At the top tip of the "2," gently pipe a small pea-sized dollop and then pull the pastry bag away so the batter ends in a point, creating a swan beak. Make as many of these as you can with the ¼ cup (60 ml) batter, 22 to 24 (that will include some extra in case some of the necks break). Bake until golden brown, 10 to 15 minutes. Set aside to cool completely.

continued

- Transfer the remaining choux paste to a pastry bag fitted with a large plain tip and pipe small 1- to 1½-inch (2.5- to 4-cm) balls, spacing them about 3 inches (7.5 cm) apart, on the remaining two sheet pans. Make as many of these as you can as you'll need 12 to 14 for the cake and you'll want to have a selection from which to choose the most perfect puffs. (Also, you can fill and serve any extras next to the assembled cake.) Bake for 15 minutes, then immediately reduce the oven temperature to 350°F (175°C) and continue baking until deeply golden brown, 30 to 40 minutes more. Remove the choux puffs from the oven and let cool just enough that you can handle them.
- Using a very sharp serrated knife, cut one of the choux puffs in half through the middle. If the interior of the choux feels at all soft, return the cut choux puffs to the oven and bake for 5 minutes more. Set aside to cool completely.

BAKE THE PUFF PASTRY

- Preheat the oven to 375°F (190°C). Line a half sheet pan with parchment.
- Take about one quarter of the puff pastry dough and roll it out to a rough 13-inch (33-cm) round on a lightly floured work surface. (Be sure that you are rolling the dough out in the right direction—that is, with the layers stacked—so you get the full effect of the "puffed" layers as it bakes.) Use a 12-inch (30.5-cm) round guide and lightly trace the circle upon the dough (do not cut through). Let the dough rest for 20 minutes in a cool place (a counter is fine unless it's very hot; in that case refrigerate it). Once rested, using an incredibly sharp knife, trim the dough into a 12-inch (30.5-cm) round. (Save the scraps for another treat.)
- Transfer the round of dough to the prepared pan. Dock the dough with a fork. Place a piece of parchment on top of the dough and place another sheet pan on top of that (which will weight down the dough while baking). Bake for 20 minutes. Remove the top sheet pan and parchment and continue baking until the dough is deep golden brown and baked through, 10 to 15 minutes more. Set aside to cool completely.

LIGHTEN THE PASTRY CREAM

- In the bowl of a stand mixer fitted with the whisk attachment (or in a large bowl with a whisk), whisk the heavy cream to stiff peaks.
- Stir the cooled pastry cream well, until loosened and smooth. Using a large rubber spatula, gently fold the whipped cream into the pastry cream. Cover and refrigerate until needed.

TO FINISH

- Fill a large heatproof bowl with ice. Set aside.
- Make the caramel "glue": Combine the sugar, lemon juice, and 3 tablespoons water in a heavy saucepan. Stir over medium heat until the sugar is completely melted. Stop stirring and continue cooking over medium heat until the caramel turns a light amber color. Immediately set the saucepan on top of the ice to stop the caramel from cooking further.
- Transfer the cooled puff pastry round to a serving platter.
- Cut off the top third of 10 to 14 puffs and set the tops aside (see photo 1). Using tongs, dip the bottom of a cooled choux puff bottom (use the best-looking ones first) into the caramel and place on the edge of the cooled puff pastry. Continue gluing choux puff bottoms around the perimeter of the puff pastry (I can usually fit 10 to 14 along the perimeter, depending on how large they puffed in the oven). Set aside one or two of the remaining cut choux puffs (cut more if necessary).
- Fill a large pastry bag fitted with a large star tip with the lightened pastry cream. Fill each of the choux bottoms lining the perimeter of the puff pastry with a healthy dollop of lightened pastry cream. Fill the two extra choux bottoms with cream as well, and set aside. Pipe the remaining lightened pastry cream onto the exposed puff pastry in the middle of the cake.
- Dip a swan neck in gold dust, if using (see photo 2). Place a gold swan neck (the base of the "2" shape) deep inside the cream of each choux puff to anchor (see photo 3). Dust and place necks into the two reserved choux puffs as well.

continued

Cut the reserved choux puff tops in half to create the swan "wings," keeping each set of wings together on the sheet pan (see photo 4). Dust each set of wings with gold dust and place them in the cream of a choux puff on the pastry so the two pieces resemble the two wings of a swan (see photos 5 and 6). Dust and place the wings onto the two reserved choux puffs as well.

In the bowl of a stand mixer fitted with the whisk attachment (or in a large bowl with a whisk), whisk the cream with the confectioners' sugar and vanilla to stiff peaks. Put the whipped cream in a pastry bag with a star tip or a St. Honoré pastry tip and pipe on top of the pastry cream in a decorative pattern (or you can dollop the cream and make a wavy pattern with the back of a spoon). Place the extra choux swans randomly on the sweetened whipped cream. Serve immediately.

Check page 16 before proceeding for additional details on ensuring your recipes are gluten free and/or vegan.

VEGAN

FOR THE PUFF PASTRY DOUGH: Replace the butter with 2 pounds (910 g) Earth Balance Vegan Shortening. FOR THE PASTRY CREAM: Use the vegan version of the Pastry Cream on page 141, but increase the sugar to 1 cup (200 g). Caramelize the sugar per the main recipe and then add the soy, coconut, or almond milk and stir to combine. Add the dry ingredients in the vegan recipe and stir until thickened. FOR THE CHOUX SWANS: Replace the butter with 4 tablespoons (55 g) Earth Balance Vegan Buttery Sticks. Replace the eggs with 2 tablespoons Ener-G egg replacer (not prepared) whisked together with ½ cup (120 ml) water until foamy and thick, whisking until there are absolutely no lumps (any clumping will result in a bit of a volcanic explosion where the lumps lie). Proceed by combining 1¼ cups (300 ml) water and the Buttery Sticks and bringing to a simmer, then adding the flour, sugar, and salt and stirring to thicken as in the main recipe. Transfer the mixture to the bowl of a stand mixer fitted with the paddle attachment and mix on low speed. Slowly add the whisked Ener-G mixture and mix until smooth. Then add sparkling water 1 tablespoon at a time until the mixture is smooth, shiny, and easily piped; I typically use 4 tablespoons. Pipe and bake as in the main recipe with this caveat: Don't pipe the puffs too high and, in fact, press the choux paste out so that it is 1 to 1½ inches (2.5 to 4 cm) wide but not mounded more than ½ inch (12 mm) high. This will result in about 24 puffs; choose the best for the pastry. These vegan puffs are more delicate than traditional choux puffs (but still very delicious). If you find them too delicate to cut (pick an ugly one to test), simply allow them to cool to room temperature, then, with your large pastry bag filled with lightened vegan pastry cream, poke a small hole into the side of the puffs and fill the choux puff with cream instead. In this case, make a small opening at the top of the pastry, on a far end, so you can insert the bottom of the swan neck. TO LIGHTEN THE PASTRY CREAM: Replace the heavy cream with 1 cup (240 ml) full-fat coconut cream. TO FINISH: Replace the heavy cream with full-fat coconut cream.

GLUTEN FREE

FOR THE PUFF PASTRY: Replace the flour with 2 pounds (910 g) gluten-free flour blend (like King Arthur Flour's Gluten-Free All-Purpose Baking Mix; Bob's Red Mill Gluten-Free All-Purpose Baking Flour; or Thomas Keller's Cup 4 Cup blend) and 6 teaspoons xanthan gum. Proceed as in the main recipe. FOR THE CHOUX SWANS: Replace the flour with 1½ cups (190 g) gluten-free flour blend and 1 teaspoon xanthan gum.

HEALTHIER

FOR THE PUFF PASTRY: Replace the flour with 2 pounds (910 g) whole-wheat pastry flour. Replace half of the butter with 2 cups (480 ml) organic unrefined virgin coconut oil that's been melted to measure and resolidified. Massage the coconut oil into the flour first until it resembles fine cornmeal and then add the remaining butter as in the main recipe. FOR THE PASTRY CREAM: Use the healthier version of the Pastry Cream on page 141. FOR THE CHOUX SWANS: Replace the flour with 1 cup (100 g) plus 2 tablespoons whole-wheat pastry flour. TO LIGHTEN THE PASTRY CREAM: Replace the heavy cream with full-fat coconut cream. TO FINISH: Replace the heavy cream with full-fat coconut cream and use organic confectioners' sugar.

CRISPY
SUGAR CONES

Caramel Sauce CHOCOLATE SHELL

MARSHMALLOWS

BUTTER CRUNCH PECAN TOFFEE

CARAMELS CARAMEL PINWHEELS

COCONUT MANGO ICE CREAM

VANILLA BEAN *Caramel Lollipops*
ICE CREAM COCONUT ICE CREAM

BANANA SPLIT ICE CREAM

Minty Ice Cream Sandwiches

TRIPLE CHOCOLATE
ICE CREAM

ICE CREAM
and
CANDY

I am an absolute fool when it comes to chocolate chip cookies acting as the vehicle that delivers ice cream safely into my pie hole. The way the cookies are firm enough to keep everything in place yet soft enough to just melt into the ice cream as you chomp away. The bigger the cookie ice cream sandwich the better, but as I've gotten older (and taller . . . and wider) the cookie sandwiches seem to have gotten smaller and smaller. Good thing I'm a dab hand at making all the elements myself! Now I can make them as piggishly large or as miniscule as I like.

For that matter, why not make your own ice cream toppings? Your own cones? Heck, let's make our own candy, too!

TRIPLE
Chocolate
ICE CREAM

{ MAKES 1 QUART (960 ML) }

Ingredients

1 cup (200 g) sugar
8 large egg yolks
½ teaspoon xanthan gum
3 cups (720 ml) heavy cream
1 cup (240 ml) brewed coffee
½ cup (40 g) unsweetened cocoa powder
2 tablespoons vanilla bean paste
¼ teaspoon salt
3½ ounces (100 g) bittersweet chocolate
   (like Lindt 90%), finely chopped
½ cup (70 g) cocoa nibs (optional)

This chocolate ice cream is so damn decadent, I can't take it. Honestly, it's out of control. Or more aptly, I get out of control when it's around. It's, well, chocolaty. And rich. And chocolaty. Oh, goodness gracious. Now I need to go make some.

Procedure

- Prepare your ice cream maker according to the manufacturer's directions; often that means freezing the insert bowl at least 24 hours in advance.
- In a medium bowl, whisk together the sugar, egg yolks, and xanthan gum until light and fluffy. Set aside.
- In a large heavy saucepan, combine 1 cup (240 ml) of the cream, the coffee, cocoa powder, vanilla, and salt. Whisk until combined and smooth. Transfer the egg mixture to the saucepan and whisk to combine. Place over medium-low heat and whisk until the mixture thickens enough to coat the back of a wooden spoon. Remove from the heat.
- Add the chopped chocolate to the hot custard and let sit undisturbed for 3 minutes. Whisk to combine the chocolate. Pour the mixture through a sieve into a large bowl. Cover the bowl with plastic wrap and refrigerate the mixture until completely cool, 2 hours to overnight.
- Add the remaining 2 cups (480 ml) cream to the chilled custard and whisk to combine. Transfer the chilled mixture to the ice cream maker and follow the manufacturer's instructions to process and finish. Prior to transferring the finished ice cream from the ice cream maker to the freezer, carefully stir in the cocoa nibs, if using.

Check page 16 before proceeding for additional details on ensuring your recipes are gluten free and/or vegan.

HEALTHIER AND VEGAN

Omit the ingredients in the main recipe entirely and do the following instead to make 1 pint (480 ml):

1 cup (240 ml) unsweetened vanilla cashew milk
8 ounces (225 g) firm silken tofu (water packed, not boxed), drained (see page 13), at room temperature
½ cup (100 g) granulated sugar, or ½ cup (80 g) organic granulated palm sugar for the healthier version
½ cup (120 ml) organic agave syrup
½ cup (120 ml) hot brewed coffee
½ cup (40 g) unsweetened cocoa powder
3½ ounces (100 g) bittersweet chocolate (like Lindt 90%), melted
3 tablespoons organic grapeseed oil
2 tablespoons vanilla bean paste
1 tablespoon cacao butter, melted
½ teaspoon xanthan gum
¼ teaspoon salt
½ cup (70 g) cocoa nibs (optional)

- Prepare your ice cream maker according to the manufacturer's directions; often that means freezing the insert bowl at least 24 hours in advance.
- Put the cashew milk and tofu in a blender and blend until smooth. Add the sugar, syrup, coffee, cocoa powder, melted chocolate, oil, vanilla, cacao butter, xanthan gum, and salt and continue blending until very smooth. Pour the mixture through a sieve into a large bowl. Chill for 1 hour. Transfer the chilled mixture along with the cocoa nibs, if using, to the ice cream maker and follow the manufacturer's instructions to process and finish.

HEALTHIER AND VEGAN

Omit the ingredients in the main recipe entirely and do the following instead to make 1 pint (480 ml):

1½ cups (360 ml) unsweetened vanilla cashew milk
8 ounces (225 g) firm silken tofu (water packed, not boxed), drained (see page 13), at room temperature
½ cup (100 g) granulated sugar, or ½ cup (80 g) organic granulated palm sugar for the healthier version
½ cup (120 ml) organic corn syrup or organic agave syrup
3 tablespoons organic grapeseed oil
2 tablespoons vanilla bean paste
1 tablespoon cacao butter, melted
½ teaspoon xanthan gum
¼ teaspoon salt

- Prepare your ice cream maker according to the manufacturer's directions; often that means freezing the insert bowl at least 24 hours in advance.
- Place the cashew milk and tofu in a blender and blend until smooth. Add the sugar, syrup, oil, vanilla, cacao butter, xanthan gum, and salt and continue blending until very smooth. Pour the mixture through a sieve into a large bowl. Chill for 1 hour.
- Transfer the chilled mixture to the ice cream maker and follow the manufacturer's instructions to process and finish.

GLUTEN FREE

The ice cream is already gluten free.

GLUTEN FREE

The ice cream is already gluten free.

I'm not scared of my ice cream appearing dotty. So many people these days want the flavor but not the evidence of what made it. Not me. I want people to know that I spent a boatload of money on the microscopic innards of the vanilla bean. One way I get the most bang for my buck is by buying vanilla bean paste. I don't know about you, but I'm awfully tired of spending $20 on a dry and wrinkled pod trapped under glass, which has to be rehydrated and resuscitated. Instead I just pop open a bottle of vanilla bean paste and I'm ready to go.

Vanilla Bean ICE CREAM

{ MAKES 1 QUART (960 ML) }

Procedure

- Prepare your ice cream maker according to the manufacturer's directions; often that means freezing the insert bowl at least 24 hours in advance.
- Fill a large bowl with ice. Set a second bowl, slightly smaller, on top of the ice and nestle it in so it won't tip. Pour the cream into the second bowl. Set aside.
- In a large heavy saucepan, whisk together the sugar, egg yolks, and xanthan gum until pale. Whisk in the milk, vanilla, and salt until combined. Place the saucepan over medium-low heat and whisk constantly until the custard thickens enough to coat the back of a wooden spoon, about 5 minutes.
- Pour the custard through a sieve into the bowl containing the cream. Whisk to combine. Cover the bowl with plastic wrap and refrigerate until completely cool, 2 hours to overnight.
- Transfer the chilled mixture to the ice cream maker and follow the manufacturer's instructions to process and finish.

Ingredients

2 cups (480 ml) organic heavy cream
⅔ cup (130 g) sugar
7 large egg yolks
½ teaspoon xanthan gum
2 cups (480 ml) organic whole milk
2 tablespoons vanilla bean paste
¼ teaspoon salt

a note from my sweet tooth

"What the hell is xanthan gum doing in the ice cream recipe??" I know you're thinking it. Run to your freezer and pull out a pint of Ben & Jerry's. What do you see on that ingredient list? Xanthan gum. You already know that it acts as a thickener in gluten-free baking. In case you thought it was a deeply disturbing chemical, let me just assure you that compared to most things, it's actually pretty natural and is created by the fermentation of glucose, sucrose, or lactose. It's used in commercial salad dressings as a thickener and an emulsion agent (it keeps the dressing from separating so the herbs and yummy bits stay suspended). It's used in toothpaste as a binder (see—not just in gluten-free stuff!). In ice cream, it helps keep ice crystals from forming, leaving the ice cream smooth and luxurious. So there are myriad reasons to keep a supply of xanthan gum in your pantry. You never know when you'll need to make a super smooth, homemade ice chunk–free ice cream or whip up a batch of toothpaste.

Banana *SPLIT* ICE CREAM

{ MAKES 1 QUART (960 ML) }

Ingredients

2 cups (480 ml) heavy cream
6 ripe bananas
½ teaspoon lemon juice
¾ cup (150 g) sugar
6 large egg yolks
½ teaspoon xanthan gum
1 cup (240 ml) whole milk
1 tablespoon vanilla bean paste
½ teaspoon salt
1 cup (170 g) semisweet chocolate chips
    (optional)
1 cup (165 g) hulled and diced strawberries
    (¼-inch/6-mm pieces; optional)
1 cup (165 g) diced pineapple (¼-inch/6-mm
    pieces), drained (optional)
½ cup (75 g) salted roasted peanuts, roughly
    chopped (optional)

My Omi spoke one word of English and it's questionable whether it was English at all. Whenever she came to visit us in the States, we'd bring her to Gifford's Ice Cream parlor and my tiny German grandmother would have us order her a banana split. After her first bite, she'd break out her one word, "Vunderfool." That's "wonderful" to you and me. Even if you couldn't quite work out what she meant, one look at her face would provide evidence of her utter happiness with the treat before her. This is my ice cream love letter to my beloved Omi. It really is vunderfool.

Procedure

- Prepare your ice cream maker according to the manufacturer's directions; often that means freezing the insert bowl at least 24 hours in advance.
- Fill a large bowl with ice. Set a second bowl, slightly smaller, on top of the ice and nestle it in so it won't tip. Pour the cream into the second bowl. Set aside.
- Puree the bananas in a food processor along with the lemon juice until smooth. Set aside.
- In a medium bowl, whisk together the sugar, egg yolks, and xanthan gum until the mixture lightens and ribbons.
- In a medium-sized heavy saucepan, combine the egg yolk mixture, milk, vanilla, and salt. Whisk over medium heat until the custard thickens enough to coat the back of a wooden spoon about 5 minutes. Add the pureed bananas and whisk until combined.
- Put the banana custard mixture through a sieve into the bowl with the cream, using a rubber spatula to press through as much of the banana as possible. Whisk to combine. Cover the bowl with plastic wrap and refrigerate until chilled, 2 hours to overnight.
- Transfer the chilled mixture to the ice cream maker and follow the manufacturer's instructions to process and finish. Prior to transferring the ice cream from the ice cream maker to the freezer, carefully stir in the chocolate chips, strawberries, pineapple, and peanuts, if using.

Check page 16 before proceeding for additional details on ensuring your recipes are gluten free and/or vegan.

HEALTHIER AND VEGAN

Omit the ingredients in the main recipe entirely and do the following instead to make 1 pint (480 ml):

6 ripe bananas, unpeeled, frozen overnight
½ teaspoon lemon juice
½ teaspoon xanthan gum
¼ teaspoon salt
1½ cups (360 ml) full-fat coconut milk
½ cup (120 ml) organic agave syrup
1 teaspoon vanilla bean paste
½ cup (85 g) semisweet chocolate chips (optional)
½ cup (85 g) hulled and diced strawberries
    (¼-inch/6-mm pieces; optional)
½ cup (85 g) diced pineapple (¼-inch/6-mm
    pieces), drained (optional)
¼ cup (35 g) salted, roasted peanuts (optional)

- Peel the frozen bananas and place in the bowl of a food processor along with the lemon juice, xanthan gum, and salt. Puree until smooth. With the processor running, slowly add the coconut milk, agave syrup, and vanilla. Immediately stir in the chocolate chips, strawberries, pineapple, and peanuts, if using. Transfer the mixture to a freezer-safe container and freeze until solid.

GLUTEN FREE

The ice cream is already gluten free.

HEALTHIER AND VEGAN

Omit the ingredients in the main recipe entirely and do the following instead to make 1 pint (480 ml):

8 ounces (225 g) firm silken tofu
    (water packed, not boxed), drained (see
    page 13), at room temperature
1½ cups (360 ml) full-fat coconut milk
½ cup (100 g) granulated sugar, or ½ cup
    (80 g) organic granulated palm sugar
    for the healthier version
½ cup (120 ml) organic agave syrup
3 tablespoons organic grapeseed oil
1 tablespoon cacao butter, melted
1 tablespoon vanilla bean paste
1 tablespoon coconut extract
½ teaspoon xanthan gum
½ teaspoon salt

- Prepare your ice cream maker according to the manufacturer's directions; often that means freezing the insert bowl at least 24 hours in advance.
- Put the tofu and coconut milk in a blender and blend until smooth. Add the sugar, agave syrup, oil, cacao butter, vanilla, coconut extract, xanthan gum, and salt and continue blending until very smooth. Pour the mixture through a sieve into a large bowl. Cover with plastic wrap and refrigerate until completely chilled, 2 hours to overnight.
- Transfer the chilled mixture to the ice cream maker and follow the manufacturer's instructions to process and finish.

COCONUT ICE CREAM

{ MAKES 1 QUART (960 ML) }

I freely admit to having hated coconut for nearly thirty years, and I will also admit that I was an idiot for denying myself the enjoyment of such a marvel of nature and all its myriad incarnations, from shredded, to milk, to cream, to oil, to sugar; the manner in which coconut can be used as both flavor and texture is nothing short of a miracle. I am now a true convert to the coconut lifestyle. If you find yourself unable to open yourself to its beauty, try this recipe as a gateway.

Ingredients

2 cups (480 ml) organic heavy cream
1 tablespoon coconut extract
⅔ cup (130 g) sugar
7 large egg yolks
½ teaspoon xanthan gum
2 cups (480 ml) full-fat coconut milk
1 tablespoon vanilla bean paste
¼ teaspoon salt

Procedure

- Prepare your ice cream maker according to the manufacturer's directions; often that means freezing the insert bowl at least 24 hours in advance.
- Fill a large bowl with ice. Set a second bowl, slightly smaller, on top of the ice and nestle it in so it won't tip. Pour the cream and coconut extract into the second bowl. Set aside.
- In a medium-sized heavy saucepan, whisk together the sugar, egg yolks, and xanthan gum until pale. Whisk in the coconut milk, vanilla, and salt until combined. Place the saucepan over medium-low heat and whisk constantly until the custard thickens enough to coat the back of a wooden spoon, about 5 minutes.
- Pour the custard through a sieve into the bowl containing the cream and coconut extract. Whisk to combine. Cover the bowl with plastic wrap and refrigerate until completely chilled, 2 hours to overnight.
- Transfer the chilled mixture to the ice cream maker and follow the manufacturer's instructions to process and finish.

OPTIONS

GLUTEN FREE
The ice cream is already gluten free.

This, my sweet friends, is a tropical samba on your taste buds. Mango and coconut make for beautiful dance partners. The coconut is as creamy and dreamy as it's ever been. And mango boogies through that decadence with its bright fruitiness. Whether you need a cool reprieve during the heat of summer or a reminder of summer's sumptuous warmth on a frigid winter's eve, this is the stuff that'll make all your tropical dreams come true.

Procedure

- Prepare your ice cream maker according to the manufacturer's directions; often that means freezing the insert bowl at least 24 hours in advance.
- Fill a large bowl with ice. Set a second bowl, slightly smaller, on top of the ice and nestle it in so it won't tip. Pour the cream and coconut extract into the second bowl. Set aside.
- In a medium-sized heavy saucepan, whisk together the sugar, egg yolks, and xanthan gum until pale. Whisk in the coconut cream, mango puree, vanilla, and salt until combined. Place the saucepan over medium-low heat and whisk constantly until the custard thickens enough to coat the back of a wooden spoon, about 5 minutes.
- Pour the custard through a sieve into the bowl containing the cream and coconut extract. Whisk to combine. Cover the bowl with plastic wrap and refrigerate until completely chilled, 2 hours to overnight.
- Transfer the chilled mixture to the ice cream maker and follow the manufacturer's instructions to process and finish. Prior to transferring the ice cream from the ice cream maker to the freezer, gently stir in the mango pieces.

Coconut MANGO ICE CREAM

{ MAKES 1 QUART (960 ML) }

Ingredients

2 cups (480 ml) organic heavy cream
1 tablespoon coconut extract
½ cup (100 g) sugar
8 large egg yolks
½ teaspoon xanthan gum
1 cup (240 ml) coconut cream
1 cup (240 ml) mango puree
1 tablespoon vanilla bean paste
¼ teaspoon salt
1 mango, peeled and cut into
    ¼-inch (6-mm) cubes

OPTIONS

GLUTEN FREE
The ice cream is already gluten free.

COCONUT MANGO ICE CREAM

*Check page 16 before proceeding for additional details on
ensuring your recipes are gluten free and/or vegan.*

HEALTHIER AND VEGAN

Omit the ingredients in the main recipe entirely and do the
following instead to make 1 pint (480 ml):

8 ounces (225 g) firm silken tofu (water packed, not
    boxed), drained (see page 13), at room temperature
1½ cups (360 ml) full-fat coconut milk
¾ cup (180 ml) mango puree
½ cup (100 g) granulated sugar, or ½ cup (80 g) organic
    granulated palm sugar for the healthier version
½ cup (120 ml) organic agave syrup
3 tablespoons organic grapeseed oil
1 tablespoon cacao butter, melted
1 tablespoon vanilla bean paste
1 tablespoon coconut extract
½ teaspoon xanthan gum
¼ teaspoon salt
1 mango, peeled and cut into ¼-inch (6-mm) cubes

- Prepare your ice cream maker according to the
  manufacturer's directions; often that means freezing
  the insert bowl at least 24 hours in advance.
- Put the tofu, coconut milk, and mango puree in a
  blender and blend until smooth. Add the sugar, syrup,
  oil, cacao butter, vanilla, coconut extract, xanthan gum,
  and salt and continue blending until very smooth. Pour
  the mixture through a sieve into a large bowl. Cover with
  plastic wrap and chill for 1 hour.
- Transfer the chilled mixture to the ice cream maker and
  follow the manufacturer's instructions to process and
  finish. Stir in the mango pieces before transferring to
  the freezer.

Vanilla Bean Ice Cream
(PAGE 195)

Banana Split Ice Cream
(PAGE 196)

Caramel Sauce
(PAGE 204)

Coconut Mango
Ice Cream
(PAGE 199)

Coconut Ice Cream
(PAGE 198)

Salted Caramel Ice Cream
(PAGE 202)

Crispy Sugar Cones
(PAGE 205)

Salted CARAMEL ICE CREAM

{ MAKES 1 QUART (960 ML) }

---------- Ingredients -----------

2 cups (480 ml) heavy cream
1 cup (200 g) sugar
¼ teaspoon lemon juice
2 cups (480 ml) whole milk
7 large egg yolks
½ teaspoon xanthan gum
½ teaspoon salt

You could argue that anything "salted caramel," much like any dessert that includes bacon, is so early aughts. It's done. Finished. Hackneyed and yesterday's fad. But while I agree that we're better off with the bacon left out of sweets (I'd rather just eat it crispy alongside some L&T), I'll stand by salted caramel until the end of time. Like chocolate and vanilla, salted caramel deserves to enter the Flavor Hall of Fame permanently.

························· Procedure ·······························

- Prepare your ice cream maker according to the manufacturer's directions; often that means freezing the insert bowl at least 24 hours in advance.
- Fill a large bowl with ice. Set a second bowl, slightly smaller, on top of the ice and nestle it in so it won't tip. Pour the cream into the second bowl. Set aside.
- In a large heavy saucepan, combine ¾ cup (150 g) of the sugar with ⅓ cup (75 ml) water and the lemon juice. Stir over medium heat until the sugar is completely dissolved. Stop stirring and continue cooking over medium heat until the color of the syrup is medium amber. Remove the caramel from the heat and carefully pour in the milk; stand back, as the mixture will bubble up vigorously. Once it's stopped bubbling, about 10 seconds, stir to combine the ingredients.
- In a large bowl, whisk together the egg yolks, the remaining ¼ cup (50 g) sugar, the xanthan gum, and salt until the mixture appears light. Continue whisking the yolks while carefully adding 1 cup (240 ml) of the hot caramel to temper. Transfer the tempered yolk mixture back to the saucepan with the remaining caramel and whisk over low heat until the mixture thickens enough to coat the back of a wooden spoon about 5 minutes. Pour the mixture through a sieve into the bowl containing the cream. Whisk to combine. Cover the bowl with plastic wrap and refrigerate until completely chilled, 2 hours to overnight.
- Transfer the chilled mixture to the ice cream maker and follow the manufacturer's instructions to process and finish.

202
LET THEM EAT CAKE

Check page 16 before proceeding for additional details on ensuring your recipes are gluten free and/or vegan.

HEALTHIER AND VEGAN

Omit the ingredients in the main recipe entirely and do the following instead to make 1 pint (480 ml):

1 cup (200 g) granulated sugar, or ½ cup (100 g) granulated sugar plus ½ cup (80 g) organic granulated palm sugar for the healthier version

¼ teaspoon lemon juice

1½ cups (360 ml) unsweetened vanilla cashew milk

8 ounces (225 g) firm silken tofu (water packed, not boxed), drained (see page 13), at room temperature

¼ cup (60 ml) organic corn syrup or organic agave syrup

3 tablespoons organic grapeseed oil

2 tablespoons vanilla bean paste

1 tablespoon cacao butter, melted

½ teaspoon xanthan gum

½ teaspoon salt

- Prepare your ice cream maker according to the manufacturer's directions; often that means freezing the insert bowl at least 24 hours in advance.
- In a medium-sized heavy saucepan, combine the sugar (if making the healthier version, use only the granulated sugar here) and ⅓ cup (75 ml) water and the lemon juice. Stir over medium heat until the sugar is completely dissolved. Continue cooking over medium heat until the color of the syrup is medium amber. Remove the caramel from the heat and immediately and carefully add 1 cup (240 ml) of the cashew milk and, if making the healthier version, the palm sugar; stand back, as the mixture will bubble up vigorously. Once it's stopped bubbling, continue stirring until combined.
- Put the tofu and the remaining ½ cup (120 ml) cashew milk in a blender and blend until smooth. Add the caramel, syrup, oil, vanilla, cacao butter, xanthan gum, and salt and continue blending until very smooth. Pour the mixture through a sieve into a large bowl. Cover with plastic wrap and refrigerate until completely chilled, 2 hours to overnight. Transfer the chilled mixture to the ice cream maker and follow the manufacturer's instructions to process and finish.

GLUTEN FREE

The ice cream is already gluten free.

Caramel *SAUCE*

{ MAKES 2½ CUPS (600 ML) }

Ingredients

1 cup (220 g) dark brown sugar, packed
1 cup (200 g) granulated sugar
½ cup (1 stick/115 g) unsalted butter, cut
    into very small pieces
½ cup (120 ml) light corn syrup
¼ cup (60 ml) sweetened condensed milk
1 teaspoon vanilla bean paste
1 teaspoon salt

It's all well and good that you made homemade ice cream, but what's the point if the toppings aren't just as good? Well, I've got you covered. Let's start with the caramel, shall we? I can't live without a generous dousing of caramel on my sundaes.

Procedure

- In a medium-sized heavy saucepan over medium heat, combine the brown sugar, granulated sugar, butter, corn syrup, condensed milk, vanilla, and salt and stir constantly with a wooden spoon until the sugar is completely dissolved. Attach a candy thermometer and continue stirring until the caramel reaches 245°F (120°C; the firm ball stage).
- Transfer to a jar, cover, and refrigerate until needed, up to 1 month.

OPTIONS

Check page 16 before proceeding for additional details on ensuring your recipes are gluten free and/or vegan.

VEGAN

Replace the butter with ½ cup (115 g) Earth Balance Vegan Shortening. Replace the condensed milk with ¼ cup (60 ml) full-fat coconut milk.

GLUTEN FREE

The caramel sauce is already gluten free.

HEALTHIER AND VEGAN

Replace the granulated and brown sugar with 2 cups (320 g) organic granulated palm sugar. Replace the corn syrup with organic agave syrup. Replace the sweetened condensed milk with ¼ cup (60 ml) either nonfat sweetened condensed milk or full-fat coconut milk.

I'm totally down with people who choose the cake cone or bowl option at an ice cream joint. Okay. I'm lying. There's no reason to choose anything other than a sugar cone. Or, if on offer, a waffle cone. Because let's be honest here, you're already eating a cow's worth of cream, so why not up the ante and go for the crispy sweet vessel?

{ MAKES ABOUT 1 DOZEN SMALL SUGAR CONES }

Procedure

- In a large bowl, whisk together the milk, vanilla, and salt until combined. Sift the sugar and flour over the mixture and whisk to combine, making sure the mixture is smooth. Cover the bowl with plastic wrap and refrigerate for 20 minutes to rest.
- Add the sparkling water to the batter and stir together.
- Spray a 6-inch (15-cm) frying pan liberally with nonstick cooking spray. Spread ¼ cup (60 ml) of the batter into the pan, using an offset spatula to nudge the batter into as perfect a 6-inch (15-cm) round as you can manage. Cook over medium-low heat until the bottom is golden brown, about 4 minutes. Carefully flip and cook the other side until golden brown, about 2 minutes.
- Gently lift the round from the pan and quickly manipulate it into a cone shape, pinching the bottom to seal. Set aside to harden. Wipe the pan down before respraying with nonstick cooking spray and adding the next round of batter. Continue cooking and shaping the cones until all of the batter is used.

Ingredients

1 cup (240 ml) whole milk
1 teaspoon vanilla bean paste
½ teaspoon salt
½ cup (100 g) sugar
½ cup (70 g) all-purpose flour
2 tablespoons sparkling water

CRISPY SUGAR CONES

Check page 16 before proceeding for additional details on ensuring your recipes are gluten free and/or vegan.

VEGAN

Replace the milk with 1 cup (240 ml) full-fat coconut milk (the coconut milk should be very thick; if it appears very runny, remove the lid and place in the refrigerator uncovered overnight, to thicken). Add 1 teaspoon Ener-G egg replacer (not prepared) along with the sugar and whisk the mixture until it ribbons.

GLUTEN FREE

Replace the flour with ¼ cup (40 g) plus 2 tablespoons finely milled brown rice flour, 2 tablespoons sweet white sorghum flour, 1 tablespoon tapioca starch, and ¼ teaspoon xanthan gum.

HEALTHIER

Replace the milk with 1 cup (240 ml) full-fat coconut milk (the coconut milk should be very thick; if it appears very runny, remove the lid and place in the refrigerator uncovered overnight, to thicken). Replace the sugar with ½ cup (80 g) organic granulated palm sugar. Replace the flour with ½ cup (50 g) whole-wheat pastry flour.

a note from my sweet tooth

Regarding the chocolate shell, the decision between vegan shortening and coconut oil is really a matter of taste. While refined coconut oil gives you the perfect consistency, those who have an intense aversion to coconut might be able to detect the very slight coconutty taste that lingers with the oil. If you're that person, opt for the shortening.

I'm that kid. The one who would take an itsy bitsy scoop of ice cream and unload an entire bottle of Magic Shell on it, hoping I'd have just enough frosty stuff to harden the lake of goo swimming in my bowl. Something about that slightly salty, hard chocolate coating ticked all my "I'm eating something scrumptious so I'm going to do a happy dance" boxes as a kid. Had I bothered to read the ingredient list on the bottle, I wouldn't have cared less that the stuff was laced with ingredients only to be found in an orbiting International Space Station lab. Today, it does bother me. So I'm happy to have a recipe in which the ingredient list is short and naturally sweet.

Chocolate SHELL

{ MAKES 1 CUP (240 ML) }

Ingredients

8 ounces (225 g) bittersweet chocolate (at least 60%), finely chopped
1 tablespoon organic refined coconut oil or vegetable shortening
Pinch of salt

Procedure

- In a large heatproof metal bowl, combine the chocolate, oil, and salt. Place the bowl over a saucepan of simmering water (to make a double boiler). Stir continuously until the chocolate is completely melted. Let cool to room temperature and cover with plastic wrap. Keep at room temperature or refrigerate. The mixture will harden.
- In order to use on ice cream, place the bowl over a large saucepan filled with 1 inch (2.5 cm) of simmering water, making sure the water doesn't reach farther than halfway up the bowl. Keep the water on a simmer, stirring the chocolate mixture, until completely melted. Spoon the sauce over ice cream while fluid. It will harden within a few seconds of hitting the ice cream to form a shell.

OPTIONS

Check page 16 before proceeding for additional details on ensuring your recipes are gluten free and/or vegan.

GLUTEN FREE & VEGAN

The chocolate shell is already gluten free and vegan (assuming you've used a vegan chocolate).

HEALTHIER

To increase the health factor, use organic chocolate and coconut oil.

MINTY ICE CREAM Sandwiches

{ MAKES TWELVE ICE CREAM SANDWICHES }

Ingredients

FOR THE MINT CHIP ICE CREAM
2 cups (480 ml) organic heavy cream
½ teaspoon natural peppermint extract
2 cups (480 ml) whole milk
1 cup (40 g) fresh mint, coarsely chopped
⅔ cup (130 g) sugar
7 large egg yolks
½ teaspoon xanthan gum
1 teaspoon vanilla bean paste
½ teaspoon salt
3 ounces (85 g) bittersweet chocolate,
    grated

FOR THE CHOCOLATE COOKIES
1½ cups (210 g) all-purpose flour
1 cup (85 g) unsweetened cocoa powder
½ teaspoon salt
1 cup (2 sticks/225 g) unsalted butter, at
    room temperature
1 cup (200 g) sugar
1 large whole egg
1 large egg yolk
1 teaspoon vanilla bean paste

Gone are the days when "green" meant mint. Our evolved food culture has shown us that dye doesn't make the flavor but rather the flavor makes the flavor. And it doesn't hurt when you mix in a little chocolate. And it really doesn't hurt when you sandwich the stuff with more chocolate. So let mint be mint without the false emerald adornment. And if you're a true friend of the stuff, give it a chocolate cookie hug.

Procedure

MAKE THE MINT CHIP ICE CREAM
- Prepare your ice cream maker according to the manufacturer's directions; often that means freezing the insert bowl at least 24 hours in advance.
- Fill a large bowl with ice. Set a second bowl, slightly smaller, on top of the ice and nestle it in so it won't tip. Pour the cream and peppermint extract into the second bowl. Set aside.
- In a large heavy saucepan, combine the milk and mint. Bring to a simmer. Remove from the heat and let steep for 20 minutes. Pour the milk through a sieve set over a bowl, discard the mint, and return the milk to the saucepan.
- In a large bowl, whisk together the sugar, egg yolks, and xanthan gum until pale. While whisking the milk, add the egg yolk mixture to the pan, along with the vanilla and salt. Continue whisking until combined. Place the saucepan over medium-low heat and whisk constantly until the custard thickens enough to coat the back of a wooden spoon about 5 minutes . Pour the custard through a sieve into the bowl containing the cream and peppermint extract. Whisk to combine. Cover the bowl with plastic wrap and refrigerate until completely cool, 2 hours to overnight.
- Transfer the chilled mixture to the ice cream maker and follow the manufacturer's instructions to process and finish. Prior to transferring the ice cream from the ice cream maker to the freezer, gently stir in the grated chocolate.

MAKE THE CHOCOLATE COOKIES
- Preheat the oven to 350°F (175°C).
- In a bowl, combine the flour, cocoa powder, and salt. Whisk for 30 seconds to combine.

continued

- In the bowl of a stand mixer fitted with the paddle attachment, mix the butter and sugar until light and fluffy. Add the whole egg and mix to combine. Scrape down the bottom and sides of the bowl. Add the egg yolk and vanilla and mix to combine. With the mixer running on low speed, add the flour mixture and mix until just combined. Divide the dough in half, shape each half into a disk, and wrap each piece with plastic wrap. Refrigerate the dough for 20 minutes.
- Roll out each piece of dough on a piece of parchment paper to a 9-by-12-inch (23-by-30.5-cm) rectangle. Transfer the two parchments with dough onto two sheet pans. Using a fork, dock the dough. Bake until just cooked through (make sure not to let the edges get crisp), 10 to 15 minutes. Let cool completely.

ASSEMBLE THE SANDWICHES

- Take the ice cream from the freezer and let sit at room temperature until just soft enough to spread, 5 to 10 minutes.
- Using a small offset spatula, spread the ice cream in an even layer over one of the chocolate cookie rectangles. Carefully top the ice cream with the second chocolate cookie rectangle. Wrap the sandwich with plastic wrap and freeze until just set, about 1 hour.
- Run a sharp knife under hot water and dry completely. Using the hot knife, cut the large ice cream sandwich into twelve individual sandwiches.

Check page 16 before proceeding for additional details on ensuring your recipes are gluten free and/or vegan.

VEGAN

FOR THE MINT CHIP ICE CREAM: Omit the ingredients in the ice cream recipe entirely and do the following instead:

> 1½ cups (360 ml) plain almond milk
> 1 cup (40 g) fresh mint, coarsely chopped
> 8 ounces (225 g) firm silken tofu (water packed, not boxed), drained (see page 13), at room temperature
> ½ cup (100 g) sugar
> ½ cup (120 ml) organic agave syrup
> 3 tablespoons organic grapeseed oil
> 1 tablespoon cacao butter, melted
> 1 teaspoon vanilla bean paste
> ½ teaspoon peppermint extract or oil
> ½ teaspoon xanthan gum
> ½ teaspoon salt
> 3 ounces (85 g) bittersweet chocolate, grated

- Prepare your ice cream maker according to the manufacturer's directions; often that means freezing the insert bowl at least 24 hours in advance.
- In a small saucepan, combine the almond milk and mint and bring to a simmer. Remove from the heat and let steep for 20 minutes. Pour the almond milk through a sieve into a blender and discard the mint leaves. Add the tofu and blend until smooth. Add the sugar, agave syrup, oil, cacao butter, vanilla, peppermint extract, xanthan gum, and salt and continue blending until very smooth. Pour the mixture through a sieve set over a large bowl. Refrigerate until completely chilled, 2 hours to overnight.
- Transfer the chilled mixture to the ice cream maker and follow the manufacturer's instructions to process and finish. Prior to transferring the ice cream from the ice cream maker to the freezer, carefully stir in the grated chocolate.

FOR THE CHOCOLATE COOKIES: Replace the butter with 1 cup (225 g) Earth Balance Vegan Shortening. Replace the egg and egg yolk with 1 large egg's worth of flaxseed meal mixed with water (see page 12).

GLUTEN FREE

FOR THE MINT CHIP ICE CREAM: The ice cream is already gluten free. FOR THE CHOCOLATE COOKIES: Replace the flour with 1 cup (160 g) finely milled brown rice flour, ⅓ cup (45 g) sweet white sorghum flour, 2 tablespoons tapioca starch, and 1 teaspoon xanthan gum.

HEALTHIER

FOR THE MINT CHIP ICE CREAM: Follow the vegan recipe for the ice cream but replace the sugar with ½ cup (80 g) organic granulated palm sugar. FOR THE CHOCOLATE COOKIES: Replace the flour with 1½ cups (150 g) whole-wheat pastry flour. Replace half of the butter with ½ cup (120 ml) coconut oil (melt to measure then let resolidify). Keep the remaining ½ cup (1 stick/115 g) unsalted butter.

As much as I love a good chewy candy, I find myself completely addicted to the crunch of toffee. Not too challenging a crunch, but one that gives way to a buttery crispness and, hopefully, if I'm really lucky, there's a touch of chocolate and roasted pecans to come along for the ride. So I find it quite convenient that I can make a batch up lickity split, just to my specifications. Now you can too.

Butter CRUNCH PECAN TOFFEE

{ MAKES 2 POUNDS (910 G) TOFFEE }

Procedure

- Line a sheet pan with parchment paper and spray with nonstick cooking spray.
- In a large saucepan, melt the butter over low heat. Stir in the sugar, vanilla, and salt. Continue stirring until the sugar is completely melted. Clip on a candy thermometer and increase the heat to medium-high, continuing to stir until the mixture turns amber and the temperature reads 300° to 305°F (150°C; the hard crack stage). For a while, the mixture will look as if it's separated, but as you continue stirring and the temperature rises, it will start to come together. Immediately pour the toffee onto the prepared sheet pan. Let sit, undisturbed, for 5 minutes.
- Sprinkle the chocolate chips evenly over the warm toffee and let sit for 5 minutes.
- Using an offset spatula, gently spread the now melted chocolate into an even layer over the toffee. Immediately sprinkle the pecans over the chocolate. Let the toffee cool completely.
- Break the cooled toffee into small pieces. Store in an airtight container for up to 2 weeks.

Ingredients

2 cups (4 sticks/450 g) unsalted butter
2 cups (400 g) sugar
1 teaspoon vanilla bean paste
1 teaspoon salt
1 cup (170 g) bittersweet chocolate chips
1 cup (110 g) chopped pecans, lightly toasted

OPTIONS

Check page 16 before proceeding for additional details on ensuring your recipes are gluten free and/or vegan.

VEGAN

Replace the butter with 2 cups (450 g) Earth Balance Vegan Shortening.

GLUTEN FREE

The toffee is already gluten free.

HEALTHIER

Replace half of the butter with 1 cup (225 g) Earth Balance Vegan Shortening. Replace the sugar with 2 cups (320 g) organic granulated palm sugar. Be very aware that palm sugar burns easily, so make sure to stir constantly throughout the process and turn the heat to only medium-low instead of medium-high. It will take a bit longer for the toffee to come to temperature, but this will help keep the mixture from burning.

MARSHMALLOWS

{ MAKES 8 LARGE SQUARE MARSHMALLOWS }

Ingredients

4 envelopes unflavored gelatin
1 tablespoon vanilla bean paste
3 cups (600 g) sugar
1 cup (240 ml) corn syrup
½ teaspoon salt
Blue gel food coloring (optional)
1 cup (100 g) confectioners' sugar

No matter that marshmallows are simply puffs of sugar, they are the stuff of happiness, of convivial campfires and sticky fingers. Without them, a steaming cup of cocoa would be a sad cup of sweet sludge. Without them, Lucky Charms would no longer be magically delicious and s'mores just wouldn't be the same.

Procedure

- Line a 9-inch (23-cm) square baking dish with parchment paper, creating a 2-inch (5-cm) overhang on all four sides. Spray with nonstick cooking spray.
- Put the gelatin and vanilla in the bowl of a stand mixer fitted with the whisk attachment. Add ¾ cup (180 ml) water (it should cover the gelatin completely). Give the mixture a gentle stir to combine, then let stand. The water will saturate the gelatin while you make the sugar syrup.
- In a large saucepan, combine the sugar, corn syrup, and salt. Stir the mixture over medium heat until the sugar is completely melted. Stop stirring, attach a candy thermometer, and increase the heat to medium-high. Heat the mixture to 240°F (116°C; the soft ball stage), then remove from the heat.
- With the mixer running on medium speed, slowly pour the hot sugar syrup down the side of the mixing bowl into the gelatin mixture. Once all of the syrup is added, increase the mixer speed to high and mix until the mixture is white and fluffy and has quadrupled in volume, and the stand mixer bowl is cool to the touch.
- Using a large rubber spatula sprayed with nonstick cooking spray, transfer the marshmallow mixture to the prepared pan. Spray a small offset spatula with nonstick cooking spray and smooth out the top of the marshmallow.
- Dip a wooden skewer into the food coloring and swirl the coloring into the marshmallow. Set the marshmallow aside to set, uncovered, for 4 hours or up to overnight.
- Once the marshmallow is set, sift confectioners' sugar liberally over the top of the marshmallow. Turn the marshmallow out onto a new piece of parchment and gently peel off the parchment from the bottom and sides. Coat the underside of the slab of marshmallow with confectioners' sugar. Using a very sharp knife, cut 2-inch (5-cm) squares from the block, dredging the sides of the marshmallow in confectioners' sugar to keep them from sticking to each other. Store the marshmallows in an airtight container for up to 2 weeks.

Check page 16 before proceeding for additional details on ensuring your recipes are gluten free and/or vegan.

VEGAN

Replace the gelatin with 1 tablespoon agar agar powder. In a small saucepan, stir together the agar agar and ¾ cup (180 ml) water and bring to a boil, stirring until the agar agar has dissolved. Add to the mixing bowl.

GLUTEN FREE

The marshmallows are already gluten free.

HEALTHIER

The gelatin choice is up to you: You can use the classic version's gelatin, or use agar agar, which is made from seaweed. Marshmallows require a lot of sugar, and there's nothing healthy about that. No matter what gelatin or gelatin replacement you use, replace the granulated sugar with 2 cups (380 g) of an organic and less processed variety of sugar, like Sucanat. Replace the corn syrup with ½ cup (120 ml) organic agave syrup. Leave out the food coloring.

VEGAN

FOR THE CARAMEL: Replace the butter with ½ cup (115g) Earth Balance Vegan Shortening. Replace the condensed milk with ¼ cup (60 ml) full-fat coconut milk.

FOR THE FILLING: Replace the butter with ½ cup (115g) Earth Balance Vegan Shortening. Replace the milk with 1 tablespoon full-fat coconut milk.

GLUTEN FREE

Both the caramel and the filling are already gluten free.

HEALTHIER

FOR THE CARAMEL: Replace both sugars with 2 cups (320 g) organic granulated palm sugar. Replace the butter with ½ cup (115 g) Earth Balance Vegan Shortening. Replace the condensed milk with ¼ cup (60 ml) nonfat sweetened condensed milk or full-fat coconut milk.

These aren't the caramels you know, the ones trapped in a crinkly cellophane bag in the off-brand section of the grocery store. These are a sweet revelation, a swirl of caramel nestling creamy vanilla goodness. If you present these to your guests, they'll never believe that you made these chewy jewels yourself.

{ MAKES ABOUT 2 DOZEN PIECES }

Procedure

MAKE THE CARAMEL

- Line a sheet pan with parchment paper and spray with nonstick cooking spray.
- In a large heavy saucepan over medium heat, stir together both sugars, the butter, corn syrup, condensed milk, vanilla, and salt. Attach a candy thermometer and stir until the mixture reaches 245°F (120°C; the firm ball stage).
- Pour the hot caramel evenly into the prepared pan. Tilt the pan to create a rough 11-by-13-inch (28-by-33-cm) rectangle, making sure that it's no more than ⅛ inch (3 mm) thick.
- Let the caramel cool just enough to handle (bend a corner back to make sure that it's pliable but still holds its shape). Make the filling while the caramel is cooling.

MAKE THE FILLING

- In the bowl of a stand mixer fitted with the paddle attachment, combine 1½ cups (150 g) of the confectioners' sugar and the butter. Mix until smooth. Add the milk, vanilla, and salt and mix until combined. Pinch off a piece of the filling. If it's firm yet pliable, you're ready to go. If it feels wet and not easy to handle, continue mixing on low speed, adding the remaining ½ cup (50 g) confectioners' sugar, 1 tablespoon at a time, until the mixture is firm yet pliable.
- Divide the filling in half and wrap each piece with plastic wrap.

ASSEMBLE THE CARAMELS

- Cut the caramel in half lengthwise, so that you have two 11-by-6½-inch (28-by-16.5-cm) pieces. Lift one piece from the pan and place on a work surface.
- Using your fingers, gently press the first piece of filling onto the caramel in an even layer. Switch to a rolling pin to even out the layer. Starting with one long end, roll up the caramel and filling as you would a jelly roll, as tightly as possible. With the seam facing down, use a sharp knife to cut the log into ½-inch (12-mm) pieces. Wrap each piece in waxed candy paper. Repeat with the remaining caramel and filling.

Ingredients

FOR THE CARAMEL

1 cup (220 g) dark brown sugar, packed
1 cup (200 g) granulated sugar
½ cup (1 stick/115 g) unsalted butter,
    cut into very small pieces
½ cup (120 ml) light corn syrup
¼ cup (60 ml) sweetened condensed milk
1 teaspoon vanilla bean paste
1 teaspoon salt

FOR THE FILLING

1½ to 2 cups (150 to 200 g)
    confectioners' sugar
½ cup (1 stick/115 g) unsalted butter,
    at room temperature
1 tablespoon whole milk
½ teaspoon vanilla bean paste
Pinch of salt

Waxed candy paper

Caramels

{ MAKES UP TO 2 DOZEN CARAMELS }

1 cup (220 g) dark brown sugar, packed
1 cup (200 g) granulated sugar
½ cup (1 stick/115 g) unsalted butter, cut
   into very small pieces
½ cup (120 ml) light corn syrup
¼ cup (60 ml) sweetened condensed milk
1 teaspoon vanilla bean paste
1 teaspoon salt
Waxed candy paper

Sticky. Chewy. Buttery. Salty. It's tough to deny the pull of a perfectly made caramel, one that gives a touch of resistance when you take your first bite but then gives way happily to the ministrations of your teeth. By making your own, you're guaranteed an uninterrupted supply of the stuff. If you're not too greedy, find a pretty box and drop in a few; tie it all up with a ribbon and you're a gift-giving genius.

Procedure

- Line a quarter sheet pan (measuring 9½ by 13 inches/24 by 33 cm) with parchment paper, allowing the parchment to hang over the edges of the pan by 2 inches (5 cm).
- In a heavy saucepan over medium heat, combine both sugars, the butter, corn syrup, condensed milk, vanilla, and salt. With a wooden spoon, stir constantly until the sugar and butter are completely melted. Attach a candy thermometer and continue stirring until the caramel reaches 245°F (120°C; the firm ball stage).
- Pour the caramel into the prepared pan and tip it back and forth very carefully to evenly distribute. Let sit overnight at room temperature to set.
- Lift the caramel out of the pan using the parchment overhang and place on a work surface. Spray a very sharp chef's knife with nonstick cooking spray. Cut the caramel into 1-by-2-inch (2.5-by-5-cm) rectangles. Wrap the pieces in waxed candy paper and store in an airtight container.

OPTIONS

Check page 16 before proceeding for additional details on ensuring your recipes are gluten free and/or vegan.

VEGAN

Replace the butter with ½ cup (115 g) Earth Balance Vegan Shortening. Replace the condensed milk with ¼ cup (60 ml) full-fat coconut milk.

GLUTEN FREE

The caramels are already gluten free.

HEALTHIER

Replace both sugars with 2 cups (320 g) organic granulated palm sugar. Replace the butter with ½ cup (120 ml) organic refined virgin coconut oil. Replace the condensed milk with either ¼ cup (60 ml) nonfat sweetened condensed milk (organic, if you can find it) or full-fat coconut milk.

If you've ever had a Sugar Daddy, you know that you're not dealing with just any caramel. You can't just bite into the thing and be done with it. You have to work at this caramel. It's so damn hard that it requires patience. But take your time with it and you'll have hours of delicious work.

Caramel LOLLIPOPS

·········· Procedure ··········

- In a large saucepan, combine the sugar, corn syrup, and salt and stir over low heat until the sugar has completely melted. Stop stirring, increase the heat to medium-high, and clip on a candy thermometer. Heat to 310°F (154°C; the hard crack stage).
- Meanwhile, in a small saucepan over low heat, combine the cream and vanilla and stir until it just begins to simmer.
- When the sugar syrup reaches temperature, turn off the heat and add the warm cream mixture. The mixture will bubble vigorously, so stand back until it calms. Check the temperature; if it has dipped below 275°F (135°C), warm the caramel mixture until it reaches 275°F (135°C). Remove from the heat. Add the butter, stirring constantly until it's completely incorporated.
- Carefully divide the hot caramel among heatproof small square molds (small silicone square specialty molds work well for this). Let the caramel cool slightly but not so much that it's hard. Insert a lollipop stick into each of the molds and let the caramel cool completely. Pop the lollipops out of the molds and wrap each in waxed candy paper.

{ MAKES 1 DOZEN LOLLIPOPS }

·········· Ingredients ··········

2 cups (400 g) sugar
1 cup (240 ml) corn syrup
1 teaspoon salt
½ cup (120 ml) heavy cream
1 tablespoon vanilla bean paste
¾ cup (1 ½ sticks/170 g) unsalted butter, at room temperature, cut into small pieces
12 lollipop sticks
Waxed candy paper

OPTIONS

Check page 16 before proceeding for additional details on ensuring your recipes are gluten free and/or vegan.

VEGAN

Replace the cream with ½ cup (120 g) full-fat coconut milk. Replace the butter with ¾ cup (170 g) Earth Balance Vegan Shortening.

GLUTEN FREE

The lollipops are already gluten free.

HEALTHIER

Replace the sugar with 2 cups (320 g) organic granulated palm sugar. During the cooking phase of the sugar, make sure to continue stirring after the sugar has melted, as palm sugar burns easily. Replace the corn syrup with organic agave syrup. Replace the cream with ½ cup (120 ml) full-fat coconut milk.

RESOURCES

Cookie Letter Press by Fred & Friends: Available at Amazon.com.

Springerle Rolling Pin: Available at Kingarthurflour.com, Amazon.com, and Surlatable.com.

Golden Flax Meal: Available at Kingarthurflour.com.

Versawhip 600k: Available at Amazon.com or Modernistpantry.com.

Gluten-Free Flour Alternatives: Many gluten-free flours can be found in grocery stores in a special gluten-free section or in bulk at Nuts.com.

Nut Flours: Almond flour is readily available in many specialty food stores and also at Nuts.com. Peanut flour, pistachio flour, and hazelnut flour are available at Nuts.com.

Sprouted Flour: You can find Sprouted Super Flour at Nuts.com.

White Whole Wheat Flour: You can find white whole wheat flour in many grocery stores or at Kingarthurflour.com.

ACKNOWLEDGMENTS

I'd like to thank my intrepid recipe testers, especially Al Samonte, Heike Sellers, Kiki Hong-Praslick, and the Jasmin 5!

Many sweet thanks to my literary agent, Laura Nolan, for always having my back.

All my gratitude to superwoman editor Elinor Hutton.

I don't know what I'd do without Claire Bamundo, book publicist extraordinaire and all-around fabulous gal.

Raymo, you are the best, Chicken Celeste.

And to Sandy and Louis, how much do I love you? So much.

INDEX